THE REGIONS OF BRITAIN

The South-East

THE REGIONS OF BRITAIN
Previous and forthcoming titles in the series include:

The Pennine Dales	Arthur Raistrick
The Upper Thames	J. R. L. Anderson
The Lake District	Roy Millward and Adrian Robinson
The Scottish Border and Northumberland	John Talbot White
The Islands of Western Scotland	W. H. Murray
The Peak District	Roy Millward and Adrian Robinson
The Cotswolds	Josceline Finberg
East Anglia	Norman Scarfe
Cornwall	W. G. Hoskins
The Welsh Marches	Roy Millward and Adrian Robinson
The Central Midlands	Victor Skipp

JOHN TALBOT WHITE

The South-East Down and Weald: Kent, Surrey and Sussex

EYRE METHUEN · LONDON

First published 1977

Printed in Great Britain for
Eyre Methuen Ltd
11 New Fetter Lane, London EC4P 4EE
by Cox & Wyman Ltd
Fakenham, Norfolk

ISBN 0 413 32090 1 (hardback)
ISBN 0 413 32100 2 (paperback)

The South-East

Contents

	Acknowledgements	*page* 10
	Introduction	11
1	In the Steps of the Iguanodon	17
2	The Kingdom of the Oak	36
3	Albion's Shore	60
4	The White Horse	83
5	The Forest Frontier	99
6	Iron Masters and Clothiers	127
7	The Garden of England	146
8	Boroughs and Market Towns	170
9	Ports and Resorts	193
10	The Pleasuring of London	222
	Select Bibliography	242
	Index	249

To my brother, Percy

The South-East

Illustrations

1 The south-east counties *page* 12
2 Topographical areas 18
3 Natural sculpture on Rusthall Common 22
4 Leith Hill seen from Holmbury Hill 25
5 Aerial view along the Hog's Back 26
6 Botany Bay, Thanet 28
7 The Devil's Kneadingtrough 33
8 Coppice woodlander 37
9 The Mens nature reserve 39
10 Churchyard Yew, Tandridge 42
11 Beeches on Toy's Hill 47
12 Major nature reserves 50
13 Grey heron at Northwood Hill 56
14 Neolithic flint-mines on Harrow Hill 62
15 Kit's Coty 64
16 Disc barrows on Bow Hill 67
17 The Long Man of Wilmington 71
18 Major remains of the Roman occupation 73
19 The Roman Stane Street 75
20 Mosaic floor at Lullingstone 79
21 Pevensey Castle 82
22 Saxon chancel and apse, St Nicholas, Worth 90
23 Saxon sundial, St Andrew's, Bishopstone 91

24 Medieval bridge on the Sussex Rother, Stopham 105
25 Norman lead font, Brookland church, Romney Marsh 106
26 Mural of the Last Judgement, Chaldon church 107
27 Medieval lych-gate, Boughton Monchelsea 110
28 Gatehouse of Bayham Abbey 114
29 Castles with substantial structural remains 117
30 Bodiam Castle 121
31 Medieval priest's house at Alfriston 123
32 Fireback, 1636 131
33 Sixteenth-century hall house, Smarden 134
34 Knole House and park in 1830 139
35 Camber Castle 140
36 Decorated Tudor brickwork at Sutton Place 142
37 Oast house near Sissinghurst 150
38 Shearing Kent sheep at Bethersden 155
39 Shepherd's cott near Birling 156
40 Sussex oxen and turn-wrist plough early in the 1900s 159
41 Staddle barn at Cowdray 160
42 Outwood Mill 162

43 Scotney 166
44 The cathedral and precinct at Canterbury 173
45 John Speed's map of Chichester, 1610 175
46 The market cross at Alfriston 180
47 Extract from Matthew Richardson's 'Ground Plan of Guldeford', 1739 181
48 Eighteenth-century Town Hall in Gatton Park 183
49 The confederation of the cinque ports 195
50 Watchbell Street, Rye 203
51 Medieval town planning – Winchelsea 205
52 Wooden net houses on the Stade at Hastings 207
53 Nineteenth-century town planning – Kemp Town 211
54 Victorian restoration at Hall Place, Leigh 225
55 Stephenson's locomotive 'Invicta' 226
56 The North Downs Way above Godmersham 236
57 Topiary work at Hever Castle 238
58 Jack-in-the-Green, Charing church 241

The South-East

Acknowledgements

It would not be possible for me to acknowledge by name the hundreds of people – friends, acquaintances, librarians, local officials and members of societies – who have assisted me in gathering material and ideas about the south-east. The sources have been abundant, the help unstinting. For their personal hospitality and assistance, however, I should like to thank Miss J. Draper of Bethersden, whose knowledge of the region has been so readily shared, my colleague Mrs O. Jackson, Mr & Mrs Thomas of Horsmonden, Mrs B. Serjeant of Halnaker, Mr & Mrs Hamilton of Wisborough Green, Mr & Mrs Fleck of Slinfold, Mr & Mrs Hooper of Diprose and Mr & Mrs Cassell of Sittingbourne.

Acknowledgements and thanks for permission to reproduce photographs are due to Aerofilms for plates 5, 14, 21, 30, 35, 44, 51 and 53; to the Royal Commission on Historic Monuments (England), for plate 20; to the National Monuments Record for plates 26 and 31; and to Mrs B. B. Parry for plate 36. Plate 40 is from *A Country Camera* by Gordon Winter. Illustrations 7, 8, 13, 15, 23, 25, 27, 37, 52 and 58 were drawn by Percy F. White, and the maps were drawn from the author's roughs by Neil Hyslop.

The South-East

Introduction

When my grandfather went for a day out in the country, he took the pony and cart out of the stables under the railway arch in Deptford, close to the river, and rode to Southend Pond four miles away. There the family found green fields, watercress beds, a mill pond and the Green Man. At that same time, in the first years of the twentieth century, Sir Halford Mackinder was describing the new realities of the south-east in a classic geographical study. 'In a manner,' he wrote, 'all South-Eastern England is a single urban community, for steam and electricity are changing our geographical conceptions. The wives and children of the merchants, even of the more prosperous of the artisans, live without – beyond green fields – where the men only sleep and pass the Sabbath.'*

The family excursion was soon overtaken by the pattern Mackinder had foreseen. The family moved out to new estates being built on the fields around Southend Pond. The day out at the weekend became the daily migration from home to work. That pond is now within the boundaries of Inner London and the road sign showing the border of Kent has moved on another eight miles. The landscape in the triangle of three counties, Kent, Surrey and Sussex, lying to the south and east of London, has always been influenced by the presence of the capital city but never more so than in the present century. Described by Mackinder as 'one of the most naturally compact sub-divisions of all Britain', the region has as its framework the web of roads and railways that link the Channel ports with London. The trains and buses and, finally, the personal ownership of cars, have brought the whole region within the reach of Mackinder's

* Halford J. Mackinder, *Britain and the British Seas* (Macmillan, 1906).

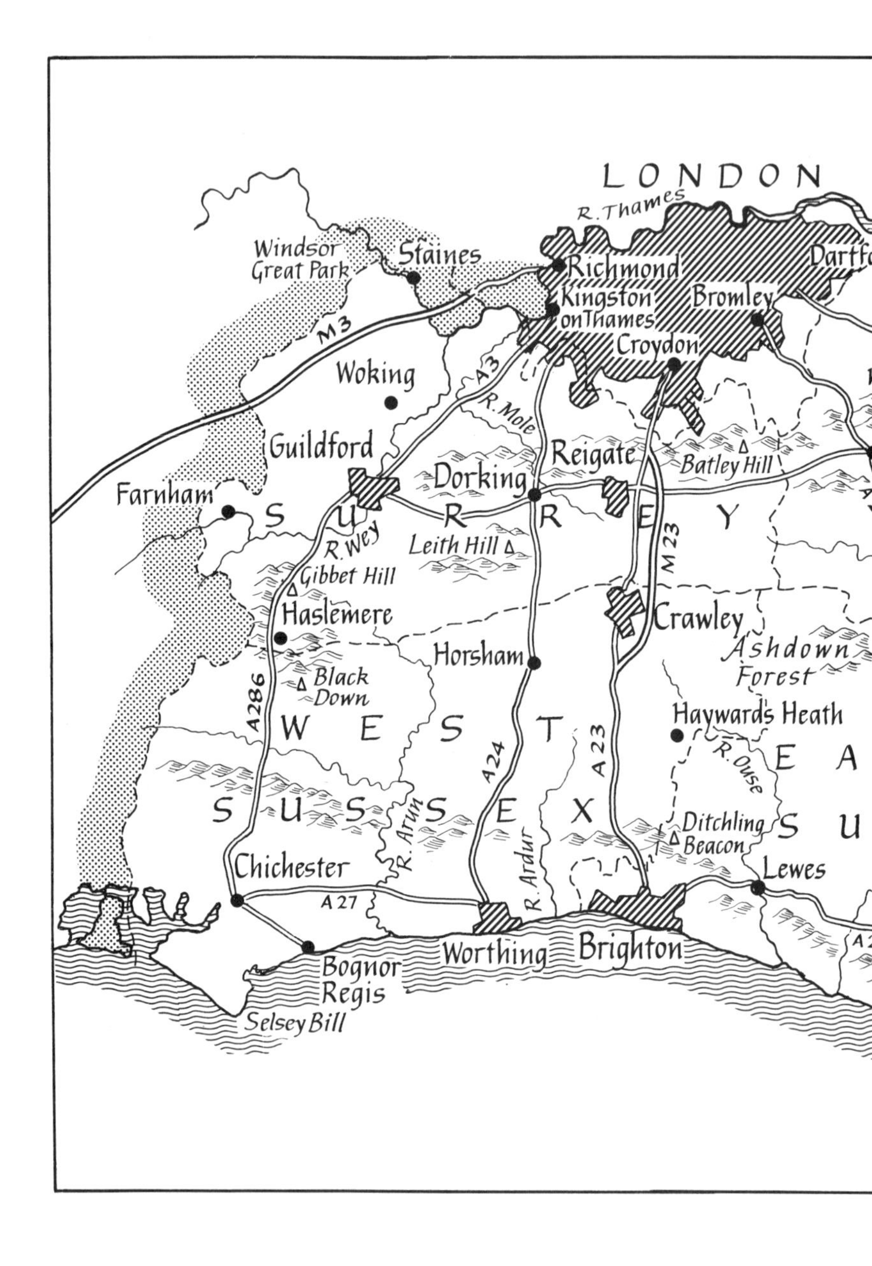

LONDON
R. Thames
Windsor Great Park
Staines
Richmond
Kingston on Thames
Bromley
Croydon
M3
Woking
A3
R. Mole
Guildford
Reigate
Batley Hill
Dorking
Farnham
SURREY
R. Wey
Leith Hill
M23
Gibbet Hill
Haslemere
Crawley
Horsham
Ashdown Forest
Black Down
A286
WEST SUSSEX
Hayward's Heath
R. Ouse
A24
A23
R. Arun
R. Ardur
Ditchling Beacon
Chichester
Lewes
A27
Worthing
Brighton
Bognor Regis
Selsey Bill

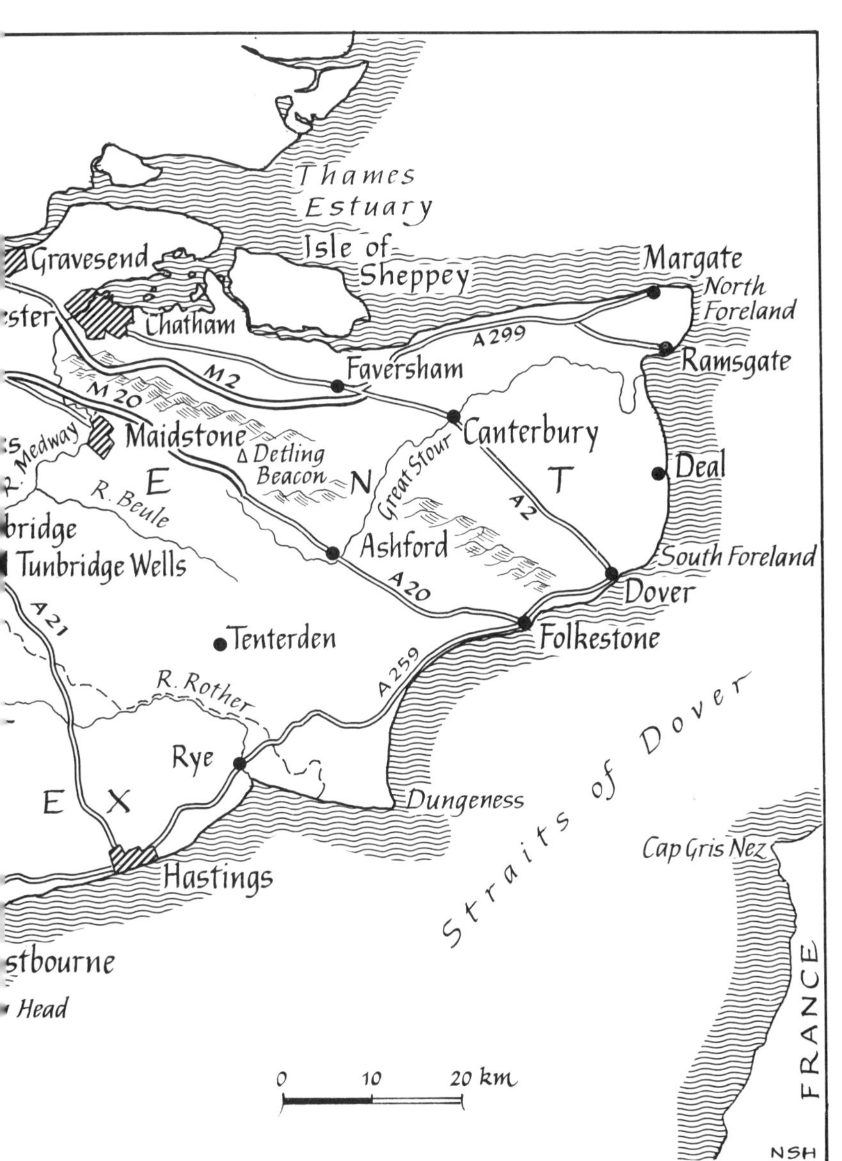

1. *The south-east counties.*

'merchants and artisans'. Surrey, for example, used to begin at the south side of London Bridge. The county cricket team still plays at the Kennington Oval. Now there is a belt of twenty-five miles of buildings before the train from Waterloo reaches open country beyond Woking.

Inevitably, the shadow of London falls across every chapter of this study. From the Roman period onwards its influence is decisive. But this book is primarily concerned with the region beyond the boundaries of the capital city; a region that holds a variety of human landscapes unmatched in England with a complex chequerboard of farm and forest, of heath and park and garden; a tapestry woven on the warp of weald, down, marsh and coast.

The natural framework of the landscape is dependent on two fundamental events. The first was the folding of its sedimentary rocks into a great dome. The second was the formation of the Dover Strait cutting through that dome, separating the island from the continental land mass. Those two events gave the region its spectacular coast, its special relationship with the continent and a variety of geological outcrop and soils remarkable in so small a compass.

The life of the region, according to Mackinder, was based on four main activities, 'the traffic from the continent, the defence of the continental angle, the cultivation of the land and the pleasuring of London'. It was in the front line of invasion, whether peaceful or bloody, whether of people or ideas. On its shoreline are some of the most significant landing places in the island history, like Sandwich Bay, where Roman, Saxon and Christian missionary each in turn found their first landfall. William the Conqueror landed at Pevensey before marching to the most famous battle in English history. The walls of the Norman castle there are contained within a Roman fort and are reinforced by gun emplacements built during the 1939–45 war; a two-thousand year span of island defence. The lone Spitfire at Biggin Hill aerodrome is part of the same martial theme as the Roman fort and the beacon fires that have given the landscape one of its chief characteristics, the defence of the highway to London. More friendly invaders seeking landfall after long journeys are the migrating birds which bring delight to the naturalists, especially at Dungeness and Beachy Head, Sandwich Bay and Selsey.

The history of the human landscape goes back literally to the beginning of settlement in the British Isles. The remains of Swanscombe man, more than a quarter of a million years old, were identified in gravels being excavated near Dartford. Since then no region of Britain has been so transformed by human activity and yet every step in the sequence from Stone Age to the pleasuring of London can be identified in the present landscape. Stone Age cave, Bronze Age burial mound, Iron Age camp, Roman villa, Saxon church and parish, all stand tribute to the peoples who came to the forested land and fashioned it for their own purpose. To a large extent, the story of the human landscape has been the defeat of the forest. Nature survives only on man's terms. The clearance of the forest reached its climax in the medieval period, which can be recalled, not just by abundant castles, churches and cathedrals but by the survival of hundreds of timber-framed buildings, the finest of any region, some dating back to the thirteenth century. In that same period was fashioned the pattern of village, farm and field that we inhabit today. Later centuries have modified it but not changed it fundamentally. The south-east is a living museum of the medieval world.

Having spent many years in the north of Britain, my return to my home territory was a journey of rediscovery. I have spent recent years exploring the region on foot, following neolithic ridgeways, Roman roads, pilgrims' ways, field paths and nature trails, assembling facts and impressions and a harvest of pleasure. If I can add to the pleasure of others who live, work or travel in the region, I shall be content. Inevitably, the evolution of a complex, humanized landscape told in such brief compass must reflect my own interests and prejudices. I mourn the necessities of omission as much as the readers will. But I hope the essential strokes of the canvas have been painted truly. The smaller brush strokes can be the reader's pleasure, in pursuing some of the references compiled in the bibliography, or, better still, in walking the pathways of discovery for themselves. No region has been more intensely studied, more written about, yet there is always something fresh to find. The landscape, like the seasons, is perpetually changing.

Despite the growth of London, the pressures of urban growth, there is a rich survival of open spaces. Surrey has a greater proportion of commons and heathlands than any other county outside the highland zone. Sussex is the most heavily wooded county in England, and Kent is the most fruitful area in the garden of England. At the very heart, near the junction of the three counties, is Ashdown Forest, an unenclosed common of heathland and woodland, an aboriginal memory, a memorial to the primeval state. The rocks underlying Ashdown are amongst the oldest in the region and there the landscape story begins.

I

In the Steps of the Iguanodon

After a wet and stormy season, the cliffs at Fairlight show their wounds. The clay becomes so saturated with water that it oozes down the cliff face like tooth-paste. Cracks appear on the paths along the cliff top and surface water pours into them, increasing the instability of the rock face. Heavy and lubricated with water, the rocks slide and slump and fall to the sea's edge. The waves smash them and the drift along the shore carries much of the material away to the east. The cliffs are retreating as they have done ever since the sea's incursion first made Britain an island about 8,000 years ago.

As the soft clays are eroded, so the layers of sandstone are undercut and tumble down in blocks, adding to the variety of boulders and pebbles to be gathered there. The cliffs rest on a solid platform of sandstone that is streaked with black seams that look like coal, so much so that bore-holes were once drilled near Bexhill in a fruitless search for coal. The black streaks are thin layers of lignite that may have been formed by logs of wood or other vegetable matter that once floated in the shallow waters of a great Wealden lake in which sands and muds were being deposited. The interpretation appeals to the imagination just as much as the words written on the present geological map of the area such as 'submerged forest' and 'footprints of the iguanodon' shown just offshore. Geology is another name for the poetry of rocks.

Not all the stones on the Fairlight shore are derived from the cliff above. There are flints from Beachy Head. There are flat stones full of fossil snails, called the winkle stone or Sussex marble. There are exotic stones from further west dragged by the constant ebb and flow of the Channel tides. But Fairlight, one of the few areas of the south-east coast not obliterated by housing, has other

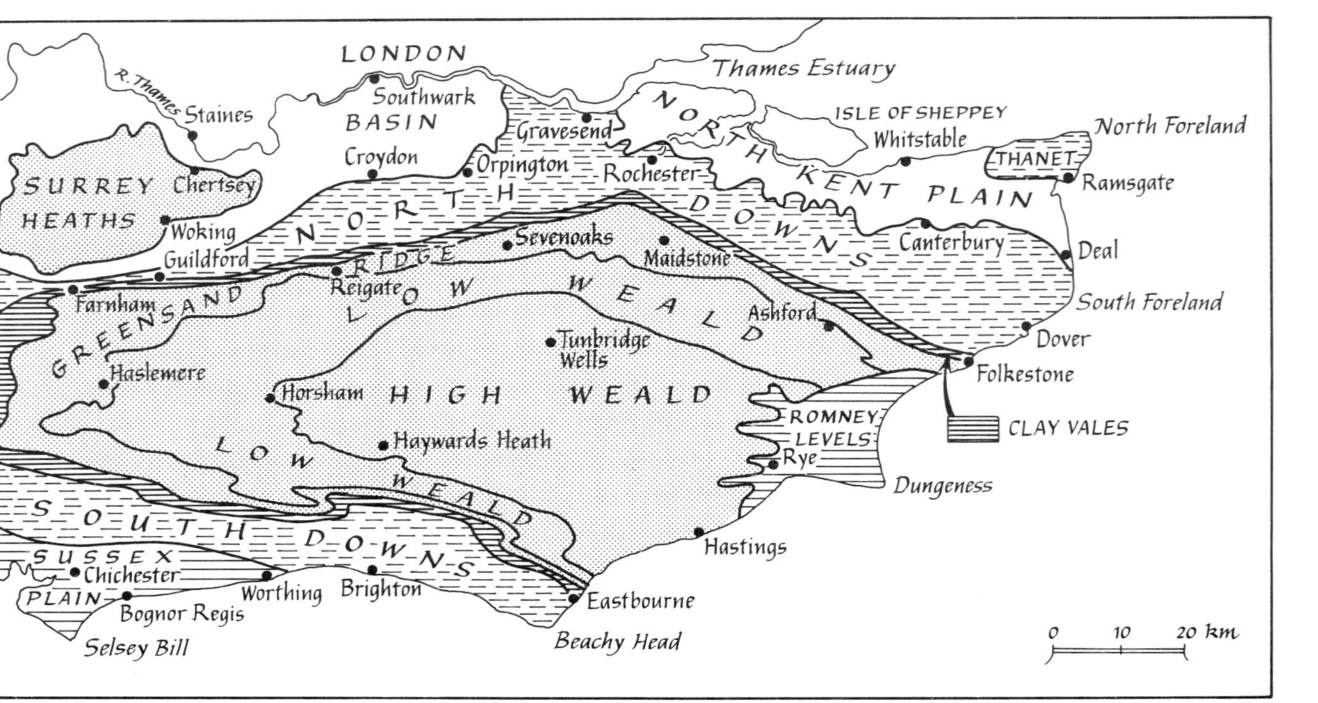

2. *Topographical areas.*

claims to fame than its unusual collection of rock specimens. There is no better place to begin the long and complicated story of the evolution of landscape in the south-east. For the Fairlight clays, formed about 100 million years ago, are the oldest rocks to make an effective contribution to the scenery. They mark the beginning of the Cretaceous system of rocks, the time of the iguanodon and the brontosaurus. Nearly all the surface of the south-east peninsula is composed of rocks younger than the Fairlight clays. It is a young region in the great time perspective of Britain's geological history.

There is one small area near Heathfield in East Sussex where older rocks from the Jurassic period appear on the surface but although they are responsible for the mining gear that extracts much of the country's gypsum supply, they make little impact on the topography. The even older coal-bearing strata of East Kent were discovered by bore-holes in 1890 and created the Kent coalfield. They are part of the platform of palaeozoic rocks that underlie the south-east. In London, they lie at a depth of about 300 metres. They tilt to the south until, at Henfield in Sussex, they are at a depth of nearly 1,500 metres.

The Fairlight clays are the lowest of the various strata that are known collectively as the Hastings Beds, which vary enormously from soft clays to tough sandstones like those that hold Hastings in a rocky grasp. They are named after the areas of their characteristic occurrence, the Ashdown Sands, the Tunbridge Wells Sands, the Wadhurst Clay. As they stretch from Fairlight westwards beyond Ashdown to Horsham, they form the High Weald, the heart and core of the entire region, containing some of its most spectacular landforms. North and south of this core, the later, younger rocks occur in basically the same sequence, with the youngest rocks at the extremities. This essential symmetry is the most extraordinary feature of the landscape. Whichever way you walk from Fairlight, the sequence is similar. To the east lie the marshes of Romney and Walland. To the west, the Pevensey levels. Beyond them are thin outcrops of greensand and gault clay flanked, in turn, by the cliffs and escarpments of the chalk country. Dover's white cliffs and South Foreland are mirror images of Beachy Head and the Seven Sisters. The North Downs match the South Downs. Even the low plateaux and marshes of the Thames estuary find their counterpart in the Sussex plain and the creeks of Bosham and Selsey.

An explanation of this symmetrical pattern of rocks was first put forward as long ago as 1806 by John Farey, who suggested that the rock strata of the south-east had been folded up into a great dome, that the top of the dome had been eroded away to reveal the oldest rocks in the middle and the youngest at the edges. The chalk of the South Downs and the North Downs were joined in a wide arc. The Hastings Beds lie in the heart of the dome. Farey's classically simple hypothesis is still accepted, still the basis of our understanding. The dome is known as the Wealden anticline.

The upheaval in the earth's crust that caused such an upfolding of the rocks was the same that created the Alpine ranges of Europe. South-east England was the outermost ripple of the earth storm that threw up the highest mountains on the continent. The movement began in the Tertiary period after most of the Wealden rocks, including the chalk, had been deposited. It did not create one simple fold. Several smaller ones have been identified, all running basically on an east–west axis in line with the major Wealden fold. These subsidiary ripples occur in Thanet, for example, along the Sussex plain from Chichester to Bognor, at Peasemarsh south of Guildford, at Henfield in Sussex. They cause minor but significant variations in the basic rock sequence.

The earth still adjusts. In 1962 an earth tremor shook houses from Guildford to Chichester and the Isle of Wight, a periodic event. Every uplift of the earth stimulates its counterpart, the process of erosion by running water, by wind and deep frosts, so that the Wealden dome has been reduced to its present comparatively low relief. That is not to say that the south-east is a plain. Far from it. The variety of its rocks has produced a similar variety of scenery and some of the steepest slopes in the country, though the summits of the hills are all below 300 metres. The rocks have done more than create a varied landscape. They have evoked a varied response from man, the settler, who has used them both directly in building and industry and indirectly in agriculture and forestry, giving the region as complex a human landscape as its physical structure.

Each rock layer not only contributes something to the present landscape, it holds the secret of past landscapes. A doctor from Lewes, Gideon Mantell, unravelled the origins of the Wealden rocks in the 1830s. To read his *Geology of the South-East of England* is to share the patient investigation and imaginative response of the earth scientists, the excitement of the pioneer discoveries – the bones of the iguanodon in Tilgate Forest, the elephant beds in the Black Rocks of Brighton. Many local museums have fossilized iguanodon footprints. They can be seen, together with the ripples in the sand, in a quarry in the grounds of Scotney Castle (K). Some relics occur in unusual places, such as the iguanodon bones in the church at Stone-in-Oxney on the edge of Walland Marsh.

A much-used layer of sandstone found within the Wealden clays has been worked in the vicinity of Horsham, though all the quarries I have seen have been disused. The Horsham stone splits into thin slabs, like a slate, and makes admirable roofing and paving stone. It is seen especially in churches and churchyards as far afield as Westerham and the Sussex coast. The lack of new quarries makes it difficult for proud owners of local cottages to maintain them. Many use tiles for the unseen part of the roof and keep their Horsham stone for the front.

The winkle stone or Sussex marble that we picked up on Fairlight's shore comes from the same Wealden clay. It was formed by beds of freshwater snails trapped by silting in the Wealden lake. It was the subject of one of the first geological studies in the region in 1684 concerning 'some form'd stones found at Hunton in Kent'. For these remarkable snail fossils do not occur only in Sussex, around Petworth, but also in Kent, particularly near Bethersden. The Paludina marble was used by the Romans for causeways and fords. I once walked every footpath in the parish of Staplehurst, a medieval web centred on the church, and found nearly every one to be paved with the marble. It was used in local buildings and its capacity to take a high polish made it a favourite decorative stone for church monuments, fonts and altars. Fireplaces in the great houses such as Knole are carved from it. Even the Marble Room at Petworth, full of Italian and other exotic marbles, has a lower course of local Sussex marble. The extraction pits, characteristically small and rectangular, litter the area between Marden and Ashford in Kent though they are not so evident in Sussex. Some of the lovely church paths have proved difficult for modern footwear and have been despoiled by tarmac while others at Tenterden have been restored as a contribution to the European Architectural Heritage Year in 1975.

There are a few places, then, where you can pick up snails that slithered around the Wealden lake one hundred million years ago. There are rather fewer places where you can hear the jargon of modern climbers, of chimneys, abseils and traverses and see their ropes festooning the rocks. But the eroded blocks of Tunbridge Wells sandstone at High Rocks and Harrison's Rocks are a nursery for the sport. Children at Hastings enjoy their mountain adventures in similar rock formations quite as much as the visit to the castle above. The bedding planes within the sandstones show them to have been formed in a great delta. The weather attacks the joints in the massive rock creating the chasms the climbers like. But it also erodes the weaker layers within the sandstone undercutting the harder bands. The effect can be spectacular as in the Toadstone on Rusthall Common or Great-on-Little in the woods near West Hoathly. The isolated pinnacle called the Chiding Stone south of the National Trust village of Chiddingstone is a similar erosional feature.

The variation between tough, resistant sandstones and soft clays gives this inner Wealden area another of its features, an alternation of high ridges and valleys. The remarkable straightness of some of the valley troughs, such as the

3. *Natural sculpture on Rusthall Common, Tunbridge Wells.*

line of the Kent Water that divides Kent from Sussex is due in part to geological faults that also have a predominantly east–west alignment. The sandstone supplies much of the local building material but the clay is even more widely used in the form of bricks. Large brick-works are found as far apart as Pluckley (K) and Ewhurst (Sy). The total thickness of the deposits in the Wealden lake was about 900 metres, the clay being the thickest layer.

A submergence of the land led to the Wealden lake becoming a salt-water bay in which sands were deposited that we know as the greensand. This rock produces some of the most delightful landscapes in the region and some of the most attractive building stone. It varies from east to west and its main beds are named after the outcrops on the south-east coast at Hythe, Sandgate and Folkestone. The name 'greensand' is rather misleading in that much of the green patina that is seen is caused by algae. A green mineral called glauconite gives the rock its geological name but its colour varies usually from rich reds and browns to white. Its rich variation can be seen in the porch at Ightham church where the different textures and hardness attain special local names such as the Ightham stone and the Oldbury stone. In this same part of Kent, especially south of Maidstone, the Hythe Beds are quarried for the Kentish ragstone that has been in use since Roman times and contributed, for example, to London's walls.

In the extensive quarry at Bedham (Sx), layer after layer is exposed, from massive sandstones used for building to fine sand and sand quarries are found throughout the region. In Surrey, around Godalming, the Sandgate Beds supply the Bargate stone, a durable stratum used in early buildings. Some of the old Saxon and Norman fonts in the area are hewn out of single blocks. Seams of dark brown ironstone occur in many areas but notably in the Folkestone Beds where they are called carstone. It is seen at its best, looking like flaked chocolate, on the Devil's Jumps near Frensham, where its toughness protects the conical hills in contrast to the fine crumbling sands that mark the paths below it. It is used decoratively in church walls as at St Martha's-on-the-Hill near Guildford and makes lovely pathways such as that of Limpsfield church (Sy).

The greensand forms a high ridge along much of its outcrop and gives the highest point of Sussex at Blackdown (919 feet), higher than any part of the South Downs, and the highest point of Surrey at Leith Hill, 294 metres. These two high points both occur towards the western limit of the region where the greensand is buckled into a great arc that sweeps from north to south along the Hampshire border and shows most clearly the complex nature of the Wealden dome. The sandstone prominences of Woolbeding Common, Blackdown, Hascombe and Leith Hill form embayments that contain areas of older Wealden strata. The greensands are simpler in their course through Kent, forming the lower but still outstanding ridge that runs from Crockham Hill to Ightham with heights occasionally over 210 metres.

I came across another unusual deposit when dipping around one of the small streams near Lenham (K) when I found small nodules of pure lime being deposited in the slowly flowing water. In some places the nodules coalesced to form white sheets of stone. Very light, easy to cut, attractive to touch, this was the tufa that the Normans used for corner work in their churches and castles, as at Leeds and West Malling. The Romans used it, too, in the lighthouse at Dover. Another deposit also found at Leeds and still worked in large pits at Nutfield (Sy) is the fullers' earth, a soft absorbent clay worked for cleaning wool.

The Upper Greensand is less prominent in the region generally and hardly appears east of Sevenoaks. Only about fifteen metres thick, it does, however, form a low ridge fronting the South Downs in West Sussex, much favoured by village sites. Between the two greensands, held like a wet sandwich, is the gault clay, so sticky, so unstable that it is locally known as the 'blue slipper'. Rich in fossils, it began as a thick mud deposited on an ancient sea floor. Easily eroded by running water, it forms low ground and broad vales such as Holmesdale. It is an important source of brick and tile manufacture. The extraction pits around Sevenoaks, for example, are a haven for wild fowl, fishermen and water sports. It forms the tumbled cliffs in the Warren at Folkestone, where the chalk slips over the saturated gault, much to the anguish of railway engineers. Its outcrop at the foot of the South Downs is very narrow and produces no vale comparable with Holmesdale.

'Chalk is king,'* wrote Sean Jennett. The two white arms of chalk that embrace the whole region, form its basic skeleton and produce its most dramatic cliffs, have evoked similar sentiments from many writers. Their softness of outline, their deep coombes and easy valleys always strike me as the female element of the landscape. The chalk marks a dramatic change in the ancient conditions in which rocks were deposited. Nearly all of the British Isles and much of the continent was submerged beneath a deep sea. 'I like to think,' wrote Jacquetta Hawkes, 'of the seas where chalk was forming, clouded with white as though from a snow-storm – a fall that lasted for thirty million years and lay to a depth of a thousand feet.'† The 'snowstorm' trapped millions of marine creatures that became the fossils of the chalk, the sea-urchins and molluscs. It is the study of

* S. Jennett, *The Pilgrims' Way* (Cassell, 1971).

† J. Hawkes, *A Land* (Cresset Press, 1951).

4. *Leith Hill and the pine-dominated Greensand ridge seen from Holmbury Hill.*

5. *Aerial view along the Hog's Back looking towards Guildford. The modern road follows the ancient ridgeway. The large arable fields on the chalk slopes contrast with the Weald in the right background.*

such fossils and their evolution that enable geologists to work out the sequence and time-scale of geological history. The chalk is divided into three main sections, the Lower Chalk which forms the low platform below the Downs, the Middle Chalk that forms the steep faces of the escarpments and the Upper Chalk that covers the plateau tops. The latter is the thickest of the series and is the main source of flints. Between the three chalk series are harder layers of chalk rock, the lower known as the Melbourne Rock. The harder chalk bands, also known as clunch, are a source of building stone found especially in the villages of West Sussex between Harting and Cocking. Generally the chalk is too easily weathered, too soft to use for building, though it occurs on the interior walls of churches. A lovely Tudor fireplace at Loseley Hall near Guildford is carved out of one single block of hard chalk.

Being a remarkably pure limestone, nearly 95 per cent calcium carbonate, chalk has been worked as a source of lime and a basis of the modern cement industry. The scars of old and new workings abound especially where the chalk is close to waterways such as the broad gaps in the Sussex Downs, alongside the Adur and the Arun. Enormous pits along the Thames estuary produce a formidable and ever-growing landscape of industry and waste, a white desert. Daniel Defoe commented two hundred years ago that 'the barren soil of Kent makes the Essex lands rich and fruitful'. The man-made canyons have become deeper and wider ever since.

A soft rock, yet chalk produces a rim of high land, the highest hills in Kent and the most impressive cliffs. The paradox is partly explained by the earth movements that folded the chalk into a dome. The most intensive folding has tilted the chalk so much at the Hog's Back as to form a high but narrow ridge. Where the tilt is gentler, as in East Kent, the chalk forms a broad plateau more than twenty kilometres wide. But chalk has a characteristic common to limestones. It is permeable and absorbs water so that surface water drains through it. This has the effect of making the chalk more resistant to erosion. It also creates an underground reservoir of water of major importance to London and other urban areas.

The most memorable visual image of the chalk is in the sheer white slab of the cliffs below the Seven Sisters. The structure of the chalk adds to the impression of an immense wall. The strong jointing gives the sea one of its points of attack which is seen to perfection on the other extremity of the peninsula at the North Foreland and Botany Bay. Erosion along the joint lines creates caves, then breaks through isolated headlands to form arches and finally stacks. The shores of Thanet supply the whole sequence, a dizzy display for the promenaders at Cliftonville, especially when a north-easter is driving the waves down the long fetch of the North Sea. You can almost feel erosion taking place. The sheer whiteness of the cliffs makes the occasional thin black bands of flint even more prominent.

Flints are so fundamental to the early history of man, so common in the walls of buildings, so attractive in their varied texture and shape – river cobbles, knapped flints, field stones – that it is surprising that their mode of origin is still something of a mystery. Flint is a form of silica and, like the chalk itself, derived from materials in the bodies of the creatures that inhabited the chalk seas. It occurs in fissures or joints of the chalk forming tabular and nodular flints. It may have been formed after the deposition of the chalk by percolating water charged with carbon dioxide. Many a knapped flint will reveal a small fossil such as a sponge inside, indicating an accretion taking place round the original fossil.

A porous crust gives the dark flint its white skin and adds to its attraction. Durable but difficult to handle, it is used in a variety of ways. The cobbles from the shore and the rivers are used as they are, with plenty of mortar to fill

6. *Coastal scenery: erosion of chalk cliffs at Botany Bay, Thanet.*

the gaps. Nodules may be split in half or even knapped down to small squares as in Elizabethan chequerwork walls. Flint flakes are frequently used for galletting to strengthen the mortar between the irregular flints. Sussex, between the Downs and the shore, is the showcase for flintwork, though the walls of Shoreham Castle in the Darent Valley (K) take some beating. I was never more aware of flints than when walking over new plough on the Downs above Boxley

(K). The whole two-mile stretch was littered with close-packed flints just as if the earth's skeleton had been laid bare by the plough.

After the deposition of the chalk in warm seas, the whole region was uplifted and folded into a land surface, marking the end of the cretaceous period. Then followed a long period of subsidence. The chalk was overlain with sands and gravels and clays. The dinosaurs gave way to birds and the first mammals. The period of Tertiary rocks began with the dramatically named Eocene or dawn of recent times. This deposition is mostly on the margins of the region. First came the Thanet Sands quarried in South London for the old Charlton glass industry. Used for gun-moulding, they may have influenced the siting of the Woolwich Arsenal. Good water-bearing strata, the sands are full of springs as at Well Hill near Chelsfield. The famous exposure of the sands at Pegwell Bay in Thanet has been spoilt by continual slumping of the cliffs.

Above the Thanet Sands are broad spreads of flint pebbles, often in a sandy matrix but sometimes cemented together by lime forming a natural concrete, a conglomerate sometimes called puddingstone. These extensive beds are named after their occurrence at Woolwich and Reading and Blackheath. Oyster shells and other fossils show the shallow marine conditions in which they were deposited. The stiff London Clay, bane of gardeners, rich in plant remains, is found in much of the London basin and also in smaller patches in the Selsey peninsula in West Sussex. It forms low hills in the Blean north-west of Canterbury but it is best studied in the eroded cliffs of Sheppey (K). A source of brick-making, the clay also contains nodules of copper, as a sulphate of iron, which were collected on the Sheppey shore for smelting. There are low mounds called 'coterells' on there marshy flats of Sheppey and North Kent which have been variously interpreted as Viking graves or artificial dry-points for livestock during flooding. They are more likely to be remnants of an eroded surface of London Clay.

Later beds of sand, clay and pebbles were deposited on top of the London Clay, notably in North-West Surrey, the Claygate Beds, the Bagshot Beds, the Bracklesham and Barton Beds. They underlie the extensive heaths and commons that stretch from the Thames down to the Hampshire border. Fine sands for polishing, ironstone for industry and some unusual deposits looking like brown toffee appear in church walls such as Chobham. Similar rocks are found in churches along the Sussex coast where the Bracklesham Beds outcrop around Selsey. You can stand by the shore of West Wittering with a retreating tide and have the sea deliver up dozens of spiral shells of turritella freshly scraped from the not-so-solid rock, the easiest fossil-gathering I know.

There are small deposits of comparatively recent origin which suggest further fluctuations in the relative positions of land and sea. Gravel beds of sand and shattered flints occur on Headley Heath (Sy) at about 180 metres and on the North Downs near Lenham (K). Among these plateau gravels are fragments of ironstone. There are several ironstone boulders on the crest of the chalk above Wye at about the same height. How does ironstone occur so far from its place of origin? A possible solution is that the whole peninsula was submerged beneath the sea by at least 180 metres. This hypothetical sea incursion has been called the Pliocene Sea. Such a submergence would have had a modifying effect on the topography of the whole region. Imagine the south-east with only the high ridges of chalk and sandstone appearing as chains of islands above the water. The study of rocks and landforms is full of such dramatic possibilities. At 60 metres on Ambersham Common (Sx), for example, on the greensand, you are suddenly confronted with a small quarry face composed of clay, sand and shattered flints. Was this yet another level of marine invasion bringing flints from the chalk to the south? The long battle between the sea and the land is still continuing. So are the efforts to understand them. The south-east, perhaps the most researched region of Britain, still has many secrets of landscape to discover. The origin of the rocks and their occurrence is only half of the landscape story. The rest is the moulding of those rocks, their erosion by running water, of rivers carving valleys, adjusting to every subtle change of geological outcrop and to every convulsion of the earth. Today's scenery marks a moment's balance between the twin forces of creation and destruction.

At first sight, the rivers of the south-east conform to the symmetry of the geological structure. They rise in the heart of the Weald and flow north and south to the Thames and the Channel respectively. The Mole and the Ouse rise in the vicinity of Worth Forest, the former flowing north through the Downs to Molesey on the Thames while the Ouse flows south through the South Downs to Newhaven. So do the Wey and the Arun but the divide between them, the watershed, is not the Wealden core but the high ridge of greensand at Blackdown. Some river courses run east and west rather than north and south. The Medway and its upper tributaries, the Eden and Kent Water, have a predominantly easterly flow. So, too, the Kentish Rother running from its source near Rotherfield to the marshes at Rye. The Sussex Rother rises in Hampshire and flows east to its junction with the Arun at Pulborough. The river pattern, then, is not a simple one but more like a trellis. The rivers seek out the weaker rock outcrops and exploit them. They erode laterally along the clay vales taking the easiest course. Yet nearly all the rivers at some time in their career to the sea flow from comparatively low ground in the inner Weald and break right through the barriers of the chalk downs, creating the gaps which give us our major routeways.

Running water would be expected to pond up against such inland cliffs rather than break through them, but perhaps the present river pattern is a memory of the ancient dome of the Weald. The rivers were initiated by water flowing off the central dome as it was upfolded. The gaps through the North and South Downs mark the earliest stages of the drainage when the rivers were flowing from a greater height and making valleys in the chalk in the usual way. As the central dome was eroded, the rivers adjusted to the different rock strata that were revealed beneath the chalk, wearing away the softer beds such as the clays quicker than the more resistant sandstones. As the land rose, so the rivers cut down deeper. As the land fell, so they slowed down and filled up their own outlets with the material they were carrying. The rivers are in competition. They steal each other's tributaries. The River Wey, for example, has 'captured' the upper tributaries of the Blackwater. The Arun has extended its catchment right across the main axis of the Weald to the foot of Leith Hill, in the process taking water supply from its neighbour, the Adur. In later adjustments to a rise in land levels or a fall in sea level, the rivers have cut through their own deposits, creating river terraces. Most striking are the terraces of the Thames which have had such a decisive influence on the siting and growth of London as well as many other riverside settlements. The level terraces, with their light, well-drained soils, were an attraction to early settlers.

On John Speed's map of Surrey drawn in 1610, he leaves part of the River Mole blank and inserts the words 'the river runeth under'. The Mole goes underground. Whenever a river flows over limestone, in this case chalk, it loses some or all of its water into the porous rock. If the rock is saturated or frozen or covered with other deposits, the river may flow on the surface but when the water is in direct contact with the chalk it forms solution hollows and more and more water finds its way into underground aquifers. More than twenty swallow holes have been found along the Mole. More than 150 such holes have been identified in the chalk of Thanet. Dry valleys, therefore, are another characteristic of chalk country. That rivers once occupied them is proved by deposits of alluvium as in the East Dean Valley north of Chichester. For much of the year, indeed, for many years, the Nailbourne between Canterbury and Dover is a dry rubble of flints bleached like the discarded skin of a snake. Yet that same stream can rise in spate and flood along its course. It flowed vigorously after the wet winter of 1974/5. So did the Lavant above Chichester. These bourne streams give rise to many legends foretelling disaster. When they flow, disaster follows. The Wandle above Croydon is another example. Heavy, persistent rain saturates the chalk, the water-table rises until it reaches the surface and the bourne streams flow.

Many dry valleys are associated with high-level gaps in the chalk downs such as the Cocking Gap. With the erosion of the chalk dome and the retreat of the chalk escarpments as they are weathered back, the water level within the chalk is lowered and, once more, ancient river valleys become dry.

Adding variety and interest to the chalk escarpments are the deep, basin-shaped hollows called coombes. The most spectacular have been associated with the Devil. He has all the best landscapes as well as the best tunes. The Devil's Kneadingtrough above Wye is the finest of all. The Devil's Dyke near Brighton is another. The Devil's Punchbowl near Hindhead is formed by a different set of geological circumstances. The Hythe beds of sandstone are undermined by springs at the junction with the Atherfield Clay which is exposed on the floor of the bowl. A small anticline to the north shuts the valley off, making an isolated basin. In part, the coombes owe their origin to similar processes as the dry valleys but their very steep profiles and general shape are reminiscent of the corries in the northern mountains that were formed during the Ice Age. The south-east may not have been covered with ice but it would have suffered severe tundra conditions with heavy snow accumulations and deep frosts. There are many deposits, especially at the foot of the coombes, which show the effect of alternating freeze and thaw and the downward movement of the soil accumulating as chalk head or coombe rock. The thick deposits of clay-with-flints on the North Downs have never been satisfactorily explained. They may be the result of decomposition of the chalk but they are 'more likely to have been assembled under sub-glacial conditions, as a mélange of local materials disturbed and partly re-sorted by local ice-caps or snowfields'.*

Resting on the shore near West Wittering on the Selsey peninsula are several massive boulders. They are made of granites, gneiss, basalt and other rocks not found anywhere in the neighbourhood. There is another collection of such 'erratics' at Hotham Park in Bognor. Others have been dredged up by fishermen in the Channel. The only agency capable of carrying such boulders from their point of origin, such as Brittany and the Channel Islands, is ice. Sussex geologists such as E. A. Martin writing earlier in this century thought of ice, perhaps

* F. H. Edmunds, *The Wealden District, British Regional Geology* (HMSO, 1954).

7. *The Devil's Kneadingtrough, a coombe in the escarpment of the North Downs near Wye, looking south across the Low Weald.*

icebergs drifting up-channel along the ice front. But smaller rocks of 'foreign' origin have been found amongst the clay-with-flints and in 'pipes' in the chalk, frost-hollows filled with later material. These are some of the many features that suggest that the full impact of the Ice Age upon the south-east region has not yet been appreciated. Throughout the region, for example, are hundreds of large boulders of crystalline sandstone known as 'sarsens', a name derived from Saracens or 'sour stones'. Known also as greywethers from their similarity to recumbant sheep, more than a hundred are grouped round the pond in Stanmer Park in Brighton. Dozens occur along the North Downs from Belmont to Meopham. There are several in Surrey, at Virginia Water and in Godstone churchyard for example, but the most famous is the Saxon coronation stone at Kingston-upon-Thames. They supplied the megaliths of pre-history. They are believed to have been remnants of a Tertiary rock strata that once covered the area but nearly all of them are smoothed and pitted and even scratched just like glacial erratics.

The variations of sea-level during and after the ice advance, the land depressed by the weight of ice and then rising with the release of its burden, are still proceeding. The formation of river-terraces was especially active at this time, the rivers being subject to great changes of régime. The raised beaches along the coast are due to this recovery of the land. The 30-metre beach is clear north of Chichester on the edge of the Goodwood estate at Waterbeach, a site which the farmer tells me has a copious supply of spring water. A lower bench at about 5 metres has been identified around Worthing. These benches and terraces are littered with the evidence of early man and the animals he hunted. Some of the best evidence used, for example, by Gideon Mantell, has been lost by soil slump and interference by man as at Black Rock.

There is yet another unseen piece of this post-glacial jig-saw. Stand by the famous meanders of the Cuckmere gap and try to imagine the valley as a deep water inlet stretching far inland like those of south-west England. Bore-holes have shown as much as 25 metres of recent river-deposits filling in older river beds under the present river mouths. The last major sea incursion, called the Flandrian transgression, took place when early man inhabited the region. The river mouths were submerged, the coastal forests drowned and the tides reached the inner Weald. The rising sea finally breached the land-bridge that linked Britain with the continent about 8,600 years ago. The island history began.

The physical gulf is ever widening. The London Clay cliffs of Herne Bay are retreating at an average of more than one metre a year while the chalks of Thanet and the Seven Sisters are being worn away at only a slightly lower rate.

Coastal erosion has been swift enough even in historic times to remove settlements along the Sussex shore between Brighton and Selsey. The land that is lost on the headlands is compensated for by the new areas of created land, the new deposition of Dungeness and the marshes. The physical changes in what Kentish people like to call 'the sixth continent' show the persistence and subtlety of such processes, how they affect and are affected by the works of man. Twelve thousand years ago, before the formation of the Channel, the Romney area was about twenty metres above the present level. Depression of the area took place in Neolithic times. Creeks reached far inland. Later uplift of the land is shown by deposits of trees in a thick peaty layer. Further depression was followed by yet another uplift still taking place when the Romans were occupying the region. Their ports, like Lympne, were on a distinctive shoreline cut in the older Wealden rocks. The shingle spit of Dungeness anchored to Fairlight was beginning to grow towards the east causing an accumulation of silt between the ness and the shore. Marshland developed on the shallow silty deposits, shallow enough for reclamation to begin. The Rhee wall was built.

Despite the storms and floods that culminated in the loss of Winchelsea in the thirteenth century, the growth of the shingle spit and the reclamation of the Romney, Walland and Guldeford levels has been continuous. The River Rother changed its outlet several times, moving from the western extremity of the marsh near Hythe to the present artificial cut near Rye. The growth outwards of the shingle ridges is shown by the site of Henry VIII's castle at Camber, now well inland. In recent years a succession of lifeboat sheds on the ness itself has tried to keep pace with the seaward accumulation of shingle. The silting up of these marshes, as with those of Pevensey and the Wantsum by Thanet, is due partly to the natural changes in sea level and partly to the erection of containing walls by man. As with the construction of sea defences, groynes and breakwaters, man tries to stem the natural processes of erosion and becomes an agent of landscape change. This is most apparent in one of the 'youngest' landscapes in the region, the East Head spit near West Wittering, a rare dune area now controlled by the National Trust. The changes in the spit have been recorded since 1786. In 1963, storms breached the spit and the dunes were almost destroyed. New dunes have been created by bulldozers. Wooden barriers have been built to stem the violence of the wind, new grasses have been planted to stabilize the sand and public access is limited so that this rare and almost entirely re-created landscape can survive. The imprint of gull's feet in the fresh blown sand of East Head is the most recent statement of the geological story that began 100 million years ago in the footsteps of the iguanodon.

2

The Kingdom of the Oak

John Evelyn, ardent tree-planter and inspirer of many sylvan landscapes in the south-east, put the oak first amongst trees. He spoke approvingly of the idea of an Order of the Royal Oak with, naturally, a green ribbon for decoration. The oak, he wrote, 'so often saved and protected the whole nation from invasion and brought it so much wealth from foreign countries'. The wooden walls of England were fashioned from the oak forests of the south-east peninsula. Two thousand prime oaks were needed for one first-rate ship of the line. Despite his penchant for formality in parks and gardens, Evelyn approved the broad-spreading common oak which supplied timbers for ships and houses. Source of fuel, of food for livestock, home of more organisms such as galls, grubs and fungi than any other tree, the oak is the symbol of the region.

Some of the great oaks remain. Those that Samuel Palmer drew in such loving detail when he was living at Shoreham still survive in Lullingstone Park where the deer roamed until the last decade. Gnarled and broken with age and the ravages of lightning and man, the immense trunks dominate the chalk slopes. Another stunted survivor is the Elizabeth oak in Greenwich Park, already large enough in the sixteenth century to shelter the future queen in its trunk whilst, according to legend, Henry and Anne Bullen danced around it. Pope's oak in West Grinstead Park, where he composed 'The Rape of the Lock', the Bear Oak at Penshurst, Ratner's oak at Rolvenden and the enormous tree that stands by the entrance to Headcorn churchyard are all objects of veneration. The County Oak at Ifield near Crawley was cut down 'to the regret of all classes' in 1844 but its timbers supplied the vestry screen in the local church.

My favourite oak story is that associated with the Domesday Oak in Godinton

Park (K), now a heap of timber to the north of the house. After standing for a thousand years, the great tree groaned and split asunder just as war was declared on 3 September 1939. Half of it broke away, the rest falling later that evening.

The oak was one of the early colonisers with the retreat of the ice sheet. As the weather warmed, so the greenery reestablished itself from the south. With pine, birch, hazel, elm and alder, the tundra gave way to forest. After the variations of climate, the sub-arctic, the boreal, the Atlantic and the sub-boreal

8. *Coppice woodlander in the Weald near Capel.*

phases, the oak became firmly established and finally flourished as the dominant tree. Sussex naturalists estimate that it once covered nearly three-quarters of that county. It adapted itself to chalk downland, to dry sandy soils, to heavy clays and it can still be seen in all these varied habitats. On the heavy clays, the common oak, *Quercus robur*; on the drier soils, the sessile oak; between them, many hybrid species exist. Even on the piney heaths of Surrey, Blackdown, for example, oak dominates the older woodland areas. Oak woodland represents the climax vegetation in the region. Even without the evidence of pollen analysis from peat bogs and lake deposits, its extent can be judged by the place names that are related to it, from Acrise in East Kent, to Ockley in Surrey and Oakhurst in the Selsey Peninsula.

The clearance of the oak forest began long before the Saxons settled and named their villages. Pure stands of oak are comparatively rare, yet, according to forestry statistics, it is the dominant tree in all three counties. In Surrey, the Scots pine comes a close second, in Sussex and Kent, the beech. In spite of urban growth and farming, the south-eastern counties are amongst the most wooded in Britain. Their forest cover is above the national average and Sussex is the most heavily wooded county in England, with estimates up to 22 per cent. From most of the famous vantage points such as Leith Hill, Crundale or Chanctonbury, the impression is of a woodland landscape, an illusion assisted by the amount of hedgerow timber which accounts for about a third of the region's total supply.

Much of the remaining oak woodland is in the form of standard-with-coppice, oak trees forming the upper storey, the lower storey being trees that have been cut down to the stock in order to produce abundant poles. This is a type of woodland management that is probably as old as monastic settlement, as in the Abbey Woods above Lessness Abbey (K). Coppicing, from the French *couper*, to cut, is especially associated with the south-east. Chestnut and hazel were the main trees, although hornbeam, birch and oak itself were used in a similar way. This gave a regular supply of poles and fencing and fuel. The annual auction of cants or corners of coppiced woodland is still carried out, usually in November, and the successful bidders have to cut the coppice and clear it up by the following April. This is traditionally carried out on a seventeen-year cycle in order to get thicker, taller poles for the hop-gardens, though some is cut earlier for paling. Coppiced timber supplies charcoal for industrial use and many a Kentish woodman remembers supplying charcoal for gas-masks in the 1939 war.

Oak is not favoured by modern commercial growers due to its slow growth and tendency to spread, though the oaks planted by William Robinson, the famous cottage gardener, at Gravetye (Sx) are straight enough. What remains of the oak forest is valuable to naturalists and needs protection. One area that approaches the aboriginal condition lies below the greensand scarp near Wisborough Green (Sx). A large part of its 150 hectares has been bought by the Sussex Trust for Nature Conservation. Faced with the encroachment of quarrying, the Trust seeks to buy the rest to save the largest woodland reserve of its kind in the country. Called the Mens, probably after the word 'gemeine' meaning 'common', the area is known to have been wooded since the sixteenth century and probably even earlier when it was recorded as swine pasture and a source of fuel for the early glass and iron industries. It is not a picnickers paradise, fortunately, even though there are public paths across it. The underwood is tangled and dense. The micro-climate is humid and it is this very humidity that suits the rarer fungi and lichens found there. It is the home of the Purple Emperor and the rare White Admiral butterfly, symbol of the Sussex Trust,

9. *Old oak woodland: the Mens nature reserve.*

flying high and strongly with its characteristic white markings on its dark upper wings. It feeds on flowers of bramble but the vital flora in its life-cycle is the honey-suckle which abounds in the undergrowth. The Mens has all the features of an old deciduous woodland with trees of many types and many ages. Under the oak and beech is a shrub-layer of holly, yew, hawthorn and crab-apple. Occasional birch and chestnut and rowan appear and much dead wood ideal for insects, woodpeckers and fungi.

Another patch of Sussex oak woodland is Nap Wood near Tunbridge Wells, with a similar ecological pattern on the deeper clays with holly, yew and wild cherry forming the understorey. On the higher, sandier ground, oak coppice is mixed with birch, rowan, pine and beech. The oak has been coppiced in the past for tannin and there is some evidence of coppicing amongst the alders that thrive on the iron-rich waters of the poorest drained land. Many plants here, such as the hay-scented fern, are regarded by botanists as relic species from the Atlantic period of climate about 6,000 years ago, so the tree canopy must be maintained to give them the habitat they need to survive.

A small area of woodland lies behind Woods Mill, the headquarters of the Sussex Naturalists' Trust, on wet claylands near Henfield. Though small in extent, it is illuminated by a most imaginative and instructive nature trail, a model of its kind.

At the Ham Street woods, another National Nature Reserve in Kent on the edge of the Romney Marsh, there is an area of coppice-with-standards that is being managed so as to cause a reversion to high forest, again of the damp oak woodland type. The other trees here include the aspen, the gean and the wild service tree adding unusual variety to the hornbeam, chestnut, hazel, ash and birch. From one point of view it is encouraging to read that in a new Forestry Commission plantation, at Dene Park near Shipbourne (K), the conifers are not thriving on the heavy Wealden clay and the slower-growing oak and beech are proving their worth. The Commission often plants the deciduous trees amongst the faster-growing conifers avowedly for their amenity and ecological value but the forest cover that they produce after cropping the conifers has a high economic value in the long run.

A tree that grows well on limey soils is the elegant and much-neglected ash. I doubt if there is a lovelier image of the final emergence of the new growing season than the breaking of the ash bud. It can be seen to perfection in the chalklands of Kent and West Sussex. Cobham Great Wood and Chilham Park in Kent have reputedly the tallest specimens in the country, and there is a most graceful avenue of them in the park at Doddington. The hornbeam, toughest of timbers, strong enough to provide the yoke for Sussex oxen, is widespread and especially popular in the old deer parks enclosed from the wild after the Norman conquest. It is frequently pollarded, cut not as in coppicing at the base but higher up the main trunk, to give extra growth of smaller branches. I have often seen deer eating the foliage, and the best examples I know are in Hatch Park at Mersham (K).

There are several places, on steep and inaccessible slopes, where woodland seems to have been untouched by management or livestock grazing. In White Horse Wood on the face of a chalk coombe there is a wilderness of hazel, oak, whitebeam, maple, hawthorn, yew, birch, wild service, all of low growth, all twisted and interlocked with an abandon of bramble, white bryony and elderberry. In winter, it is the spindlewood that is made conspicuous by its orange capsules. In September, the whitebeam rich with berries on a carpet of white leaves steals the scene. Always the yew, with its dark brooding, teases the imagination. But the greatest tree there is the beech, intolerant of all competitors, making an open clearing beneath its canopy. Queen of the forest, the beech was only second in importance to the oak in the ancient Wealden forest, its mast being nearly as important as the acorn to the roving herdsmen and the wildlife. Although it is regarded primarily as the tree of the chalklands, some of the best stands are found on the greensand ridge near Crockham Hill on the Kent–Surrey border. Finest of all, as acceptable to the forester as to the artist by nature of their tall, straight growth, are the beeches of Goodwood and Slindon (Sx) on the dip slope of the South Downs. Young beech dominate the Commission plantations at Friston, covering the catchment area for Eastbourne's water supply. There are reports of a virulent disease, not unlike Dutch elm disease, causing premature yellowing of the leaves, that is affecting beech trees, especially of the age of Friston's forty-year-olds.

In parts of the downland that I have watched for some years, young beech have started to emerge from the hawthorn and dogwood scrub that encroaches on neglected grassland. Given time, the beech will outshade the other vegetation and initiate a reversion to open woodland. Beech for furniture, hornbeam for yokes, the spindle for mill spindles, apple wood for machinery, chestnut for beams and poles, elms for water conduits; each tree had its special use now largely lost in an industrial age. But many have made a comeback in the revival of local craft industries and none more than the yew, prized for its decorative value. I have even seen beakers and plates made from the heartwood of yew. Together with the holly and the juniper, the yew is one of our few native evergreens. So prevalent is it along the chalk downs and the line of old routeways that some early topographers have linked it with neolithic trading routes, but its more famous association is with churchyards. Symbol of eternity, its branches were used for processions on Palm Sunday to replace the palm that is similarly planted near churches in the Eastern Mediterranean lands. In the three counties there are more than one hundred churchyard yews of immense girth and antiquity. Tandridge (Sy) lays claim to be the greatest of all with an umbrage of more than twenty-five metres. It shadows the entire south wall of the church and is trained by a series of props to form a canopy over the path to the porch. Stand by that enormous flaking trunk and you will have a sense of antiquity unmatched in the region. The church records indicate that the tree antedates the original Saxon church but most yews date from the Norman period. Tandridge has a friendly rivalry with neighbouring Crowhurst which has a yew with a ten-metre girth which puts it amongst the giants. Yews were often planted in pairs and two stand at Cudham, in line between the lych-gate and the porch. Local opinion suggests that they mark stages in the progress of the coffin from gate to porch, a sort of limbo. The parson should meet the coffin at the first yew. These yews have been concreted to preserve them, while others are bound by chains, but one of the Cudham yews was damaged by heavy snow accumulation in a late April storm.

10. *Churchyard Yew, Tandridge.*

In some parishes, the sale of yew wood was one of the parson's perks. Ideas associated with the tree are diverse, that they were linked with compulsory archery practice, a source of bows, that they formed a barrier against livestock, being poisonous. Some historians aver that they marked a pre-Christian enclosure. At Eastling (K), for example, they form a complete circle. This area of East Kent has some of the finest yew landscapes of all, even a local hostelry being named after the tree. The topiary work at Sharsted Court and Doddington is supreme in its achievement. The Romans avoided the yew, with its dark implications, preferring the box tree for their formal topiary, but the yew came back into favour in medieval times and especially in the Tudor period of formal gardening. There are over one thousand clipped yews in the maze at Hever.

The yew in its woodland setting finds its most perfect expression in Kingley Vale, a deep chalk valley in West Sussex, facing the Channel. The finest example in Europe, it is protected as a National Nature reserve. Access is easy but mercifully, unlike many of the Sussex beauty spots, the car parks have been kept at a distance. The scrubland invades, as in so many downland areas, and gives cover to numerous birds, to deer and other fauna. Orchids and other chalk flora abound but in the deeper soils of the valley bottom a grove of yew trees, estimated to be at least five hundred years old, shuts out all other flora. Outside, the sun may shine and the birds sing but within the grove is a cathedral calm, a dead silence exaggerated by the deep carpet of needles and the branches hanging down to form a complete screen. In places, the branches have taken root and young plants grow around the halo of the parent trees. Ten minutes in there and stories of witchcraft are no longer fanciful. It seems only right that up on the ridge of Bow Hill are prehistoric burial mounds, some of the best preserved in the region. A wild day in Kingley Vale is an unforgettable experience. I hoard many memories of the place, not least the sight of twelve kestrels, all in line, hovering on the rim of the valley. A lengthy nature trail threads through all of the varied pleasures of this unique reserve.

After the oak and the beech, the most common tree in the region is the Scots pine. It was one of the first colonizers as the ice-sheets waned and it is most prolific on the drier sandier soils of the sandstone hills and the pebble beds that give rise to heathlands. As such heaths and commons cover more than 10,000 hectares in Surrey alone, it is small wonder that the Scots pine cone was adopted as the symbol of the Surrey Naturalists' Trust. The Scots pine, *Pinus sylvestris,* has a rapid growth rate, as much as one hundred feet in seventy years in favourable conditions. Foresters like it for its rapid economic return. It seeds easily and, like the birch, colonizes empty spaces quickly, in disused quarries, for example, or on commons where grazing rights have ceased to be exercised. Yet few of the pine forests of the south are aboriginal. Such forests exist only in the Scottish Highlands and they are rare even there. Much Scots pine was planted at a time when Scottish landscapes were the vogue, such as the second half of the nineteenth century. Queen Victoria was at Balmoral. Pictures of red deer as monarchs of pine-studded glens stood on many a parlour wall. Estate agents capitalized on the fashion and advertised new houses in the Weald as Scotland-in-Sussex and south-west Surrey took on its present appearance as an outlier of the wild north country, without the climate. The wild deer were present, too, but mostly roe and fallow.

Even the Scots pine clumps on Ashdown Forest were planted by the lord of the manor in the 1870s. Local people, used to the heath and bracken and sparse oak and beech, viewed 'those ugly clumps' with disfavour. Some of the best specimens from Ashdown were carted off to Hever in the early years of this century to be replanted in the grounds of the newly restored castle. An earlier period of pine popularity was the restoration of the Stuarts. General Monk brought the guards from Coldstream and pines which were planted as an avenue at Greenwich linking the upper park with the Queen's House. They were felled in the last century. I have heard Sussex people call the pine the Charlie tree, but which Charlie this refers to, the Bonnie Prince or the restored monarch, I am not sure.

Scots pine, birch, heather and bracken are the familiar ingredients of almost every viewpoint from Leith Hill down to Woolbeding Common. Generally less varied in flora than the chalk country, the heaths nevertheless have a sense of openness and wild that can be very rewarding. There are minor surprises such as squirrels scattering the débris of young green cones beneath pine trees in mid-summer. They prefer the base of the cone and will nibble at dozens before finding one succulent enough to eat to the core. Blackdown, where Tennyson spent the last years of his life, owned by the National Trust since 1944, is as good an area as any to study the sandstone flora. All the young pines are from naturally sown seed. The three main types of heather make August a time of almost Highland splendour, cross-leaved heath, bell heather and the Scotch heather all in flower. Bilberry and blackberry fill the spaces, with gorse along the paths. On the steeper slopes to the east, the older deciduous woods are in evidence with oak, whitebeam and rowan. There are some remarkable hybrids of whitebeam and rowan, one of the unusual features of the excellent nature trail laid out on the hill. Feral deer are frequently seen. There is so much woodland cover around that they can travel long distances in comparative safety. From Blackdown, villages like Lurgashall (which once had common rights on Blackdown) and Fernhurst appear to be what they originally were, mere clearances hemmed in by forest. On the summit, the tracks are sandy, sometimes cutting into solid rock, but the older stock tracks leading down to lower ground cut deeply down into man-made canyons, torrents in the wet season.

Although speculative housing has invaded and occupied parts of the common land of Witley, Hindhead, Weydown and Greyswood, large areas of the greensand ridge in Surrey are controlled by the National Trust and make one of the largest areas of protected open space in the region. Even areas used for army training, marked 'danger area' on the Ordnance Survey maps, are often open to public access. From Hindhead north to Frensham there are several nature trails giving information about the varied features derived from the different strata. From the wooded summit of Gibbet Hill, the tributaries of the Wey cut north through the sandstones, in the Devil's Punchbowl hollowed out by springs sapping the softer beds of Atherfield clay. The wet, deciduous woodland at the bottom of the punchbowl is a different world from the dry pine heath above. To the north, the Bargate Beds provide a strip of rich farming land with orchards before the ground rises dramatically to the tough iron-stained beds of sandstone on the Devil's Jumps and Thursley Common. The nature reserve at Thursley includes the Warren Mere reserve developed round the old hammer-ponds of the iron industry.

To the west is Frensham and the recently established Countryside Park, centred on two large ponds once used by the monks of Waverley Abbey for fish breeding. On summer weekends the shores of these ponds are like a south-coast beach. The intense use is having a visible effect on the vegetation. The common, ungrazed for fifty years, is reverting to scrub woodland. It presents a classic problem for the management of open space. Car parks encourage access to the ponds and the most eroded paths are periodically railed off. The Scots pine is the only tree capable of giving a profitable return, so about 60 ha of pine are being developed with the ultimate intention of establishing a more varied woodland. Pine and birch are thinned out where oak saplings are appearing and especially in the wet zones where the alder is present. Birch and pine have the effect of drying out an area and killing off their competitors for space. A similar situation is found at Hothfield Common at the far eastern extremity of the same rock outcrop near Ashford (K). Controlled by the Kent Trust for Nature Conservation and the local authority, this is a rare acid peat bog and supports an unusual variety of flora. In summer it is a riot of colour with spotted orchids, bog asphodel, cotton grass, sundew and heathers. Volunteers have built a wooden causeway across the bog to give access yet keep the wet zone relatively undisturbed.

Fires are a regular hazard in summer on the dry heathlands, where temperatures in excess of 35°C are often recorded. Burning was a medieval practice when the commons were in regular use for grazing, and controlled burning may still be used to maintain an open heather-dominated complex. But uncontrolled fires, as in the summer of 1976, have ravaged many heaths, including Hothfield. The damage on Surrey heaths, such as Thursley Common, has been so extensive, with the potential loss of sand lizards, for example, and bird-nesting sites, that naturalists have estimated that it may take up to twenty years for the heather to reach maturity again and for its associated fauna to recover.

The high spot of the greensand outcrop, in more ways than one, is the sixteen kilometres along the ridge from Blackheath near Guildford to Holmwood Common, bouncing from summit to summit, Pitch Hill, Holmbury Hill, Leith Hill. Broken by deep, north–south valleys in which the streams were once harnessed for power to drive mills and forges, the forest has developed on the commons of the nearby settlements such as Albury, Shere, Ewhurst, Cranleigh, Wotton and Holmwood. Being the most popular walking area in the south-east, the tracks are churned into fine sand by horses and hikers but heather, bracken, gorse, bilberry and blackberry grow on the edge of the rides. The Scots pine is again the dominant tree and frames every view but an hour's walk along Holmbury Hill reveals at least a dozen other species – oak, birch, dogwood, hazel, spindle, whitebeam, rowan, crab apple, holly, holm oak, sweet chestnut – amongst them. The vegetation is so luxuriant that some of the famous views are becoming obscured. Two prominent Chilean pines near the summit of Leith Hill are another reminder of the recency of much Surrey woodland, a Victorian landscape rather than a primeval one. Parts of the Leith Hill area are on the Evelyn estate, for John's ancestral home was at Wotton where some of his early experiments with tree-planting were carried out.

Less spectacular than Leith Hill but gently pleasant is the greensand area on the Surrey–Kent border. Limpsfield Common was purchased by public subscription in 1972 and the land, which had had only three manorial families since the Norman conquest, came to the National Trust. The commons and charts stretch eastwards to Crockham Hill, Ide Hill and Toys Hill, all three bearing memorials to one of the pioneers in the movement for the protection of open spaces, Octavia Hill, co-founder of the National Trust. Beyond Sevenoaks lies the splendour of Knole Park, ancient deer enclosure, home of archbishops and royalty, open to the public stroller and starting-point of yet another chain of beauty spots such as One Tree Hill, Seal Chart, Oldbury Hill and Ightham Common. The word 'chart' that appears so frequently may be related to chert, a hard siliceous rock that acts as a protective capping along much of the sandstone ridge. It produces infertile soils more suited to heath than to the plough, hence the common lands.

Sussex is not excluded from these sandstone delights. Quite apart from Blackdown and Woolbeding, both National Trust areas, the same rock outcrop is the setting for three great parks, Cowdray, Petworth and Parham, Petworth being the main contender with Knole for the loveliest man-made landscape in the south-east. Trees are used as an art form, creating vistas of grassy vales, with roving sheep, deer and cattle, to make a suitable frame for the great house. The Scots pine is present but has to match its grace with chestnut avenues, beech clumps, wide-spreading oaks and limes. The pine comes into its own again on the low ridge at the foot of the South Downs, especially in West Sussex. The commons of Heyshott, Ambersham, Graffham, Lavington and Duncton all lie

11. *Beeches on Toy's Hill, one of the first open spaces given to the National Trust.*

on the upper greensand hills, but Ambersham is the gem. Emerging from the plantations of Graffham and rising to the flat summit at a mere 60 metres, the vision suddenly becomes entirely Scottish. So small on the map, so large to the eye, the great bowl of heather sweeps away to the west and the pine woods line the edges with no house in sight. The solitude is quite startling. Down by the stream that flows through the basin is a small but important area of wetland with alder and alder buckthorn in evidence. Along the ridge there are other small parcels of heathland in the hands of the National Trust, such as Sullington Warren and Washington Heath.

The Scots pine, with other conifers, has a much more favourable reception from the Forestry Commission than the oak. There are few soils where the traditional hardwood can achieve an economic return to compare with that of the softwoods. A softwood plantation will yield about three times the volume of timber, though the oak will yield for twice as long. So, for an organization which is duty bound to manage trees as an economic crop, beauty lies in a tall, straight trunk and not in the gnarled curves of a spreading oak. The Commission controls nearly 20,000 hectares of woodland in the three counties. It also exerts influence on private woodland, and at least another 20,000 hectares of the best woodland is 'dedicated' and therefore managed in accordance with Commission practice. The Commission opens up its forests to the public in the form of forest trails and has at least one ear open to public enlightenment and opinion.

Of the eighteen major areas of Commission forest, the largest are at Challock (K) and Slindon (Sx), both on the chalk. Most of the smaller forests lie within the Weald. On the chalk, beech is planted, usually with a nurse crop of conifers that will shelter the young hardwoods and yet give a commercial return before the beech are mature enough for felling. The main enemy is the grey squirrel which attacks the young growing shoots and can destroy thousands of trees. Fencing will keep out deer but no fencing can cope with squirrels. This method of mixed planting of beech and conifers has been practiced for at least two hundred years, being known at Goodwood in the late eighteenth century. The major species of conifers are Corsican pine, Lodgepole pine, Western hemlock, Norway spruce and various larches.

One large Commission forest of about 1,000 hectares is near Arundel, alongside the hardwood forest of the Mens. Nowhere is the contrast more striking between the woodland evolving over centuries and the man-made forest of the present century. Yet, in high summer, a carpet of Ladies Bedstraw, tormentil and young heather enlivens the geometrically precise rides and shows that one day the new plantings will become more 'natural' and varied even if never as exciting ecologically as the oak woodland. The King's Wood at Challock covers some of the ground that was once part of Eastwell Park, regarded by Defoe as the greatest in the south, famed for its venison, its greyhounds and its trees. Most of the grassland is under the plough and the North Downs Way cuts right through the park.

Some of the smaller woods have special interest, like the Abbot's Wood near Michelham Priory (Sx). It supplied wood to the monks and fed the furnaces of local iron works until 1828. At least twenty-eight species of tree are native and a further ten species of evergreens have been planted since 1953. Oaks have been planted with Norway spruce with an eye to the twenty-first century. The pond, once a monastic stewpond used for fish-farming, is now a wildfowl refuge. This area is also the habitat of one of the rarest of southern flowers, the spiked rampion which may have been introduced by the monks.

Tree-planting is a long-term project. It will be future generations who will appreciate the scenes that are being created now just as we cherish the landscape gardening inspired by John Evelyn and others three hundred years ago. Some of the famous landmarks like Chanctonbury Ring are now past their prime. Fortunately, enlightened people like the late Duke of Norfolk have been active in planting new beech clumps to create the landmarks of the next centuries. New species, notably conifers, have been introduced periodically and especially in the nineteenth century when botanists were scouring the New World for exotic specimens. The Wellingtonia, the Lawson's cypress, the Chilean pine and the Deodar cedar are now part of the woodland scene far removed from the old Wealden forest and belong more properly to the tradition of parks and gardens, but one of the evergreens has become so much part of the natural scene that it deserves special mention. The holm oak, *Quercus ilex*, was introduced from the Mediterranean in the seventeenth century, though I have noted it so often along the Roman roads that I wonder if it may have had an earlier introduction. As a parkland tree it infuriates gardeners by dropping its thick shiny leaves in June just as the parks are looking neat and tidy. It flourishes on limey soils and several varieties are found, for example, on the High Elms estate at Bromley (K). It is also tolerant of salty air and has been planted all round the coast. There is no resort without it. The finest avenue, called Ilex Avenue, is at Goring-on-Sea, once part of a private estate, and Victorians often planted it as a commemorative tree, as at Connaught Park in Dover.

Judging by the innumerable accounts of travellers and topographers, the greatest scenic pleasure in Sussex was not its woodland but its rolling downland grassland. The coastal areas were being spoilt by urban development so the naturalists fled to the hills to enjoy the clouds racing up the Channel with time-honoured shepherds guarding their wheeling flocks of Southdowns. The clouds still roll up, there is the same tang of salt in the air but the grasslands and the sheep have gone. Shepherds are as rare as rampions. They are still around but you have to search. Their crooks, like the famous products of Pyecombe, are antiques, more likely to be found in saloon bars and antique shops than in the field. There is more money in arable farming than in grass and the plough-up policy initiated in wartime has continued, the decline of the rabbit after 1953 compounding the change. What grassland remains is reverting to hawthorn

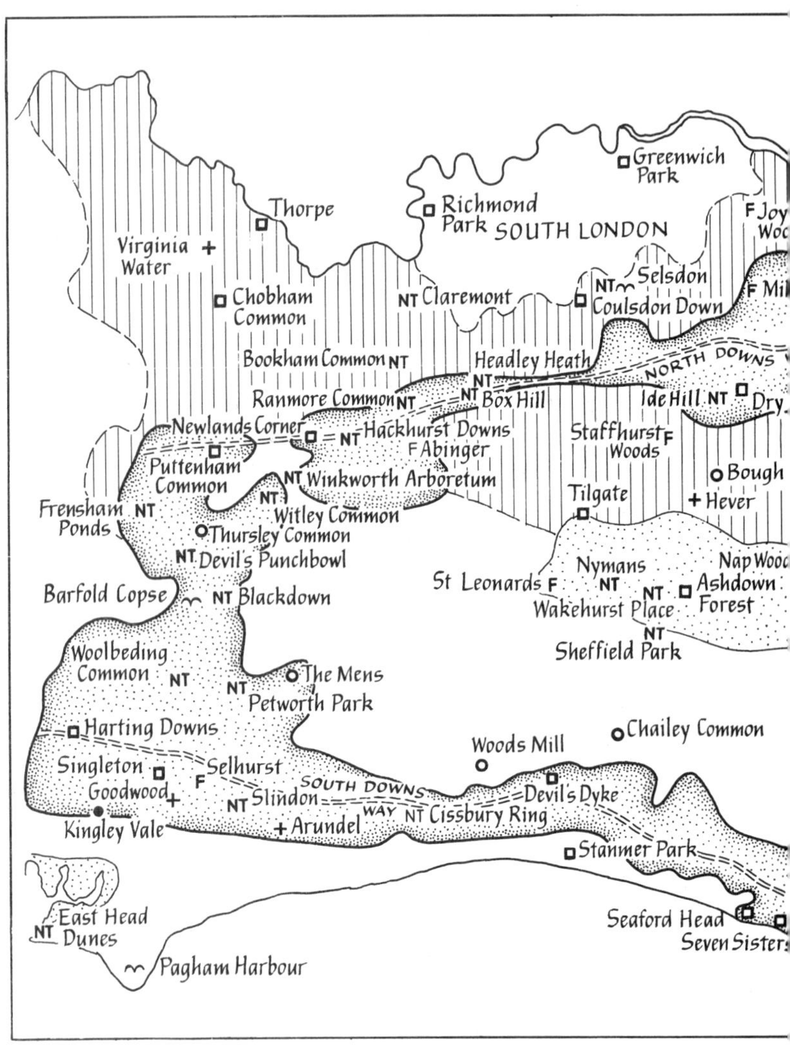

12. *Major nature reserves, open spaces, parks, forest and nature trails.*

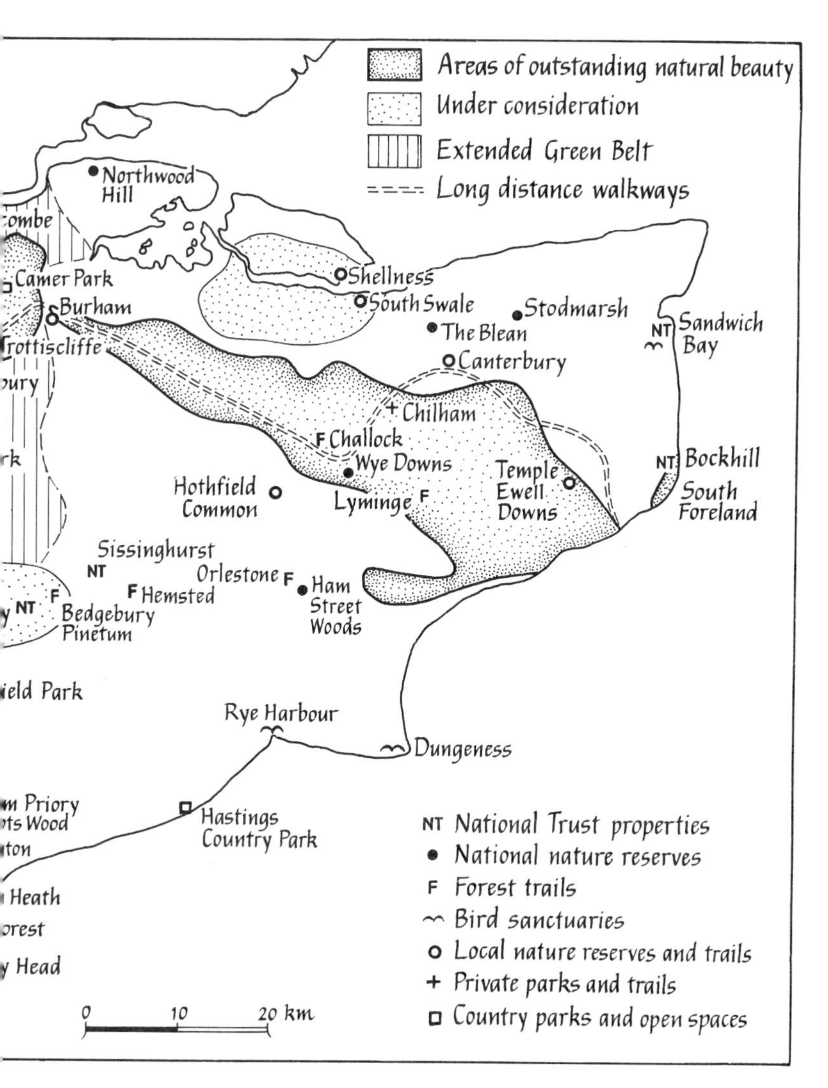

Areas of outstanding natural beauty
Under consideration
Extended Green Belt
Long distance walkways
Northwood Hill
Camer Park
Burham
Shellness
South Swale
Stodmarsh
The Blean
NT
Sandwich Bay
Canterbury
Chilham
F
Challock
Wye Downs
Temple Ewell Downs
NT
Bockhill
South Foreland
Hothfield Common
Lyminge
F
Sissinghurst
NT
Orlestone
F
Ham Street Woods
F
Hemsted
NT
F
Bedgebury Pinetum
Rye Harbour
Dungeness
Hastings Country Park
NT National Trust properties
National nature reserves
F Forest trails
Bird sanctuaries
Local nature reserves and trails
Private parks and trails
Country parks and open spaces
0
10
20 km

scrub. The short, springy chalk turf was not natural, but the result of grazing that had proceeded on and off since Neolithic man took up stock-raising.

The chalk country, when low and level, has always been ploughed. The lower chalk platform along the foot of the downs, the plateaux of East Kent, have been the largest arable areas with the biggest fields in the south-east, both in medieval and in modern times. The crest of the North Downs, plastered with clay-with-flints, was heavily wooded, but the high summits and steep slopes of the South Downs meant grassland. Both the North and South Downs have been designated as Areas of Outstanding Natural Beauty but this does not prevent fundamental changes in land use. Only where the nature reserves, like Kingley Vale, and country parks, like the Seven Sisters, have been established does chalk grassland survive as an ecological entity. Left alone, it reverts to scrub and, ultimately, to woodland. The grass cannot be left to itself, and the return of rabbits in recent years cannot restore the sward for they cannot touch the scrub layer.

The most extensive area of grassland remains in East Sussex stretching from Wilmington, above the Long Man, south to the coast at Seven Sisters and Beachy Head, broken only by Friston Forest and, even there, chalk flora survives in the forest rides. The chalk escarpment at Windover Hill is becoming coarse and tussocky but it soon gives way to the National Nature Reserve of Lullington Heath. South of the forest is the country park of Seven Sisters and the Cuckmere Valley and on either side of the chalk cliffs are the protected areas of Beachy Head and Seaford Head. These 7 kilometres are the perfect outdoor laboratory for a study of chalk flora. The adaptation of the plants is not just to a lime-rich soil but also to exposure to strong salt-laden winds and to grazing and treading. Around the much-trodden summit of Beachy Head, all but the daisy have given up the struggle but a few hundred yards downslope there is knapweed, scabious, eyebright, gentian, proliferous pink, common catsear, hawkweed, milkwort and the round-headed rampion all keeping their flowering heads close to the ground. On the cliff edge, Viper's Bugloss stands firm while the yellow-horned poppy, rock sea lavender, samphire, wild carrot and wild parsnip thrive on the bare cliffs. Trefoils, vetches, ground ivy, salad burnet, wild thyme, marjoram, basil, rock rose, centuary can all be found along the nature trail indicated at the information centre on the headland. The fruit-bearing trees and shrubs are another source of food for migrating birds but many of the trees are scorched by sea gales, the outer branches burnt with salt spray.

On the disturbed ground, especially along verges of tracks, the hemp agrimony raises its tall pink head and on Lullington Heath the chalk flora is mixed with flowers such as heathers and bedstraws that prefer an acid soil. This is the special feature of the reserve which is using mowing techniques to control gorse and other high vegetation. Once the grassland is restored to a low level, sheep and New Forest ponies are introduced to crop the grass and maintain its close sward. The same technique is used on Kingley Vale but the scrubland has been cut in strips so that the plant succession can be studied, and a suitable habitat maintained for whitethroat, linnet, yellowhammer, chaffinch, willow warbler, stonechat, redwing and many species of butterfly and moth.

The round-headed rampion, the 'pride of Sussex', is now comparatively rare although it can be found along the Downs all the way from Uppark to Eastbourne. Ditchling Beacon and the Trundle are two areas where it can usually be found in the late summer. There are seldom more than one or two flowers in evidence but its discovery is a great source of pleasure. It is often found with scabious and can easily be missed. The cowslip is another casualty of the plough but there are some places such as the slopes of Mount Caburn where it can literally turn a greensward into a yellow carpet, pricked out with wild violets.

Most people keep a special affection for wild orchids and maintain a knowing silence about their favourite habitats. In one particularly scrubby field along the Pilgrims' Way, I kept a check on the sequence of orchids for several weeks in spring and early summer and was not at all amused to find a large picnic party spread out right on top of a particularly fine display of musk orchids and twayblades. The chalk is the most prolific habitat though the wetlands such as Romney Marsh have their special species such as the late spider orchid. One of the best areas is Queen Down Warren near Hartlip (K), a local nature reserve, where even the rare Lady orchid and Green Man orchid are occasionally found in spite of people picking them and the magpies and jays snapping the heads. Above Boxley and Detling there are Bee orchids, Common Spotted, Fly, Pyramidal, Fragrant, Early Purple, Man and Butterfly orchids and twayblades depending on the time of the year. Some of the species flower and die back very-quickly, especially in a dry season. Early Purple orchids are frequently found in the coppiced woodland, too, above Boxley. At Kingley Vale, the sight of four different species of orchid all in flower by the green paths is the more dramatic after the darkness of the yew wood. The Pyramidal orchid seems to last longer than most species and can be seen in comparative abundance on Juniper Hill (Sy) even in late summer.

Another happy orchid-hunting ground is the nature reserve on the Downs above Wye (K). Parts of the reserve, such as the Devil's Kneadingtrough, are closed to the public but there are many paths that give access to rich flora. As at

Lullington and Kingley Vale, the reserve is managed for the purpose of restoring and maintaining the traditional chalk grassland which is especially rare on the North Downs. Apart from mowing, burning is used to remove the tough tor grass and sheep are brought in regularly to graze. Apart from the chalk flora, including seventeen species of orchid, there is 40 ha of old woodland with ash, hazel, whitebeam, yew, beech, hawthorn, blackthorn, dogwood, spindle and wayfaring tree present so there is a varied fauna including shrews, mice, voles, weasels, foxes, badgers, and occasional deer. The view from the reserve is one of the finest in Kent with the Low Weald taking the eye as far as the coastal marshes. The view has made this a favourite spot for visitors and persistent treading is causing erosion on the steep paths down the chalk face, but the existence of an information hut and a warden helps to keep the situation under control.

There is even less open grassland in Surrey, so much of the downland from Guildford to Box Hill being wooded. Twelve km of woodland from Albury Downs, through Netley Heath and Ranmore Common marches parallel with the greensand ridge to the south so the open spaces on Colley Hill, Box Hill and Netley Heath are of special importance. The area around Box Hill has been intensively studied by students at the field centre at Juniper Hall, one of the pioneer establishments of the Field Studies Council. Geographers, botanists and historians use this as a base. The main beauty spot of Box Hill has more than its fair share of litter and problems of over-use but the close-cropped sward of Juniper Hill to the north presents as fine a display of flora as you could wish, each species adapting itself to the varying depth of soil. To the west, on the bare chalk cliff overlooking the River Mole, is a unique woodland where yew and box dominate. In places the trunks lie almost at right angles to the slope due to soil slip but the trees adapt. The box is no longer common in the region and is seldom found as a well-formed tree. I have seen several in churchyards and a fine specimen in a garden at Teynham Street (K) but Box Hill, in keeping with its name, has the best example of box woodland. The tree is very brittle and branches fall easily. Being out of reach of grazing, this may be another example of aboriginal woodland.

The county authority in Surrey has a commendable concern for amenity and issues a comprehensive map of all the county's open spaces. They are well sign-posted, too, and many have been developed with nature trails. On the dip slope of the chalk, hemmed in by rail and road and housing, the country park of Coulsdon Common and Farthing Down offers a wide variety of flora. The area is actually controlled by the City of London Corporation which owns other outlying spaces as at Wickham and Addington on the Kent–Surrey border. Another suburban surprise is the small bird sanctuary in Selsdon Wood (Sy) owned by the National Trust. Given half a chance, many species of wild-life adjust to a suburban world. Fox, squirrel, badger, weasel, stoat all operate on the fringes of urban areas using railways, parks and commons as their highways. They often find more food and security in town than in country. We all have our favourite stories about foxes loping down the high street, of squirrels scrumping in the back garden. New stories are being added, such as roe deer enjoying a lunch of rosebuds, of heron picnicking on the fishpond, of hedgehogs learning to run away from traffic.

Deer are a major hazard for forester and gardener. The heaths and woods of West Sussex and South-West Surrey give plenty of cover and enable quite long-distance movement. I have seen feral deer laying up in wheat fields, trotting across the South Downs Way, thrashing their antlers in broad daylight. I have even encountered red deer on Box Hill. Roe, fallow, muntjac have all been reported wild in fair numbers. Most of them have come from stock escaping from deer parks, increasingly so with the number of parks unable to maintain their perimeter fences, or their herds. Most of the deer remaining in deer parks are fallow or Sika, although there is a fine herd of red deer in Richmond Park, the loveliest wildscape in the London area. Deer still roam in Knole, Mersham-le-Hatch and Boughton Monchelsea in Kent, at Parham, Buxted and Petworth in Sussex but these are mere remnants of the vast Norman chases that were enclosed from the Wealden wilderness for the sport of lords temporal and spiritual.

Together with deer as 'beasts and fowl of the warren' were the rabbits, an estimated one hundred million of them.* Introduced by the Normans for sport and commercial gain, they helped subsidize the expense of the deer parks. The word 'warren' on the present-day maps is usually an indication of a rabbit enclosure close by an ancient deer park. Even in the eighteenth century specially constructed warrens, in pits or mounds, proved twice as profitable as cows, but the laymen's way to an easy profit was killed off by imported rabbits and the removal of game restrictions in the 1880s. Myxamotosis finally ended the thousand-year farming of rabbits, though there has been a notable revival in the last decade. According to the National Farmers Union in Sussex they are once more a menace.

On the whole, the landscape of the south-east is a tamed, man-made garden.

* J. Sheail, 'Changes in the Supply of Wild Rabbits, 1790–1910', *Agricultural History Review*, Vol. 19 (1971).

The nearest approach to the wild exists along the sea shore, on the cliffs, marshes and dunes. It is there, on the sea's edge, that the most rewarding moments for the naturalist can be experienced. Imagine a hard day in February, the wind curling across the Halstow marshes, nothing to break its cold vigour on the long blow down the North Sea. Somewhere out on the mud-flats the Brent geese are honking and a ship moans on its way up the estuary. Suddenly the long, angular shape of a bird drifts in on an air current and hovers with violent wing-beats over a copse of tall, bare elms. The long legs lower delicately, the wings

13. *Grey heron at Northwood Hill.*

are stilled and the bird drops in an ungainly attitude into a large nest on the uppermost branches. In the course of the morning, fifty more birds sail in, often taking more than one attempt to land. Others are chased away from nests by the occupant and a raucous *mêlée* ensues. The herons are back. There are more than one hundred nests in the Halstow heronry, one of the largest in Britain. I have seen them floating over the marshes as late as October and it is not unusual to see as many as fifty standing motionless in the pastures to seaward. The elms, the dominant tree of the marshes, are dying. The Nature Conservancy is felling them selectively in order to encourage the heron to nest in the oaks and ash nearby. Breeding pairs are currently about one hundred and forty.

Another herony, the oldest recorded in Britain, is in the woods at Chilham Legend has it that if the herons do not return to their sanctuary by St Valentine's day, the owner of the estate will meet a terrible fate. Much of Chilham Park is open to the public but that does not include the heronry. Herons can be seen in every part of the region, especially on the levels by the Sussex rivers and the coastal flats. Anywhere with water and a fish supply can be feeding ground for them and they are quite at home on the new reservoirs inland, such as Bough Beech.

A flock of five hundred Brent geese wheeling over the creeks of Sheppey and Faversham is just as memorable as the heronry. The Medway area and the Swale are amongst the most important wildfowl haunts in the country. The varied habitat of salt-marsh, mud-flat, meadow and open water attracts mallard, teal, widgeon, pintail, pochard, shoveler, tufted duck, common scoter, eider, red-breasted merganser, shelduck and other waders, who do not seem to be put off by the power stations and oil-refineries that ring the horizon. They are a feast for the ears as well as the eyes. Walking along the sea-wall on the Isle of Harty, listening to shelduck and Sandwich tern, lapwing and oyster-catcher, curlew and redshank, pronouncing their variations on the same haunting theme, so common to marshland birds, brings a sense of remoteness and solitude so rare in the region. There are moments, too, of sheer surprise. Looking for cormorants on a September day on the Cliffe marshes, I found six flamingoes standing serenely in an old extraction pit near the cement works. There are nature reserves and sites of special scientific interest all along the estuary and further round the coast at Sandwich Bay within the shattering sound of the hovercraft terminal and again at Denge Beach under the shadow of the nuclear power station. The conjunction of modern industrial technology and wildfowl is a recurring theme. Forming a link between coast and estuary is the channel of the Wantsum and the Stour. The frequent inundations of the pastures is a reminder that this was once an arm of the sea dividing the Isle of Thanet from the mainland. Sea birds join with land birds, especially during migration, to make this a bird-watcher's paradise. 160 hectares of alluvial marsh and lagoons, the result of mining subsidence from the disused Chislet colliery, form another National Nature Reserve east of Canterbury on the Stour. The aquatic plants are as important as the birds. The same land–sea conjunction is found at the reserve at Ham Street. The coppice woods on the old cliff line behind Romney Marsh has woodpeckers, jays, jackdaws, blackbirds and thrushes as well as the more exotic fauna from the marsh and the shingle shore. Other highways from sea to land are the broad Sussex rivers. The Sussex Naturalists' Trust has purchased four fields in the Amberley Wild Brooks, another area often flooded in winter.

Sedge warblers, reed buntings, snipe, wagtails, lapwings and redshanks abound, feeding on the wet-zone plants.

Perhaps the most exciting bird reserve in Sussex is Pagham Harbour, just north of Selsey Bill. 280 hectares of inter-tidal flats were made into a reserve in 1965. The area had been reclaimed for farmland in 1891 but the sea broke through in 1910 and now the basin is cherished not only for its native birds but for a rare colony of Little Terns that nest on the artificially created shingle banks and islands. Cord grass, sea purslane, reed beds and the surrounding pastures give nourishment to migrant birds. More than 290 species have been recorded, the last stop before heading across the Channel. I was there on a memorable day in 1975 when bird-watchers were out in force after reports of rare species such as the Isabella shrike, the yellow-breasted warbler and the crested tit. There were other exotica that day, including a parakeet on the mud-flats, but my favourite sighting was the first of the Little Terns hovering offshore, heads down, plummeting into the water then rising with a crab before returning to the nesting site. Their high-pitched, unmistakable cry is the surest harbinger of summer returning.

The south coast lies on the path of many migration routes. Dungeness and Rye Harbour rival Pagham. 171 species have been ringed at Dungeness and about 140 at Sandwich Bay. Mid-September days on Beachy Head have their magic, too. Low over the crowds and the cars, the martins and swallows move in thousands down the valleys to follow the white coast, circling round and round before the final exodus, while people sit in deckchairs quite oblivious to the superb natural ritual overhead.

New reservoirs at Bough Beech and Bewlbridge, and lakes in parks all offer temporary havens to passerine birds. On one pearly grey January morning at Bough Beech, near the Kent–Surrey border, I saw mallard, widgeon, gadwall, pochard, tufted duck, Bewick swan, snipe, red-throated diver and two snow-geese. Six heron stood silent in the pastures whilst a cormorant preened its wings on a marker buoy in the middle of the lake, all this wonder seen from a road-side. Most heartening of all is the adventurous use of a worked-out gravel pit near Sevenoaks. Man-made islands and a specially constructed shoreline full of little bays and headlands give the loafing sites and privacy needed for wildfowl. The study of the birds' stomach contents led to the planting of suitable grasses and plants which resulted in an increase in ten years from 17,000 to 100,000 wildfowl. At least 189 species winter on this most successful reserve, due to the vision of an enthusiast like Dr Harrison and the enlightenment of a local industrial concern on the outskirts of a busy market town.

Another man-made habitat that the birds have adopted as their own is the extensive water surface and banks of the reservoirs on the Thames flood-plain between Heathrow Airport and the Thames at Walton, now mostly within the new, extended boundary of Surrey. Although they lack the shallow shelving shorelines most suited to wildfowl, rich green algae and floating plants are a useful food supply. The list of native and passerine birds seen on the reservoir reads like a complete catalogue from a bird-watcher's guide and includes most of the terns, the uncommon as well as the common grebes, divers, ducks and geese. On one count, for example, in 1969, the majority of smew recorded in Britain were on these reservoirs. Above all, they have become the roosting area for gulls, more than a quarter of a million, mostly black-headed, but including rarer species such as Iceland and Glaucous gulls. They are amongst the most important bird-gathering areas in the whole country. The Thames itself benefits from this proximity and a rich bird-life is found throughout its length, including such unlikely places as the old Surrey Dock in the heart of London where the wildfowl have taken over where commerce has left off.

3

Albion's Shore

'And nearby stretches out the island of the Albiones,' wrote a pioneering Greek navigator in the sixth century before Christ. The sailors and traders of the Mediterranean had made contact with the remote land of the Hyperboreans, the people beyond the north wind, living in a land rich in metals, swathed in mist. The journey beyond the Pillars of Hercules was still a daring feat when another Greek sailor from Massilia ventured forth in the fourth century BC and rounded the island that reminded him of Sicily by its triangular shape. 'The promontory nearest the mainland called Kantion,' said Pytheas, 'is said to be distant about eleven miles, at which point the sea forms a current.'* Kent and its narrow Channel crossing had entered written history.

The name Kent has a Celtic origin, recorded nearly eight hundred years before its neighbouring counties of Sussex and Surrey received their names. Kent has had several interpretations, canto meaning white, a reference to the chalk cliffs, or 'cant', a corner or angle, a word still used by masons and woodmen. 'Albion', too, was once linked with 'albino' in early dictionaries, but now it is regarded as a Celtic word of obscure meaning. A pity that such cherished illusions should be shattered but the name Albion is very popular in the south-east, attached to hotels and pubs along the coast. I like to imagine weather-beaten men, crunching an olive, drinking wine, sailing up the Channel on a summer's day and admiring the sun bouncing off the white cliffs, inventing new names to put in their log books, ready to tell tall stories of little-known islands on their return to warmer havens. The shoreline they skirted was beyond the present coast, such has been the erosion of the cliffs. Their landfalls may lie under the sea.

* As quoted by S. Casson, *Greece and Britain* (Collins, 1943).

The Celtic people that the navigators encountered, their 'many kings and potentates who live for the most part in a state of mutual peace', have left their mark on the landscape as well as the language, a mark that we can recognize even after another two thousand years of occupation has obliterated so much evidence. The Celts, in turn, were the inheritors of a region that had been peopled for more than 300,000 years. The earliest evidence of man was brought to light by industrial activity at Swanscombe. The region's most important archaeological site lies amongst the rubbish dumps that fill in old gravel workings along the Thames estuary. The treasure hunt began with a London dentist who, in 1935, found part of a human skull deep in the gravels of the Thames thirty-metre terrace, typical of the sites that have proved most prolific in early tools and weapons. Another piece of the same skull came to light no less than twenty years later, together with more than 60,000 flint implements, including hand-axes, primary flakes and fashioned flakes. The remains of elephant, rhinoceros, bear, lion, horse, deer, ox, wolf and hare filled out the picture of a warm climate enjoyed by groups of Old Stone Age hunters about 300,000 years ago. The skull that begins the human story in the region has pride of place in the Natural History museum in London. In the same museum are the materials found at nearby Crayford where the skeleton of a rhinoceros was discovered with flints stuck into it. Other sites in the Thames gravels were excavated at Frindsbury and Cuxton and in the chalk quarry at Baker's Hole near Northfleet. A collection of more than one thousand hand-axes from North Kent are in the National Museum of Wales. Looking today at the vast holes that the cement and gravel companies are still making along Thamesside, I wonder how many thousands of flints and bones and fossils are being pounded into building materials.

Wherever there are marine or river terraces there is the chance of finding traces of early man. On the raised beaches at Slindon (Sx) a workshop floor littered with hand-axes and flake tools was found beneath the Coombe rock deposits, one of several such sites in West Sussex.

Some of these sites, such as Swanscombe, are more rewarding in the museums than in the field. But there are places where the distant past has a physical presence that can prompt the imagination in a way that no museum can achieve. Say 'Stone Age' and an echo of childhood says 'caveman'. Go to Oldbury Hill high on the greensand ridge east of Sevenoaks and thread through the oak woods and the coppiced chestnut to the north rim of the hill where the view opens out over the orchards and pastures of Holmesdale. The tough layers of sandstone have been undercut by weathering and eroded along the joints of the rock to form natural caves. The roof is a tough, cherty sandstone, the floor a cold,

14. *Neolithic flint-mines and an Iron Age enclosure on Harrow Hill. In the background, lynchets of an ancient field pattern lie beneath the present large fields.*

damp stone once covered, no doubt, with rushes or skins. The site has been affected by later quarrying but enough has been found to prove human occupation about 100,000 years ago. In the nearby church at Ightham, above the commemorative plaque to Benjamin Harrison, local grocer and archaeologist, is a flint tool, which he called an eolith, the dawn stone. He claimed it to be the first tool known to man. Artifacts from the site are in Maidstone museum.

The Wealden sandstones have their caves, too. Microliths, now in Tunbridge Wells museum, were found on the floor of caves by High Rocks. There are other sites, such as West Hoathly, where similar conditions existed. In face of advancing ice and climatic conditions such as those experienced in Greenland today, Stone Age man retreated or endured, living within the severe bounds of his environment, and made his marks which are but scratches on the surface of history. He literally scratched, to dig the flints that were essential to his existence. There were flints in abundance on the surface of the chalk country and even on the greensand as at Ambersham Common but the best flints were the unweathered ones found at depth. So he mined for them. Flint mines have been identified and, in some places, reconstructed on the Sussex downs, at Cissbury, Harrow Hill, Blackpatch Hill, Church Hill and Stoke Down. The pits were up to fifteen metres deep with galleries radiating from the shaft, supported by the usual pillar type of working. The marks of deer picks, the smoky smudges of primitive lamps, even burials, have been found in them. In time, the earth caved in, the pits filled up and the surface evidence is merely of hummocks and hollows, more easily identified from the air than the ground. In most cases, as at Cissbury and Harrow Hill, they occur within the earthworks of later camps, showing the sites to be occupied at intervals over thousands of years.

There are many underground caverns and passages in the chalk of the region, at Chislehurst and Blackheath in south-east London, at Guildford and Farnham, and even within sound of the sea at Margate. Some of these cave systems have as much as forty kilometres of tunnelling within them. There are hundreds of smaller pits, the notorious dene-holes that pock the downland surface and slump regularly under the thin tertiary capping of rocks above the chalk. Local legends link them with hiding places from the Danish raiders, with druidical worship and with other fanciful fears of the past but there is no real evidence that they are of great antiquity. William Lambarde, in his *Perambulation of Kent*, quotes the opinion of local inhabitants in the sixteenth century that 'these were in former times digged, as well for the use of the chalke towardes building, as for to marle their arable lands therewith'. But he also revived the view that they were used by Germanic tribes as places of secret retreat 'in the times both of civil dissention, and foreine invasion'. The holes are still known as Dane holes in some areas. Generally six to nine metres deep, many of the holes are covered with new housing, with disastrous results to garden and house alike after a very wet season.

With the waning of the ice-sheets and the warmer, damper conditions that ensued, the forests advanced and the early colonizers found suitable sites on the sandy tracts of the greensand heaths. The land was drier there and the forest thinner, more easily cleared. The caves at High Rocks were still occupied and a rock shelter at Balcombe in the Sussex Weald was in use. But the characteristic dwelling was the pit. A post, a framework of branches, a covering of bracken, grass and skins made a home for the mesolithic inhabitants. Such homes with their pottery and flint tools have been identified around Farnham and Abinger in Surrey, at Peacehaven and Seaford in Sussex. The excavations at Abinger, carried out by Dr Leakey in 1950, have been preserved in the grounds of the manor house. A shallow pit dug one metre into the ground, up to five metres wide, leads to a ledge on which burnt stones and charcoal were found, a cooking hearth perhaps. More than one thousand flints were found in the material filling the pit. Pollen analysis at Albury (Sy) and Iping Common (Sx) shows a clearance of hazel woodland and the development of heathland. Man was already affecting the vegetation. New tools appeared such as the Frensham 'point' and the Thames 'pick' from Lower Halstow.

With the people of the New Stone Age, the landscape began its human transformation. 'The neolithic agriculturists initiated a process of deforestation which has not ended.'* The introduction of animal herding and crop farming led to a

15. *Kit's Coty, Megalithic tomb near Maidstone.*

drying out of soils and the increase of grassland. Man the cave-dweller became man the builder. A revolution in technical skills led to an increased command of the environment at a time when the last ice-age had waned and the Channel separated the island from the continent. At the end of that era were erected the most dramatic antiquities in the region, the megalithic monuments, the great stones.

* G. J. Copley, *An Archaeology of South East England* (Phoenix House, 1958).

The collection of chamber tombs made from enormous sarsens, slabs of crystalline sandstone, found around the Medway Valley is one of the most important groups in Britain. There are at least seven such tombs, the most famous being Kit's Coty, recorded in many an early topographical print. The name is derived in part from the Celtic 'coat' or 'coed' meaning 'woodland' and was first recorded by Lambarde, who preferred the belief that it was a memorial to the Celtic King Categerne rather than the tomb of the Saxon Horsa. The upright stones roofed by a capstone are about two thousand years older than either the Celtic or the Saxon chieftain and were once part of a long barrow. More extensive in their remains are the Coldrum Stones, a long barrow ten kilometres west of Kit's Coty near the village of Trottiscliffe. There are many sarsens in this area, including some under the walls of the parish church. The six standing slabs of stone making the chambered tomb stand on the edge of a chalk bluff. Thirteen more stones, including a possible capstone, lie on the ground below, undercut by quarrying. There are a further nineteen stones forming an oval enclosure to the west of the chamber. A similar arc of stones had been seen at Kit's Coty but they were dispersed in the nineteenth century. Skeletal remains from these long barrows are found in the oddest places such as Trottiscliffe church itself.

Below Kit's Coty is a clutter of stones of varying sizes known locally as the Countless Stones, which had the reputation of helping infertile women. It is known officially as the Little Kit's Coty but no obvious structure can be seen. A mile south of Coldrum are two other groups, the Addington Long Barrow and the Chestnuts. One of the barrows is cut through by the lane to Addington church, several stones lying half-buried by the roadside, forming an oval about sixty metres long. The stones of the Chestnuts are larger and a little imagination is needed to reconstruct the tomb but excavations in 1957 proved the existence of a burial chamber of massive sarsen slabs with an east–west alignment and blocking stones at either end. The cremated remains of at least nine people were found and the dating was confirmed as Neolithic but with continuing use into the early Bronze Age, contemporary with the more famous structures of Stonehenge. The Chestnuts are on private ground and only visible from the road. Although there are affinities with the west of Britain, the Medway group of megalithic tombs may be linked by their structure with Denmark and North Germany.*

Between Coldrum and Addington, linking the three tombs, is a footpath

* Glyn Daniel, *The Megalith Builders of Western Europe* (Hutchinson, 1958).

forming the parish boundary. Along this path are several sarsen stones hidden in the undergrowth. Local antiquarians in the last century wondered if they had discovered a Sacred Way of the early Bronze Age. Other suggestions were made of avenues, something like Carnac in Brittany, striding across the kilometres between Kit's Coty and Coldrum. Fanciful perhaps, but there are hundreds of sarsen stones in the area, especially along the Pilgrims' Way. The White Horse stone, for example, is as large as the slabs in the tombs and stands by the Way. Some of the stones almost certainly were part of other tombs, such as the group that now rest in the front gardens of a private housing estate at Cobham. A pile of small sarsens were used to make the grotto and phoney tomb in the grounds of Cobham Hall, an eighteenth-century folly repeated at Belmont (K), Virginia Water (Sy) and Claremont (Sy). The tombs were systematically robbed and sometimes just blown up to clear the ground wanted for crops. The Countless Stones were thrown down in 1773. Many sarsens have been used for memorials, such as the group round Meopham Green. My favourite is the one in Godstone churchyard to the memory of Walker Miles, erected by the rambling clubs of London. The same famous rambler is commemorated on Leith Hill tower. The frequent association of sarsens with churches as at Cobham, Challock, Trottiscliffe (K) and Ditchling (Sx) might suggest that pagan enclosures existed on the sites adopted by the Christian converts.

The long earthen burial barrows that were the most conspicuous monument of the Neolithic people occur infrequently on modern maps and even more infrequently on the ground. The plough-up of the grassland has removed many, although a dozen are still recorded at the eastern and western ends of the Sussex Downs. One of the best examples is Bevis' Thumb, couched along the roadside near East Marden (Sx). Isolated examples occur elsewhere, such as Julliberries' Grave across the Stour from Chilham (K). The open grasslands, especially of the South Downs, are the richest archaeological book for the casual walker to read. A ten-kilometre trek, for example, from the familiar landmark of the two windmills, Jack and Jill, above the village of Clayton, to Lewes in the east, passes a number of tumuli, burial mounds, a Bronze Age settlement on the Plumpton Plain, a fort on Ditchling Beacon, a circular earthwork at Streathill and four areas of ancient field systems and cross-dykes, according to that invaluable companion, the Ordnance Survey map. The amateur may walk with more hope than reward. What the plough has not destroyed, the colonizing scrub has obliterated, but all is not lost. Some of the tumuli are identifiable as small mounds, usually round, some elongated. Field systems emerge in low sunlight as baulks of turf, faint terraces and breaks in the slopes. The hill-forts have had a better fate, their deep entrenchments cutting circles on hill summits. The deep trenches of the cross-dykes in the dips, that may have marked territorial boundaries between the forts, are usually clear. The routeway itself is the clearest handiwork of the ancient peoples of the Bronze and the succeeding Iron Age. It was their trading link between Wessex and the south-east coast. We have to turn, once again, to museums such as the Barbican at Lewes, to find out more about the life of these early traders in metal, of axes, and daggers, jet buttons, amber beads, faience work, pendants and amulets, flint tools and weapons. Small farmsteads with circular huts were excavated at Plumpton. At Itford Hill above Beddingham, a

16. *Disc barrows on Bow Hill in the Kingley Vale nature reserve.*

hamlet of thirteen huts was found. The pits revealed evidence of barley and the remains of sheep and oxen. Weaving sheds and storage huts completed the picture of life about one thousand years before Christ.

A closer look at the burial mounds shows changes from the early long barrows to bell barrows and disc barrows of later periods, such as those on Bow Hill near Kingley Vale. More than 270 barrows are listed as Ancient Monuments, more than two hundred of them in Sussex. Of the twenty or so in Surrey, the best example is at Barrow Green near Oxted but most occur on the Surrey heaths and are difficult to identify. Most prolific in their contribution to museums are the hoards dropped or hidden by Bronze Age traders, from Bognor and Worthing, from Farnham and Kingston (Sy), at Minnis Bay and the Isle of Harty (K), on Addington golf course (Sy) and a sand-pit at Bexleyheath (K). The distribution of all known Bronze Age finds shows the densest area of occupation to be the chalklands of Sussex, the north-east shores of Kent and the Thames Valley. There are sparse finds on the greensand hills but the Inner Weald emerges on the map as a no-man's-land.

With the Iron Age and the many surviving hill-forts and camps, more than fifty in the region, we begin to recognize a more formal, organized occupation of the land. Many of the forts, as on Wimbledon Common and at Keston (K), are known locally as Caesar's Camp. A Roman origin is given to any earthwork that looks like a camp. A new dictionary of the Sussex dialect* asserts that 'anything beyond living memory is called "Roman"'. This is true for more than Sussex. In fact, Roman materials have often been found in or near these camps and in many cases they were in use during and after the four centuries of the Roman occupation. Some of them, such as Ightham (K) and Mount Caburn (Sx), were strengthened by additional earthworks against the attack of the invading Romans. They were the settlements of the native Celtic tribes, the people who gave names to the rivers such as Thames, Ouse, Avon and Tarrant that persist in our landscape language. Look for an Iron Age camp and you often find the name 'bury' – Cissbury, Chanctonbury, Oldbury, Albury, Hollingbury, Anstiebury, Holmbury, Bigbury. The name 'bury' was imposed by later invaders, the Saxons, but the relationship is clear.

The most famous group of hill-forts lies along a well-trodden route on the Sussex Downs. The present South Downs Way is deflected from the ancient alignment of the Ridgeway so as to take in the camp sites of Cissbury Ring and Chanctonbury Ring, the rings being a reference to the ramparts that enclose them. The double rampart of Cissbury, tracing the outline of a chalk spur, encloses thirty hectares. It was occupied about 250 BC and was refortified towards the end of the Roman period. The flint mines within it are, as we have seen, from a much earlier period. Chanctonbury, one of the outstanding landmarks of the Downs, is a smaller fort, capped by an eighteenth-century plantation. The cross-dykes to the west of the fort are clear, an outer defence or a boundary ditch for the occupants of the fort. The Trundle, a natural viewpoint for Gorgeous Goodwood, encloses twelve and a half acres and an earlier neolithic causeway camp. The double rampart of the Iron Age camp is deeply cut into the chalk, a popular circular walk for the many visitors, with unimpeded views inland and over the coast, a superb defensive site. Both here and at Cissbury,

* H. Hall, *A Dictionary of the Sussex Dialect* (new augmented edn, Gardner's of Bexhill, 1957).

excavations show that timber revetments had strengthened the earth banks and dissuaded potential attackers.

Just as spectacular in its setting on the summit of an isolated chalk hill is Mount Caburn, a name with an Arthurian ring. It dominates the gap that the River Ouse cuts from coast to interior. The tumuli on the hilltop ridge and the Celtic fields on the lower slopes are nearly as clear as the camp itself. This natural eye for a defensive site is repeated at the Devil's Dyke north of Brighton. The fort occupies all the promontory of the hill with the deep trench of the dyke on one side and the escarpment of the downs on the other, only the west approach being vulnerable. Several large hill-forts lie within the Wealden interior. The Iron Age people penetrated the forest in their search for iron deposits both in the clays and the sandstones. Three fine examples of promontory forts occur close together on the summit of the greensand ridge in Surrey, at Anstiebury, Holmbury and Hascombe. New excavations have shown the earthworks to be cut deeply into solid rock, the excavated material being used to heighten the banks. Another well-preserved fort lies in the heart of the Weald, near the junction of three counties, at Dry Hill. The panoramic view that these forts commanded is now hidden by tree cover, a reminder of the many changes that have occurred in the vegetation.

Largest of the forts is Oldbury, covering fifty hectares of the greensand ridge in Kent, using the same area that Palaeolithic man had inhabited. The earthworks are so extensive that it is difficult to envisage the whole place at first sight. Two deep valleys cutting from north to south through the ridge give the site a natural defence strengthened by earthworks and complex gateways. The ancient track that bisects the camp from east to west, linking the two main gates, was followed by the coaching road until the eighteenth century. The hut circles and grain-pits of the inhabitants are now covered by chestnut coppice and oaks but a small, spring-fed pond remains at the centre. Like Cissbury, Oldbury is a National Trust site, with a picnic area and car-parks carefully hidden below the western ramparts. The fort was taken by the Belgae, last of the three waves of Iron Age invaders, from the previous Wealden tribes and they, in turn, had to build further defences in a vain attempt to keep the Romans out as they marched from the coast to London. The Roman legions also stormed the fort at Bigbury, just to the east of Canterbury, another site on the old Ridgeway. Other large forts can be seen at Holwood Park, at Squerries Park near Westerham, at High Rocks near Tunbridge Wells, at Saxonbury near Rotherfield (Sx) and on Wimbledon Common.

Another distinct alignment of camps follows the south coast with views out to sea, such as Hollingbury in the hilly suburbs of Brighton and Highdown Hill behind Ferring. Several of the camps are precariously perched on the cliff line itself, such as the East Hill of Hastings and one near Beachy Head. No doubt other camps once existed on the cliffs of yesteryear that now lie under the sea. The most interesting archaeological experiment of recent years that is throwing new light on to the life of the Iron Age people is taking place just beyond the western boundary of the region, at Butser Hill in Hampshire. The farming techniques of the period are being reconstructed, grazing Soay sheep, growing woad and early species of barley. The native huts have been rebuilt and even a medieval pillow-mound for rabbits restored, although this would not have been part of the Iron Age landscape.

One of the problems of downland farming, past and present, is the lack of surface water. Artificial basins cut in the chalk surface, puddled with clay to hold water, are many, though few are in use and most have dried up. The origin of the dew-ponds is obscure and their dates disputed but some have been used as the meeting point of Saxon parishes and, by implication, must have been in use during the Iron Age. The downlands' most unusual antiquity is equally baffling. The Long Man of Wilmington with his two parallel staves is cut into the face of a shadowed coombe in the escarpment by the village of Wilmington, a simple, ritual figure. Tumuli stand on the crest behind him. Since 1873, the outline of chalk has been reinforced with yellow bricks. More than sixty metres in length, the figure is monumental in scale, possibly the work of the Iron Age Celts who were responsible for other hill figures in Britain.

By the time of the construction of the hill-forts, the pattern of routeways was well established. That we can trace them mostly on high ground may be due to the comparative difficulty of passage through the thicker forests on the heavy clay soils of the low ground. The geological structure follows an east–west trend. So do the routeways. The most famous is the Ridgeway along the South Downs, linking fort with fort, flint mines and fields. It enters the region by Harting Downs and marches with the chalk crest for the best part of 130 kilometres to Beachy Head, descending into the river gaps at crossings that can only be conjectural. The northern Ridgeway is nowhere so clear. Fragments appear on the Ordnance Survey maps. On the ground they appear as a track between two low embankments. The clay-with-flint capping of the North Downs would make a more difficult surface than the bare chalk of the south and thicker woodland covered the area. But the track certainly existed and was still in evidence when the Saxons colonized the area, for many of their parish boundaries use the Ridgeway. The most distinctive section followed the Hog's Back, west of Guildford, to its meeting with the highway through Farnham. A walkable stretch of five kilometres lies between Boxley and Detling (K). Above Folkestone, the Ridgeway is mapped as the Pilgrims' Way but for most of its length the Pilgrims' Way follows the foot of the North Downs.

17. *The Long Man of Wilmington.*

The Pilgrims' Way was a name that came into currency in the eighteenth century. That the route was used by pilgrims travelling from Winchester to Canterbury is not disputed. But pilgrims from the north and London would have used the route used by Chaucer's company of story-tellers down the Dover road from Southwark. Hilaire Belloc, who timed his perambulation to end at the precise day of Becket's martyrdom, preferred to call it the Old Way. Others have called it the Shire Way but the modern maps persist with Pilgrims and no doubt it will always be known as such. At least that has the merit of distinguishing it from the other ancient Ways. It enters Surrey as the Ridgeway but where that route leads up to the Hog's Back, the Pilgrims' Way drops to the lower ground and follows a low ridge of greensand, a dusty, grey path linking the churches of Seale and Puttenham, crossing the River Wey south of Guildford, on to Tyting and Albury before regaining the lower slopes of the chalk escarpment. And there it stays, poised between the steep chalk downs and the wet clay vale, forming a boundary between the grassland and scrub to the north and the ploughlands to the south. As it reached the river gaps like the Darent and the Medway it looped north and used fords and ferries or the rare bridging points such as Rochester. From Eastwell, for example, it turned north and followed the top of the Downs to Chilham before the descent into Canterbury. Much of that route is now used by the North Downs long-distance walkway marked by white acorns. From Canterbury to Dover, the new walkway zig-zags across the chalk plateau, although the old route still follows the foot of the chalk as far as Folkestone.

One of the notable features of the Pilgrims' Way, especially in its Kentish course, is that it passes to the north of most villages and churches. The villages are a later addition to the landscape but there is a striking continuity of paths, lanes and rights-of-way linking the villages, suggesting another ancient route running parallel with the more famous way. The ways pass megalithic tombs on the Medway and there can be little doubt that the Pilgrims' Way is a road as old as the Bronze Age, perhaps even older, part of the spider's web of roads that radiated from Stonehenge and the Wiltshire Downs to all parts of southern England, a Neolithic traders' way, linking west coast and east coast. There is no comparable track along the foot of the South Downs though there are small sections of a similar pattern such as the field path from Alfriston to West Firle. Another notable alignment in Sussex follows the greensand outcrop from Ashurst through Henfield and Hurstpierpoint to Streat. The words 'Roman road' appear on one mapped section. The Romans certainly used it but it was probably in use before they arrived.

The search for iron opened up many other routes and the many roads of East Sussex that follow the Wealden ridges inland from Rye and Udimore, for example, may have been in use then. North–south routes are more difficult to define, though the Ridgeway west of Hindhead may be part of one. The focusing of routes crossing the Medway at present-day Tonbridge is suggestive of an earlier pattern.

The north–south tracks cut across the grain of the country and often create deeply sunken lanes especially where they climb up hills. The holloways, as they are called, are not just eroded by time. Older routes than these are not deeply

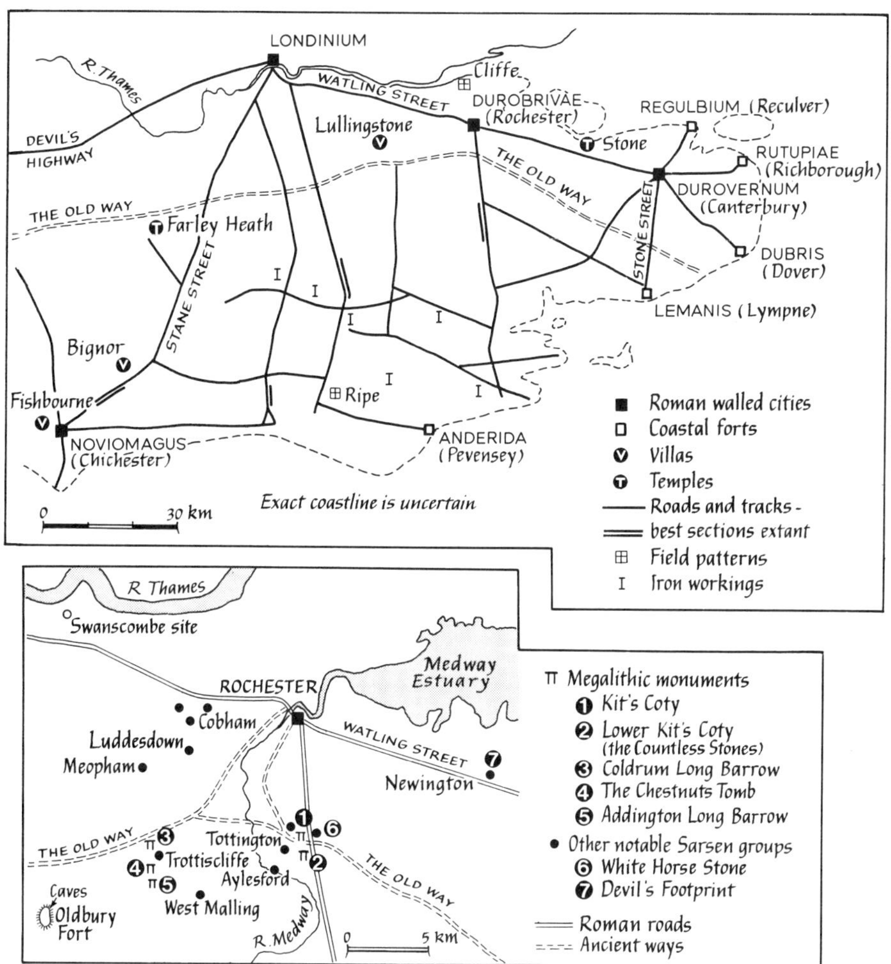

18. *Major remains of the Roman occupation. Inset: Pre-Roman sites in the Medway area.*

worn. Time and heavy cargoes may wear down the rocks but it is the action of running water, of funnelling winds down a sandy track, that shape them. There are several along the greensand ridge from Leith Hill in Surrey to Wrotham in Kent that are as much as eight metres below the level of the adjacent fields. The warren of narrow, gorge-like lanes at Iping and Woolbeding in Sussex are passable only by the lightest traffic. The down-cutting of the surface only stopped when the lanes were surfaced.

The last of the Iron Age invaders, the Belgae, were already in touch with Roman civilization and had a more advanced technology than the earlier Wealden people. They cleared much of the chalk downland for their settlement and their farms. They cleared the drier, sandier soils of the Surrey heathlands, forerunners of our present commons. They worked metals and traded across the Channel, and the adornments of their civilization brighten the cases of many museums. In the British Museum is the Richmond dagger, the ceremonial shield from Battersea, pottery, buckets, and household goods from Aylesford and Swarling. Other burial goods at Deal, Allington, Faversham, Folkestone and Walmer give evidence of settlement established on the lower ground, the river valleys and the coastal plains, and mints had been established at Selsey and Rochester. These were the native Celts bracing themselves for the Roman invasion, sometimes as allies, sometimes as slaves. But they outlasted the Romans. 'In Surrey, most of the Belgic material dates from after the Roman occupation.'* They may even have established settlements at such key sites as Chichester and Canterbury which were later developed by the Romans. The Chichester dykes, lineal earthworks, kilometres long that cut deep trenches north of Chichester, may be their work. They produced works of great artistic distinction such as the human mask moulded on the handle of a bucket found sticking to the wheel of a modern tractor at Boughton Aluph (K). The oak forests were their essential fastness where they sought refuge during foreign invasions. The oak tree was an object of veneration, the sacred groves the site of their ritual.

Set in the outer wall of the Council House at Chichester is a large inscribed stone that had been dug up near the site in 1723. The inscription, translated, runs 'To Neptune and Minerva this temple is dedicated for the welfare of the divine house by the authority of Tiberius Claudius Cogidubnus, king and legate of Augustus in Britain'. The Romans had arrived and found allies. Cogidubnus, king of the local Celtic tribe, the Atrebates, was proud of his Romanized title. The area of Selsey and the Manhood peninsula was settled.

About eight kilometres north-east of Chichester, close by the windmill on Halnaker Hill, haloed by the embankment of a small hill-fort, are the plantations of Slindon Forest. The signpost at the gateway points dramatically to Stane Street. The Roman road marches straight as an arrow on its metalled surface. Raised above the ground level, cambered so as to drain off surplus water, the road still looks fit for a Roman legion. It has legions now, of visitors following the nature trail laid out by the Forestry Commission. After two kilometres of

* G. J. Copley, *An Archaeology of South East England* (Phoenix House, 1958).

forest, the road breaks into open ground, a broad track of pounded flints, lined by gnarled trees, smothered by chalk flora. As it digs deeply into the incline by Gumber corner, a glance back over the shoulder shows the spire of Chichester cathedral, comforting as a compass point, in direct line with the Street. Set your face to the hill and climb again up to the heathland past the camp and tumuli on Bignor Hill to the summit of the Downs. The illusion looking north is still of a great forest as it must have been for the legionaries on their first day's march from Noviomagus Regnensium. The Ridgeway runs enticingly east and west

19. *The Roman Stane Street north-east of Chichester.*

but we race down the escarpment by deeply cut tracks through the chalk to the Roman villa at Bignor, with its superb mosaics. This section of the Street, dating from the first century, is the best-preserved in the region and now owned by the National Trust. The walking is so good that you look longingly ahead to continue in Roman footsteps but the street becomes a modern highway by Pulborough and Billingshurst towards the Mole Gap. There is another untouched section of Stane Street at Rowhook where a modern inn stands just at the junction with another Roman Road that led north-west to the temple site on Farley Heath.

Stane Street drives on through Ockley forming one side of that village's lovely green and aims to the right of Leith Hill and the hill-fort at Anstiebury.

Another five-kilometre section is followed by bridleways and Pebble Lane between Mickleham and Epsom, the aggars and flint surface being intact in several places. Then the suburbs of London close in and Stane Street becomes the A24 past Nonesuch Park on to Morden and Merton and London Bridge.

With such strict determination and skilled engineering, the legions conquered. Each street was equipped with posting stations or 'mansiones'. Two have been found at Hardham and Alfolddean just twenty and forty kilometres from Chichester. Others were probably sited at Dorking and Merton, breaking the march to London into five equal stages. Roman materials have been found at each place; coins and burials and other traces of Roman occupation line the entire route. Another road started in the vicinity of Brighton, a supply port possibly south of the existing shore. Part of its course across the downs can be seen between Pyecombe and Clayton. Its flint surface was robbed during the construction of the Hassocks–Burgess Hill turnpike in the early nineteenth century where it was crossed by another road running east–west along the greensand at Streat. The line is clear on the modern road system, through Blindley Heath and Godstone on to Croydon and Streatham. 'Street' or 'streat' in a place-name is often an indication of a Roman road and proof was given at Streatham by telephone engineers finding the original surface.

The straight road through Edenbridge (K) whets the appetite and, sure enough, five kilometres south the Roman road is picked up at Holtye Common. The actual Roman surface was revealed on the Sussex side of the border. Six metres wide, still bearing wheel marks, the surface is made of cinder from iron foundries in the area. Large slabs of cinder and stone are slumped in the stream to the south and may mark a Roman fording site. Similar slabs were used in a ford near Stream Farm, Iden Green, using Bethersden marble. Another paved ford can be seen in the Kent Ditch near Bodiam. Changes in river level since Roman times have covered the fords in fresh deposits and then cut down into them. These fords are part of the Roman road that linked Hastings and the iron-working area to Rochester in the north, forming the main road through Staplehurst and a deeply sunken track at Chart Sutton before entering Maidstone as Stone Street.

The cinder-surfaced street at Holtye leads southwards across Ashdown Forest to Lewes. Northwards it rises over the North Downs by a Roman villa and temple site at Titsey on to Beckenham. For much of its course it forms the boundary between the counties of Surrey and Kent. Using a ruler and a little imagination, local archaeologists in a London borough reasoned that that same Roman road would have cut through a hill called One-Tree Hill. An excavation in the public park proved them to be right. No one searching for Roman roads and, incidentally, enjoying some remarkably good walking, can find a better companion than I. D. Margery's *Roman Ways of the Weald*, the result of a lifetime's dedicated research. There are, however, some roads outside the scope of his book, such as the road from Dover to Sandwich which is particularly well preserved just north of Dover where it is followed by the North Downs Way, and the Devil's Highway that approaches from Silchester in the west across the Bagshot heaths to a Thames crossing at Staines, then known as Pontes.

Of the major highway, Watling Street, the main spine of Roman power in Kent, everything or nothing, depending which way you regard it, remains, for it is still the main highway and has therefore been mostly obliterated by later road engineering. A section through Greenwich Park, built before the diversion over Blackheath, was proven recently during pipeline operations, in direct line with the straight road over Shooter's Hill. The roads were the arteries of conquest-linking ports with cities, supplies with market. On them grew the major centres of Roman power – Canterbury (Durovernum), Rochester (Durobrivae), London (Londinium) and Chichester. The road axes and the gateways that they built form the basic ground pattern of the modern cities. The wall alignments in each case follow the Roman enclosures and, in parts, the actual Roman materials can be seen. Roman foundations have been proven even to medieval city walls. London's fragments, at London Wall and by the Tower of London, are more complete than anything in the other cities where the walls were largely rebuilt in the medieval period, but a small section of ragstone and brick of Roman construction is above ground level in the Quenin Gate of Canterbury. Rochester's walls were built in the third century in front of a previous rampart and are being exposed by redevelopments in the city.

Canterbury's wall encloses fifty hectares, the largest Roman settlement in the region, marginally larger than Chichester with forty hectares. Whereas Chichester perpetuates the basic Roman street pattern with its simple cross of North Street, South Street, East Street and West Street, Canterbury's existing High Street runs parallel with the original alignment of Watling Street. A short stretch of road still bears the name, in line with Beer Cart Lane. The original London Gate was proved by excavation to be to the west of the existing Westgate.

There are few surface remains of the cities. Foundations of walls, hypocausts and tesselated pavements have been preserved in a small permanent display under the new shops in Longmarket in Canterbury. Roman buildings have been found in Chichester, and although most of the evidence is in the Guildhall

Museum, a recent dig in cleared ground in the north-west quadrant has revealed further building *in situ*, the deep hollow of an amphitheatre lying to the east of the town in a small park. In all three cities, Roman materials have been quarried for later building. 'The thin red bricks have found their way into one wall after another and still form part of the fabric of the place.'* Nowhere is this more striking than in the walls of St Martin's church near the ruins of St Augustine's Abbey.

What wonders may lie buried about three metres below present ground level can be judged by recent excavations in Dover, the Roman Dubris, by the Kent Archaeological Rescue Corps, working on the sites of the new by-pass and town centre redevelopment near Market Street. The discoveries led the group to call Dover another Pompeii, such was the splendour of the painted house they uncovered, the walls standing to two metres being boldly decorated with trees, fronds and other designs. Superimposed on the house and destroying part of it was the stone wall of a later Roman fort of the third century. Barrack blocks, granaries, drains, sewers and water mains have all been identified. Hundreds of tile fragments stamped CLBR showed that Dubris was a naval base of the Classis Brittannica, the Roman fleet of the Channel.

Wooden harbour walls of the Roman period have been found under the East Kent bus station. Guarding the haven is one of the most exciting Roman structures in Britain, the Pharos, high on the east cliff within the present castle garth. Thirteen metres of its nineteen metres are original Roman work of the first century. Chalk and flint rubble is faced with greensand and tufa blocks and strengthened with bonding courses of bricks. This one building would make Dover worth visiting. It is unique. A second pharos stood on the west cliff but its foundations are lost under the redoubts.

In the countryside, the native tribal groups of the Cantii and the Atrebates carried on ploughing and herding, much of their grain and cattle going to supply the Roman soldiery and Rome itself. More than thirty Romano-British farm sites have been traced on the Mid-Sussex downs alone, and a Romano-British field system is intact on Farthing Down (Sy). The heart of the rural scene was the villa, with its house, outbuildings and estate. At least thirty-four villas have been recorded and more are being discovered such as Darenth and Horton Kirby in the Darent Valley (K), an area where Roman villas are as numerous as present-day villages. The villa at Horton Kirby may have been even larger than the one so well preserved at nearby Lullingstone.

* W. Townsend, *Canterbury* (Batsford, 1950).

Park palings dug in the eighteenth century at Lullingstone smashed through a Roman mosaic floor but serious investigation did not take place until 1949. Under the cover of downwash soil and rubble were buildings that showed a sequence of occupation from the first century until final destruction by fire in the fourth century, spanning the whole of the Roman epoch. The Christian symbols found in one of the rooms show the early conversion of the owners from pagan worship. Built of flint and chalk blocks, bricks and tiles, the first villa,

20. *Mosaic floor uncovered at the Roman villa of Lullingstone in the Darent Valley.*

including a ritual burial of an infant in one wall, was abandoned about AD 200 but rebuilt and extended with complex bath systems, a large granary and mosaic floors. The centre-piece is a floor depicting Bellerophon killing the Chimera, surrounded by dolphins and the symbols of the four seasons. The site is controlled by the Department of the Environment.

An even finer representation of the seasons was found at Bignor when a ploughman ripped into a mosaic of a dancing girl in 1811. The picture of Winter that was uncovered then has often been portrayed but there are many other fragments remaining in buildings including workshops and a smithy that were grouped around a courtyard. Much of the two-ha site has been infilled but the best rooms have been preserved and opened to the public by the present owner. Bignor, like Lullingstone, was the seat of a wealthy man, with extensive quarters for farm animals and slaves.

Greatest of the villas is Fishbourne. Discovered as recently as 1960 during water-main-laying operations, the site at the head of the Fishbourne creek to the west of Chichester proved to be one of the most important in Britain. Its mosaic floors of simple, geometric design are the earliest yet found. Beginning as a military settlement, Fishbourne developed into a palace, possibly for the same Cogidubnus whose name appears on the Minerva stone in Chichester. At its full extent, the villa had four wings ranging round a formal garden, now being reconstructed and planted with appropriate shrubs. There were twenty-three rooms in the north wing alone, which has been converted into a full-scale museum of Roman life. The mosaics at Bignor may be finer and made with fragments of chalk, sandstone, tile, limestone and glass but Fishbourne was adorned with stonework from all over the classic world. Such affluence was also known at Lullingstone, where two busts were made of Pentelic marble from Greece.

The three villas open to the public are typical of the favoured sites – the coastal plain of Sussex, the lower slopes of the hills behind Portslade, Brighton and Dover, the North Kent coast, the river valleys of the Medway, the Darent, the Wey and the Mole and the foot of the chalk escarpment. Good water supply, well-drained soils, fertile land adjacent, the Romans and the Romanized Britons chose well. Some of the best materials from south-eastern sites are in the Roman room of the British Museum, including the wall plaster with Christian devices from Lullingstone. Bowls, pendants, bracelets, flagons, pottery and hundreds of coins have helped to establish the detailed chronology of the Roman occupation of four centuries.

Both at Titsey and Darenth, there was evidence of fulling and dyeing cloth on the Roman sites. Ashtead (Sy), Cranleigh (Sy) and Plaxtol (K) were all centres of tile manufacture. Tile yards on a commercial scale existed at Reigate (Sy), potteries at Farnham (Sy) and glassworks at Chiddingfold (Sy). Roman remains in Surrey are sparse as compared with the other two counties, though coin hoards have been found at Croydon and Cobham, and the outlines of a Roman temple have been preserved on Farley Heath close to the spur road from Rowhook to Guildford.

Evidence of highly organized farming, with field systems quite different from the contemporary Celtic fields, have been identified at two places, one on the low chalk plateau of Cliffe on the edge of the Hoo marshes (K) and another on the level land around Ripe in Sussex north of Alciston. In these two places, you follow field-paths and tracks that do not wind in the usual serpentine fashion, for it is all straight lines and right-angles. The distances between the parallel tracks are multiples of the Roman land measurement unit of an actus, 120 Roman feet. This may be an example of centuriation, a land-settlement planned by Roman surveyors, possibly for the garrison at Rochester. Ripe is about sixteen kilometres from the Roman base at Pevensey and its comparative isolation and the fact that two such examples exist so far apart suggest that there are other such areas waiting to be identified.

The most extensive Roman structures still extant are devoted neither to gods nor to commerce but to conquest and defence. The camp discovered at Dover is one of five coastal forts in the region. Reculver and Richborough stand at either end of the Wantsum Channel, built when Thanet was an island and the Wantsum a sea-lane. Lympne and Pevensey were built on the shore of a wide bay of the Channel now silted up. The five forts were part of a chain of nine built in the third century as protection against the raids of Saxon and Friesian pirates who were already probing the outer defences of the Empire. The period of construction accords with the time when Carausius, a native in charge of the Channel fleet, set himself up as Emperor, and the forts may have served the ironic purpose of protecting his independent empire from the certain wrath of Rome.

The forts of the Saxon Shore, as they are collectively known, have had varied fates. Reculver is merely an earthwork eroded by the sea, remarkable mostly for the Saxon church within its perimeter and the caravans outside it. Richborough has also suffered from the sea but now the land to the east is marshland and the site has a sense of brooding solitude that is not even broken by the towers of the power station over on the present shoreline. Richborough was effectively the first Roman settlement in Britain, the main supply base, worthy of an immense monument called the Great Foundation. The base of that monument is one of the many features of this complex site in which at least three different periods of fort construction can be seen. The existing walls are those of the last rebuilding in the third century. Physically the remains are less exciting than the forts of the Romans' northern frontier but the museum on the site contains one of the most important collections of Roman material in the region.

Lympne has been destroyed by landslips. Hunks of Roman wall lean drunkenly down the slope towards the old shoreline but their size, their setting and the area they cover show how important the place now called Stutfall once was. Pevensey is the most memorable of them all. Like Lympne, it is now cut off from the sea, though the pastures to the south are sodden with standing water.

Unlike the other forts which bear the expected Roman regularity of outline, Pevensey is shaped in a rough oval following the contours of the low promontory. Other forts have the remains of Saxon churches within them; Pevensey contains a Norman castle. The first Norman landing took place at Pevensey, or Anderida, its old name. The Roman enclosure with its four-metre thick walls and bastions became the outer bailey of the Norman stronghold. The stonework is a fascinating amalgam of local sandstones, Eastbourne greensand, flints, ragstones, ironstones and brick. The Romans built to last. The Saxons laid siege to the place and massacred all within. The Normans transformed it to the fashion of their own military occupation.

21. *A Roman coastal fort used as the outer bailey of the Norman castle of Pevensey; the old shore line follows the wooded slope in the foreground.*

The forts of the Saxon shore were prophetic in their naming, for it was the Germanic hordes from the continent, the Angles, the Saxons and the Jutes, who destroyed the Roman power in the south-east and became the new conquerors. The English settlement transformed the landscape of the Romans and their tributary British tribes. The Britons had new masters, more numerous than the old.

4

The White Horse

Just to the north of Watling Street on the approach to Faversham is Stone Farm. In its pastures, visible from the road, is a ruined chapel. When I first saw it, it was with the expectation of the usual broken walls of ragstone and flint, perhaps a decorative window fragment slumped in the grass. But Stone had more to tease the imagination, much more. There were well-cut blocks of ragstone and tufa with bonding courses of tile on a flint foundation. The entrance to the chapel was marked by a single slab of hard greensand. It was Roman work, a mausoleum or martyrium. I learnt later that Roman coins of the third and fourth centuries had been found in the soil, fragments of painted wall and the buried skeleton of a child.* The walls of a Christian church rose directly from the Roman foundations. Incorporated in the walls was a large sarsen stone – a Saxon church of the seventh century on a Roman temple containing even more ancient stones; destruction followed by rebirth. It was a symbol of the decline of the Roman power, the succeeding Dark Age and the evolution of the English settlement.

St Augustine arrived in Canterbury in AD 597 and was directed by Pope Gregory not to destroy pagan temples but to erect altars within them. Stone may have been the result of that injunction. There was a span of more than two hundred years between the Roman structure and the English rebuilding, years in which the landscape of the south-east underwent a fundamental change. The Saxons and Jutes came as destroyers and ended as settlers. By the time that small church had been rebuilt, much of the settlement of hamlet and village

* G. W. Meates, 'The Ruined Church of Stone-next-Faversham', *Kent Life*, March 1974.

had been established. The Venerable Bede called the invaders 'the three most formidable races of Germany, the Saxons, the Angles and Jutes'.* Traditionally, the Jutes settled Kent and the Hampshire basin whilst Saxon groups migrated into the areas now known as Sussex and Surrey. Again, according to Bede, 'from the Jutes are descended the people of Kent and the Isle of Wight'. The people of Hampshire were still called Jutes when he wrote in about AD 731. 'Their first chieftains are said to have been Hengist and Horsa. The latter was killed in battle against the Britons and was buried in East Kent where a monument bearing his name still stands.' That monument has been identified with Kit's Coty, although this is unlikely as the megalithic monument had already been standing for two thousand years. But the burial was in the vicinity, for Horsa was killed at the battle of Aylesford as the invaders were marching from their base in Thanet towards London. They had arrived at the invitation of the British King Vortigern and landed from their long ships at a site identified with Ebbsfleet, close to the first Roman base at Richborough, in AD 449. They were granted land in Thanet and soon used the island as a base for conquest. Their long march and the subsequent battles at the river crossings of Aylesford and then Crayford have been traced further to Wimbledon and Fleet in Hampshire.† They came under the banner of the White Horse, the names of the two legendary chieftains being related to stallion and mare. There are stones and woods named after the White Horse in Kent. Invicta, the crest of the county, adopts it. There are dozens of inns in all three counties bearing the sign. Yet there are no hill-figures in the chalk downs comparable with that in Berkshire, and even there the white horse is Celtic in date rather than Saxon. The emblem of the white horse remains one of the mysteries of history. So do the Jutes themselves.

'There is something more than Jutish names in Kent to this day;'‡ the dominance of the hamlet rather than the nucleated village, the unique organization of the land into lathes, the survival of customary tenure such as gavelkind, all point to the possible conclusion 'that the first great phase of the English invasion was a settlement of the Jutes'.§ These customs have been traced to the Rhine Valley, the possible source of the Jutish invaders. A common name for a region still extant in the Rhine area is 'gau', a word that may be found in the termination of place-names in Kent, notably Eastry, Lyminge and Sturry. Their original forms all end in 'ge' suggesting that they were early centres of the East Region,

* The Venerable Bede, *A History of the English Church and People* (Penguin, 1970).
† G. Ward, 'Hengist', *Archaeologia Cantiana*, Vol. LXI (1949).
‡ Ibid.
§ J. E. A. Jolliffe, *Pre-Feudal England* (Clarendon Press, 1933).

the Stour region and Lyming. The same word appears in Surrey, its earlier form being Sudergeona, the South Region. The place-names and the customs of the Jutes were overlaid and intermingled with the larger, stronger groups of Saxons. The study and interpretation of place-names is a difficult but illuminating way of analysing the pattern of settlement of the German tribes who, in the process, became known as the English. They are the first record we have of settlement and the most abiding, for the oldest aspect of a village or hamlet is its name.

'The place-names of Surrey are entirely of English origin,'* implying the complete destruction or transformation of the settlements of the native Britons who had survived the Roman imperial sway. In Sussex, too, the British names are so few 'as to suggest the virtual extermination of the local Romano-British population'.† Place-names confirm the terrible story as told by the Anglo-Saxon chronicles. The Saxon Aella and his three sons arrived on the Selsey peninsula in the year AD 477. In fourteen years they marched inland and eastwards to Anderida, on or near the site of the Roman fort at Pevensey, where the defenders were slaughtered. From that bloody progress the new Saxon kingdom emerged – Sussex, land of the South Saxons. In Kent, the invaders adopted the British name. Between the two kingdoms stretched the great barrier of the forest, Andred's Weald.

The foundation of the South Region that became Surrey is more obscure but the name implies a separate invasion force coming from the Thames Valley to the north, possibly a group of the Middle Saxons who gave their name to Middlesex. One of the first certain dates in the chronology of Surrey is the foundation of Chertsey Abbey in AD 655. Surrey was by then under the power of Wessex. The king of the West Saxons was converted to Christianity about the year AD 635. By that time, the pagan hordes had had nearly two centuries to colonize the land. The abundance of pagan place-names shows that they had penetrated from the north right into the south-western corner of the area. Tuesley, Wodnesborough and Thursley are as pagan as the days of the week. Thor and Woden live on. 'Hearg', meaning the sacred place, survives in Paper Harow. 'Weoh', another pagan holy site, is found in Willey, in Wye (K), in Whiligh and Whyly (Sx).

The native Britons, also known as the Welsh, were not entirely massacred. Some were enslaved. The missionary Wilfred's grant of land in Selsey included 250 slaves. Welsh and slave became synonymous and they are recalled in place-names such as Walton, Walworth and Wallington, all in Surrey. The language

* F. J. C. Hearnshaw, *The Place of Surrey in the History of England* (Macmillan, 1936).
† Mawer, Stenton and Gover, *The Place Names of Sussex* (C.U.P., 1929).

of the original Britons or Celts predominates in the names of rivers – Thames, Darent, Lavant, Ouse and others. In settlements they are rare. Experts have traced their elements in Crooksbury, Crutchfield, Caterham, Chertsey and Limpsfield. Penge, now one of London's suburbs, was Pen-coat, a name that would not be out of place in Cornwall today, 'coat' meaning 'wood', 'pen' meaning 'headland' or 'spur of a hill'. Fortunately, both Sussex and Surrey have been studied by the Place Name Society and Kent has been deciphered by Wallenberg. Their published volumes supply an invaluable record of detection that help us to understand the English settlement, still the basic feature of the human landscape.

We even know the names of many of the chieftains such as Haesta, Ciorra, Dyttol, Folca, Godhelm, Tota, Ipa and Diccel who gave their names to Hastings, Charing, Detling, Folking, Godalming, Tooting, Iping and Ditchling respectively. The places ending in the common element 'ing' are generally accepted as being amongst the first wave of settlements. At the time of the invasions, the rivers of the south coast formed deep inlets reaching far inland and the early settlements are closely related to the older shoreline. Places like Steyning were close to navigable water. But the site of Steyning at the foot of the escarpment of the South Downs is typical, quite apart from the question of river access, of dozens of such sites, both in Sussex and along the foot of the North Downs in Surrey and Kent. Sometimes they are on outcrops of sandstone, like Tyting (Sy), Iping and Woolbeding (Sx). In Kent especially there is a close relationship with springs at the foot of the chalk as at Kemsing and Chevening. They form a distinctive line across the county as far as Stowting and Postling in the east. Another striking alignment is along the Sussex coast – Wittering, Climping, Angmering, Ferring, Goring, Worthing and Lancing – though some of the original sites may have been to the south of the existing coastline.

Another early place-name element is 'ham' and composite forms such as 'ingham'. They are so abundant that examples are needless but the linguistic link between names such as Woking and Wokingham (in Berkshire) may show a movement of folk from the earliest site to a later 'daughter' settlement. A similar link may be inferred between Poling and Pallingham from the coast to the interior in Sussex. Further waves of settlement are marked by 'ton', as in Merton and Tonbridge, and, again, in composite forms like Beddington and Washington. The Latin 'castrum' became 'chester' as in Rochester and Chichester. The paved streets of the Romans were recorded in Stansted, Stratford and Streatham. 'Stone' may be related to Roman and even earlier sites but often, as in Chiddingstone, is a corruption of 'ton'.

Place-names are a difficult source, subject to varied interpretations and conjecture, but in some areas they are supported by documentary evidence. In Selsey, for example, the Anglo-Saxon Chronicle depicts the main events of the first Saxon landing, though it was written four hundred years after the event. The Saxons landed 'at the place which is Cymenese ora and there they slew many Weales and drove some in flight into the wood which is named Andrede's leaga'.* We have met the Weales, the enslaved Britons and the forest of Andred's Weald. Ora, a landing place, exists in the present name of Itchenor, Ycca's landing place. Itchenor, together with the Witterings, Pagham, Birdham, Sidlesham and Mundham, is recorded in a seventh-century charter conveying land to the church. Most of the places are named after chieftains. Earnley, the wood of the eagle, appears on record in 780 and Selsey, the seal island, in 715. Donnington, Dunnunca's tun, first appears in 966.

The early English settlers may have founded many sites which proved unsuited to permanent occupation. The present pattern of lowland and valley-side settlements must have been the result of decades of adjustment to the physical setting. Archaeological excavation has shown that many early pagan sites were on hill tops such as Highdown Hill or on slopes such as Poll Hill. A complete early Saxon site was excavated at Banstead showing cattle enclosures, defensive mounds and 'gruben', huts dug into the ground. The new invaders would have adopted many of the sites that the previous Roman-British inhabitants had found most suited. The close association of Roman villas and English villages in the Darent Valley, for example, cannot be coincidental. Saxon materials have been found in many of the villa sites in recent years.

A map of the early place-names shows the concentration round the coasts, up the river valleys, along the foot of the hills, the very areas that had been colonized by the Romans. Quite apart from the great Wealden forest, large areas of woodland like the Blean and the Northwood of Surrey remained. New clearances of the forest were made to establish homes for new settlers with the village names recording woodland names such as Acrise, Knockholt, Shrafholt Ockley and Womanswold. Ockley, on the Roman Stane Street, was the scene of the Danish defeat in AD 851.

There are few parts of the south-east that do not have their local stories of Danish raiders. The dene holes have been envisaged as hiding places from their ravages. The mounds on Sheppey are legendary burial places of their dead. St Alphege was a local saint martyred by them, whose name is attached to the

* Quoted by W. E. P. Done, *Looking Back in Sussex* (Faber, 1953).

church at Greenwich. But the Danish contribution to the landscape of the region is minimal. Theirs was a story of destruction, such as that of Chertsey Abbey. They landed at Sheppey in 832 and on Thanet in 851, using the islands as raiding bases. At least two earthworks have been attributed to them – large circular camps – one near Appledore and one on the Swale marshes near Milton.

There are no place-names of definite Danish origin, though Thorpe by the Thames in Surrey is typical of settlement names in the Danelaw further north. The main physical survival is the Graveney boat, found in the North Kent marshes and now preserved in Greenwich Maritime Museum. Dating from about 900, it may have been one of the long ships that Alfred's troops 'took to pieces or burned'.*

Amongst the most important settlements of the sea-faring Saxons were the havens and hythes of the coast. Along the Thames are Greenhithe, Erith and Lambeth, the lambs' hythe. Hythe itself is no longer a harbour, although close to the shore, while Smallhythe, once an outport of Tenterden, is twelve muddy kilometres from the mouth of the Rother. The original haven is still to be seen in the garden of the harbour-master's house, now a museum to the memory of Ellen Terry. That harbour was still navigable in the sixteenth century. The growth of the marshlands has left many a Saxon haven high and dry, but the extent of alluvium on the geological maps helps us to reconstruct the old shoreline and show how many inland villages were havens. Up the Ouse to Lewes, for example, the pleasure craft still ply, past the round-towered churches of Piddinghoe and Southease to Beddingham and Glynde, Malling, Iford and Rodmell, Saxon villages clustered round the old shoreline.

It is the commonplace boast of English villages that they date back to Domesday. Most of them are even older. By the time of the Domesday survey, many of them had been in existence for four or five hundred years. There had been general accounts of the English settlement, as in Bede and the Chronicles, and Anglo-Saxon charters give early evidence of ownership, but the documentation is fragmentary. The places themselves are the essential record. The final, unique richness of the Domesday record comes like a summary of six centuries of English settlement. From it we infer the evolving landscape of the previous centuries. In the survey, no less than 826 places are recorded in the south-east, with about 300 churches and a similar number of mills, another tribute to the importance of the river sites. The Saxons gave us the names of the places but the physical presence is symbolized by the village church. Most of the churches

* 'Three Major Ancient Boat Finds in Britain', *National Maritime Monographs and Reports*, No. 6 (1972).

have been rebuilt throughout later centuries but enough remains to give us actual physical contact with the early English people.

The first churches, like the dwelling-places and mills, were probably built of timber. That evidence lies beneath the present stone structures. Augustine was created Archbishop of Canterbury in AD 597 and church-building in Kent began in earnest. By the middle of the next century, Surrey was converted. Sussex did not renounce the ancient pagan ways until the end of the seventh century, led by the missionary zeal of St Wilfred from Northumbria. Yet the best examples of Saxon architecture are to be found in Sussex, and finest of all the churches stands on the once ill-defined border between Sussex and Surrey, at Worth. To drive under the noise umbrella of Gatwick airport, through the bustle of Crawley, and find, close by, the quietude of Worth, is unforgettable. At first a narrow side road, then a cul-de-sac of old houses, a lych gate and an avenue of trees lead to the porch of St Nicholas. My first reaction was of disbelief, then of happy recognition. Tall stone pilasters line the walls. A stone string-course encircles them. At the east end the round apse looks warm and comforting. The corner-stones of the walls are massive in the tradition of Saxon quoin work. High up, a twin-arched light with mid-wall shafts tells the same story. Two tall Saxon doors stand to north and south, though the south door has been disguised by a fourteenth-century entrance while the Devil's door on the north side has been infilled. Tall columns in the interior have massive stone slabs as capitals and base, framing the largest chancel arch of its period in England. Restoration in the nineteenth century, from which so many early churches suffered, was held in check by local protest. So Worth stands, almost entire and intact, as a Saxon church.

Restoration was merciless at Woolbeding (Sx) but pilasters survive on the south wall. At Stopham, near the famous medieval bridge, the tall nave, the thin walls, two massive doors and quoin stones all have the Saxon feel though experts differ as to their exact dating. Like so many churches in Sussex, it may be part of the Saxon-Norman overlap in the eleventh century when contact with Normandy was close, even before the Conquest. We are on more certain ground at Bosham, squatting by the mudflats and creeks of the Selsey peninsula. There was a small monastery here in the time of Bede but the present tower, nave and much of the chancel date from the early eleventh century. The church has been associated with Canute who tried to turn the sea back somewhere in the vicinity and the corpse of an eight-year-old girl found in excavation is claimed locally to be his daughter. King Harold prayed there before journeying to Normandy, an episode depicted, together with the church, in the Bayeux tapestry. The chancel

22. *Saxon chancel and apse of St Nicholas, Worth.*

arch has a typical horseshoe shape, slightly wider above than at the base. Stone reptiles writhe round the base of the massive columns and one of the tower windows is headed by a triangle of stone slabs, an ancient device.

There are many other notable fragments of pre-Domesday churches. Jevington on the Downs has arched heads of Roman brick and a bas-relief of Christ killing the demon of evil. The south porch of Bishopstone, west of Eastbourne, dates from the eighth century. It is crowned with a sun-dial inscribed to Eadric, with thirteen deep grooves, five long ones sub-divided. The most famous Saxon church in Sussex is Sompting. Its tall tower, lined with pilasters, is capped with

23. *Saxon sundial, St Andrew's, Bishopstone.*

a unique roof, known as a Rhenish helm from its German connections, the only one of its kind in the country. The tower arch is crudely carved and there are other early carvings, including a relief of an abbot with a crozier. One of the most interesting features of St Peter of the Vetere Ponte, now St Botolphs, standing in isolation by the old bridging point of the River Adur, is its nave measurement. The ratio of 3:1 is more commonly found in Northumbria, an echo, perhaps, of St Wilfred's influence. Its chancel arch is crude but powerful. E. A. Fisher has identified Saxon stone work in sixty Sussex churches.*

* E. A. Fisher, *The Saxon Churches of Sussex* (David and Charles, 1970).

The relics in Surrey are even more fragmentary. A chancel arch, a window, some carved stones as in the large parish church of Godalming, the tower of St Mary's in Guildford. Ashstead, Cheam, East and West Horsley, Stoke d'Abernon, Wotton, Witley, Wonersh and Albury all retain some Saxon features. The tower at Compton is as fine an example as the county can offer. The chancel walls are Saxon. The pillars of the nave are carved from chalk rock, startlingly white, leading to the unique Norman double sanctuary, one built within the other. This is a place that never fails to lift the heart with an atmosphere derived from more than a thousand years of being the focus of the village drama, the manifestation in stone of the essential continuity of English settlement. Witley, on its Wealden hump, was just another, though splendid, Norman church until this century when two early Saxon windows were discovered. The paucity of Saxon remains in Surrey is not only due to the vigour of nineteenth-century restoration. The infertility of large tracts of the county discouraged settlement, so much of it was thinly populated.

Kent, in contrast, was thickly populated, especially in the north and east. First of the converted kingdoms, it has some of the earliest known Christian structures. Bertha, Christian queen of a pagan king, built a church outside the walls of Canterbury which has been identified with St Martin's, the oldest church in Britain still in regular use. The nave of masoned blocks and courses of Roman brick, a round-headed doorway, an ancient font base beneath the Norman tub bowl, a blocked Saxon window, take us back to the very beginnings of Christianity. The walls of the church are largely built with Roman brick and the same is true of St Mary in Castro alongside the Roman pharos at Dover. Restored in 1860 and dazzlingly decorated with Victorian tiles, enough remains to make it the outstanding late-Saxon building in Kent, with the usual pilasters, tower arches and double-splayed windows. Within the enclosure of St Augustine's Abbey are three more Saxon churches of the early missionary period with only the lower courses of the walls standing, but holding within the foundations the tombs of kings and bishops; St Peter and St Paul, St Mary's and St Pancras all date from the pre-Norman era. They were levelled to the ground for the new Norman church which stood until the Dissolution. The seventh century is represented at Reculver where the twin towers of St Mary's stand within the Roman fort. A Saxon cross from Reculver is in the crypt of Canterbury Cathedral.

St Margaret's at Lower Halstow, the name signifying the 'holy place', is reminiscent of Bosham in its setting. The walls show a jumble of flint and stone and Roman tile, a Saxon window in the tower. There is Saxon work, too, at

Lydd in the marshes, at Darenth and at the two minster churches in Thanet and Sheppey.

A Saxon name and a Saxon church are not enough to reconstruct the early settlements. Apart from excavations of 'gruben' huts, we know little of the other buildings in the villages and the overall pattern of the place. Perhaps at Eashing (Sy), with a farm and a few cottages grouped casually around a small green on a flat hill above the River Wey, we get close to the feeling of the early sites. Or at Southease, with a church, a farm and a cottage round a pocket handkerchief of a green. Villages change. Even their sites change. A village may move away from its church as at East Peckham and Horsmonden. Map evidence does not emerge until the Tudor estate plans and these are comparatively rare. One of the first experiments at the Open Air Museum at Singleton was the reconstruction of a Saxon hut. The ground plan of a Saxon hall is near by, based on excavations carried out in Hampshire. Secular buildings of the Saxon period are very rare, which makes a place like Luddesdown of special interest. A solid L-shaped manor house of flint and stone on the dip-slope of the Downs south of Cobham (K), it is still occupied as a private dwelling. One of the interior walls has carved in the plaster the outline of a ship that may antedate the Bayeux tapestry. The owners claim it to be one of the oldest houses still in use. Its earliest owners must have been men of importance. A sarsen stone lies on the lawn.

What the landscape does hold intact are the boundaries of the lands that each settlement annexed from the wild for its sustenance, the divisions that became formalized by the reign of Alfred as parishes. The origin of the parochial system is uncertain but the reorganization of the church following the Synod of Whitby in AD 663 stimulated it. Yet, as shown in the Domesday survey, every settlement did not have a church. And churches varied in their status. For many years, burials, for example, could not take place at 'field' churches but only at the central minster churches from which priests ministered to widespread communities. There were only seven minster churches in Surrey. Like many other features of the landscape, the parish was the result of gradual change, of settlements growing to the point at which their lands made common boundaries with adjacent places. Their bounds were recorded in charters and folk memory. The boundaries used physical features such as rivers but also, as we have seen, Roman roads, the Ridgeway, Celtic dew-ponds, ancient stone groups, tumuli and other features of the early human scene. Within the township boundary were the lands necessary to its basic sustenance, the arable fields for corn, the hay meadows, the rough grazing for livestock, timber for fuel and building. The variety of land use is related to the variety of soils and one of the most striking features of parish organization is its relationship to geology.

The line of villages between Croydon and Guildford on the dip-slope of the chalk downs, twenty in all, each have a long strip of land running at right-angles to the grain of the country. The villages are at the base of the chalk. Their parish boundaries are typically seven kilometres long and between two and three kilometres wide, enclosing chalk down, gault clay, pebble beds and London clay. The present commons are on the heavy clays. Along the foot of the chalk escarpment, the parishes are even more elongated. Godstone and Tandridge, for example, are only a kilometre wide in places and more than eleven kilometres long, pointing like fingers from the downland crest across the greensand to the Wealden clays beyond. Before new parishes were created in the last century, these parishes reached right to the Sussex border, a distance of 18 or 19 kilometres, an extraordinary adjustment to the physical setting. On the more level lands of the East Kent plateaux, of Thanet and the Thames coastal plain, the parishes take a more compact shape, smaller on the fertile land, larger on the poorer land. Acol in Thanet has three square kilometres to support it. But the sub-divisions and amalgamations of parishes have modified the ancient boundaries.

Beating the bounds is an old custom originally intended to prevent encroachment from neighbouring parishes. The custom has been revived in many places, even in London boroughs that were once Kentish manors. For the landscape historian it can be full of surprises. Typical of the excitement and variety that can be found is that of Trottiscliffe (K), where it marches with its neighbour, Birling. It starts up on the Ridgeway on the crest of the Downs by an ancient earth bank lined with pollarded hornbeams. Descending through White Horse Wood to the Pilgrims' Way, it follows a sunken track between a hedgerow and a fringing woodland belt known as a shaw, containing hawthorn, whitebeam, blackthorn, hazel, dogwood, field maple, crab apple, privet, spindle and elderberry. The track runs by the eastern face of a Neolithic long barrow at Coldrum, then plunges through woodland towards another tomb. Sarsen stones are found all along this section of the path. There is enough in that mile to suggest that the Saxons were utilizing an even more ancient boundary for their parochial division.

A land organization that was formulated more than a thousand years ago is still the basic unit of local government. The parish pump is still clanking to good effect. Domesday gives us a thumbnail picture of many of them. Take Limpsfield, for example: 'The Abbot of Battle holds Limpsfield. Harold held it before

1066. Then it answered for 25 hides. Now since the Abbot acquired it, it is not answerable. Land for 12 ploughs. In lordship, 5 ploughs; 25 villagers and 6 smallholders with 14 ploughs. A mill at 2s; a fishery; a church; meadow, 4 acres; woodland at 150 pigs from pasturage; 2 stone quarries at 2s; 3 hawks' nests in the woodland; 10 slaves.'* Previously a Saxon royal manor, Limpsfield had been granted as a source of revenue to a Sussex abbey. The 'hide' was a unit of land assessment based on the land needed for one peasant and his family. It varied in actual measurement in different areas but has been equated roughly with 120 acres. The number of villagers nicely balances the number of hides. The church and the mill are the only two buildings recorded. The essential land within the parish, the source of its daily bread, was its ploughland. One of the Limpsfield references, that of the hawks' nests, is unique, but the ploughlands are recorded for every place. More than 1,200 are listed in Surrey, their distribution showing the importance of the two lines of settlement along the margins of the chalk. More than 3,000 ploughs are mentioned for Sussex and a similar number for Kent. The lighter downland soils, the river valleys and the plains, the lower chalk platform fronting the downs supplied the best arable land.The comparative emptiness of the sandstone hills and the Wealden clays is almost certainly a true reflection, though the Domesday record, especially in Sussex, has many gaps.

Plough, meadow and woodland: the essential pattern does not differ fundamentally from the scene which is familiar to us today. In the parishes running across the Vale of Holmesdale, the meadows are by the river banks on the heavy gault clay soils while the larger arable fields stretch out across the lighter soils of the lower chalk platform. The steep downland slope supplies rough grazing. Woodland lies both on the chalk crest and on the greensand. The large, arable fields, frequently devoid of hedgerows, still have the visual impact of an open-field system and it is not surprising that the evidence of common arable fields is found on just such areas, as at Wrotham and Kemsing. The Roman ploughlands at Cliffe mentioned in the last chapter became the open arable fields of the Saxon township and were not finally enclosed until the nineteenth century. Similar large arable fields, cultivated in common, were found in East Kent and along the foot of the Sussex downs.

The water mill was the prime source of power, its major role the production of flour. There were few settlements without a mill and some townships had several. Along the Ravensbourne, a small stream flowing into the Thames at

* John Morris, *Domesday Book : Surrey* (Phillimore, 1975).

Deptford, eleven sites were known. Most of them can be identified today and the names of four are preserved in local street names. Fisheries were an important source of food. They were recorded along the Channel coast at Brighton, Rodmell and Southease, herrings at Sandwich and Luddenham, with eels a speciality on the Thames, the Wey, the Medway, the Arun and the Ouse. Saltpans, for the extraction of salt from sea water, existed on shallow shorelines, at Rye and Bosham, on the Kent side of Romney, on the Swale marshes and the Wantsum channel.

Centres of administration and commerce were already developing to the status of boroughs, two in Surrey, seven in Sussex and eight in Kent. Several of the boroughs were on Roman sites and nearly all were on or near the coast. Guildford was the furthest inland. Southwark was the southern bridgehead to London. Rochester, Canterbury, Fordwich, Sandwich, Dover, Hythe, Romney and Seasalter marked the main belt of population down the Dover road and the south-east coast of Kent while Hastings, Pevensey, Rye, Steyning, Lewes, Arundel and Chichester stood guard along the South Saxon shore. Hastings for centuries maintained some semblance of independence from either kingdom, being in comparative isolation on a ridge of high land with marshes to west and east.

The forest belt across the heart of the region was already penetrated by Roman roads and settled by ironworkers. Early churches like Worth and Capel stood in clearings on the major trackways. Clearances were extended to give grazing areas for the settlements all round its perimeter. We saw that Limpsfield had woodland to support 150 pigs. Some of that pannage was in outlying areas south of the village. Lewisham, a manor near the Thames, had grazing rights for swine in Cowden, forty kilometres away on the Sussex border, but on the direct route of a Roman street that may still have been usable even after centuries of neglect. Thanet had rights at Tenterden and the royal manor of Milton had land at Marden. Anglo-Saxon charters show that the manor of Wye, with its main ploughlands at the foot of the North Downs, had outlying grazing areas in many parts of the Weald, at Cranbrook and Hawkhurst and even further afield on the Romney Marsh. These early clearings were called denns, the element 'den' being present in hundreds of place-names. There were fifty-two such denns recorded in Domesday and many more probably existed but were omitted from the record. The existence of a further three half-denns may indicate that grazing rights were shared on a stint basis, a custom still followed in some northern wastes. In Cumbria, pastures are still stinted; the grazier is entitled not to a portion of land but to a certain number of animals.

The 'den' element is almost absent in Surrey but there are other names such as 'hurst' and 'fold' that mark the later period of inland settlement. Some of the Kentish dens had developed into something more than mere clearances for grazing by the eleventh century. The settlers had the adjacent forest for arable land and more permanent villages. Benenden, Newenden and Rolvenden all had plough teams recorded and Rolvenden, at least, had a church of its own. In the first years of the English occupation, it seems likely that the Weald was a common grazing area, the *communis silva* of all the folk. In succeeding centuries, the concept of the ownership of specific areas as subsidiaries of distant manors evolved. The hamlet is very much a part of this piecemeal subjugation of the forest. The early pioneers were freed from tithes and other customary duties of the time. The forest meant comparative freedom. The outlying denns and hursts and folds supplemented the lands within the parish boundaries. They added to the complexity of the landscape. 'Such is the ground plan of the Kentish manor,' wrote Jolliffe, 'a central hall, an archipelago of islands of demesne, inland and outland, blocks of pasture in the southern forest belt, marsh pasture upon the Thames, Stour or Romney.'* The elongation of Surrey parishes like Tandridge right into the heart of the Weald may be another type of adjustment to the same need, bringing the outlying waste into the cohesion of the parish.

In spite of such encroachments, the Weald was still the great waste stretching from the Hampshire border to the coast, the home of wild animals and beasts of the chase, an attraction to royal hunting parties. Domesday records the existence of private hunting parks. There was one at Stoke near Guildford, possibly the present-day Stoughton. In Sussex, there were enclosures at Rotherfield, Eridge, Walburton (near Arundel), Waltham (near Amberley) and Wiltingham near Hastings. There were three Domesday parks in Kent, at Wickham (possibly Wickhambreux), Chart and Leeds, the last named still existing, though no longer with a deer herd. These chases may have been marked by a boundary ditch with paling. Though some of the parks may have been of Norman origin, others may have supplanted existing royal chases of the Saxon kings. Amongst the duties of Saxon thegns was the erection of hedges on the kings' estates. These were dead-hedges of brushwood, known as deer-hayes, which made temporary enclosures into which the deer and other beasts were driven.

Most of the hunting parks were on the edge of the Weald. They made small but significant inroads into the territory of the oak and the wild deer. 'From the early documentary history of our forest, it would appear that the herds were originally turned at large into it, under the charge of swineherds without any

* J. E. A. Jolliffe, *Pre-Feudal England* (Clarendon Press, 1933).

mark, limit or restriction,' wrote Furley in his monumental study of the Weald.* The Saxon settlements were poised in a great arc round its perimeter. The pioneers and the iron miners had already penetrated its depths, creating small communities in clearings. The attack on the last forest frontier was about to begin.

* R. Furley, *A History of the Weald of Kent* (1871).

5

The Forest Frontier

Just to the south-east of Reigate, the claylands of the Surrey weald rise gently to a height of nearly four hundred feet at Outwood Common. There is a large green, a pond, a small Victorian chapel and a straggle of cottages tucked away in wooded lanes. Part of the common is a patch of oak woodland, now National Trust property. On one side of the green is a seventeenth-century smock mill, one of the earliest and best-preserved specimens of its kind. From the mill, an old road cuts south by the parish boundary with Horne, its banks rich with flowers, wood anemones celandine, and Herb Robert. Between the banks, the hollowed surface is beaten into the most glutinous surface imaginable. Tracks like this made the Weald a fearsome place for travellers well into the nineteenth century. Even oxen found it hard going. In the ditch at the side of the grey slush there are thin layers of sandstone and limestone exposed, thin but tough enough to have created this small topographical variation on the Wealden scene. The setting gives the impression that man has not quite imposed himself. Nature is not quite conquered. Outwood looks like a frontier settlement.

All about it are other places with forest names, Charlwood, Whitwood, Kingswood, Forest Row, Ashurst, Crowhurst, Cowden, Crippenden, Crawley, Horley, Holtye. Most of them entered the written record in the rent rolls and charters of the twelfth and thirteenth centuries. They mark the late colonization of the Weald, the conquest of the last frontier. We have already seen that forest clearances were known long before Domesday and place-names with elements such as 'den', 'hurst', 'ley', 'field' and 'wold', all woodland clearances, were established by the Saxons. But the majority, especially the group of 'folds' in Surrey, were settled in the two centuries following the Norman Conquest. The first reference to Cowden, for example, is in about 1100, Chiddingfold, 1130, Ashurst 1164, Charlwood 1199, Crawley 1203 and Alfold 1228. There was a general increase of settlements in the inner Weald, which formed a comparative wilderness between the three counties. The forest frontier was crossed.

The Wealden edge was not just a physical frontier, it was a legal divide. Lambarde said that the Weald was 'contained within very straight and narrow limits', a view that was confirmed by Hasted two hundred years later, who wrote that 'there have been several who have contended that all that part of Wrotham which lies below the chalk is in the Weald of Kent, as no tithe of wood was paid there. The general received opinion is that the Weald begins at the next sand hill above Fairlawne.'* In some areas, as at Westerham, the Pilgrims' Way was taken as the boundary; in Hasted's words, again, 'the woodland lying to the southward of the Pilgrims' Way is exempt from tithe by prescription'. There was a close relationship between geology and the legal definition of the Weald. It encompassed the area on rocks older than the chalk. The thin, poor soils of the greensand ridges and the Wealden sandstones, the heavy, clay soils of the interior; these were the areas where the forest still dominated.

In time, the outlying dens grew into settled hamlets and villages. The plough followed the grazier in a sequence not unlike that of the American continent in more recent times. Ewhurst, for example, was a chapelry of Merton and became a parish in its own right in 1304. Fernhurst, a chapelry of Easebourne (Sx), separated in the fourteenth century. Edenbridge was originally an appendant chapel of Westerham. And the process continues. Milland (Sx), a chapelry of Trotton parish, became a parish in 1862. Newchapel, the tall, thin spire rising from the wet, flat land near Lingfield, was consecrated in 1865, a parish created from the southernmost portions of Godstone and Tandridge. Seen in this perspective, the new town of Crawley and the airport of Gatwick are the final stages in the process that began with the medieval tenant farmers.

Despite this process spanning a millennium, the view from Blackdown needs little visual imagination to reconstruct the earlier landscape. Lurgashall, Fernhurst, Chiddingfold, Dunsfold still appear as pastoral enclosures. Beyond are Crimbourne and Hawkhurst Court, hidden in the oak forest of the Mens near Bedham. Just as striking are the greens that most of these places embrace. Village greens may be found in earlier settlements such as Meopham (K) and Stelling (K), but the persistence of greens in so many of the later medieval places makes it tempting to interpret them as the original clearances around which the

* E. Hasted, *History and Topographical Survey of the County of Kent* (1797–1801).

pioneers erected their dwellings. Further east, in Surrey, there is a particularly fine group at the foot of the sandstone ridge – Ewhurst Green, Forest Green, Mayes Green and Ockley. There is no comparable group in Kent, where the village greens are scattered widely and appear on every type of land, though they are most apparent in the Weald as at Offham and Shipbourne, both on the greensand, and at Matfield, Benenden and Horsmonden on the Wealden sandstones. The trim, rectangular green at Horsmonden has the look of a planned space and marks a new site of the village settled on the heath two miles from the original site by the church. The green is still called the Heath.

Many greens are found in association with hamlets bearing the name 'forstal' and 'lees'. The lees are found especially round old hunting parks and chases, such as Challock Lees and Boughton Lees near Eastwell. Forstals, literally the land in front of the stall or steading, are frequent in Kent and give rise to such delightful corners as Little Chart Forstal and Lenham Forstal. Other examples of late settlements with greens are found in the woodlands of Seal Chart such as Godden Green and Bitchet Green. The early use of such greens may be indicated by such names as Knockholt Pound. Pounds and forstals show a link with a livestock economy.

There are in all about 37 village greens registered in Kent, 56 in Sussex and no less than 85 in Surrey.* They average about one hectare in size and vary from small patches of grass surviving in front of the pub at Trottiscliffe, nibbled away by roads and front gardens, to the rambling common of Stelling Minnis with thirty-six hectares. Heyshott in West Sussex has a similar straggling area of rough grazing leading right through the village linking the downs with the common. Dunsfold (Sy), with its great oak and old quarry pits, now converted into ponds, is similar. The exact status and ownership of greens is still in dispute. Even after the registration of the commons in 1965, many greens, such as Stelling Minnis and Coldred, have been claimed by private owners exercising manorial rights.

The green is the unifying feature of many places, the centre of fair and festival. It was the nursery of cricket and many a Cricketers' Inn stands proudly on the perimeter. It has been claimed that the Battle of Crecy was won on the village greens of England, where the bowmen practised their lethal art. A most unusual survival in Kent is the tilting at the quintain at Offham. During the annual summer festival, the young horsemen of the village still drive their lances at full tilt towards the black-dotted board swinging on its white pole, a sport that dates

* W. G. Hoskins and L. D. Stamp, *Common Lands of England and Wales* (Collins, 1963).

back, so they claim, to Roman times. But if I had to put one example of a green above all others it would be Wisborough Green in the Sussex Weald, where church, pubs, shops and houses settle round the irregular outline of the green in happy informality.

Village, hamlet and farm, we all have our images that are evoked by these familiar words, but the exact definition is difficult. Historians like Jolliffe have suggested that the hamlet and the farm group are more typical of Kent and parts of East Sussex and Surrey than the village and attributes the fact to a possible Jutish origin as distinct from the larger, nucleated villages usually associated with Saxon settlement. Furley quotes a statute of Edward I which ordered eight men to appear for each 'entire vill', six men for each 'half vill' and four men for each hamlet.* The word 'vill' is of Roman origin and signified a large residence with farm buildings and stall associated, much like the estate at Lullingstone or Bignor. The meaning of the words changes with time and it may be more rewarding to look closely at a present parish where there is a diversity of settlement, Marden, for example, which we have already encountered as the outlying den for the royal manor at Milton. Marden, the pasture for mares, was recorded in the Domesday survey. The largest settlement is in the centre of the parish with a large church, mostly rebuilt in the thirteenth century, a small market-place with shops, a lock-up and mounting steps. Round it are no less than sixteen hamlets, small groups of buildings dominated by half-timbered farmhouses – Wanshurst Green, Chainhurst, Pagehurst, Pattenden, Underling Green and Tilden, all being first recorded in the thirteenth and fourteenth centuries. Marden may have been just one of the many hamlets that grew into special prominence because of its central position. But it seems more likely that it was the original settlement from which the others developed as more of the surrounding woodland was cleared. There are at least thirty more farms in the parish of even later date than the hamlets. A similar relationship may be found in the adjacent parishes of Staplehurst, Smarden and Headcorn.

Yet another stage in the piecemeal colonization of the Weald may be indicated by the frequent occurrence of twinned names such as Great and Little Pattenden, the little being an offshoot of the greater farm. In these parishes on the clay, there is no remnant of the forest. The impetus for its clearance was the doubling of population between the Norman Conquest and the fourteenth century. The need for more farming land was further complicated by the custom of gavelkind which led to the division of holdings. Another factor was the in-

* R. Furley, *A History of the Weald of Kent*, Vol. 1 (Igglesdon, 1871).

creasing demand for revenue by overlords which led to many large manors being sub-infeudated, broken up into smaller manors. Lewisham, for example, once an estate of Alfred, the Saxon king, had six sub-manors by the end of the thirteenth century, including Brockley, Sydenham, Catford, Bellingham and Shrafholt, though it had only the one parish church, St Mary's, at the centre.

This complex pattern of settlement was supported by an even more complicated field system. Today's jig-saw of field and forest, of close, garth, and shaw, has its origin in the same period. 'The landscape of East Kent seems to have been woven on a broad loom . . . the landscape of the Weald, on the other hand, seems to have been embroidered in minute detail.'* The larger fields, the comparatively open farmscapes of the chalk plateaux, the Sussex plain and the river valleys were already established in Saxon times. The Wealden assarts, a Norman word for an area taken in from the waste for farming, were a later development. The sense of the forest still hemming the assarts is particularly strong where the broad strips of woodland known as 'shaws' survive. They are characteristic of much of the North Downs around Wrotham, for example. In Pluckley and Little Chart on the clay, they form more than 10 per cent of the total area. They were even taxed separately from the enclosed fields and often form the line of rights-of-way from village centre to outlying pastures.

Gavelkind tenure involved dispersion and fragmentation, as at Wingham, 'if an inheritance is divided into two or three portions where there are heirs, and each makes his messuage upon his portion'. In such a quotation we can see the small hamlets emerging. The fragmentation led to some holdings becoming too small to support a tenant and estates were 'disgavelled', as on the extensive lands of John of Cobham, to halt the process. In later centuries, there was an active purchase of parcels of land, leasing of neighbouring land and other efforts to consolidate and enlarge farms. The process has been the subject of detailed and fascinating research by landscape historians, notably A. R. H. Baker.†

In Surrey, the typical holding 'comprised a messuage, a few fields and crofts and a number of unenclosed parcels of land lying within larger fields'. These larger fields, cultivated in severalty, i.e. by several tenant-farmers, were on the good land. Evidence of the common arable field system survived in parts of Sussex until the last century. Alciston, for example, had three such fields, the west, the middle and the east 'leynes'. One field had no less than four hundred separate parcels of unenclosed land, some tenants having less than half an acre.

* A. R. H. Baker, 'Some Fields and Farms in Medieval Kent', *Archaeologia Cantiana*, Vol. LXXX (1965).

† A. R. H. Baker and R. A. Butlin, *Studies of Field Systems in the British Isles* (C.U.P., 1973).

The area still looks open, lacking hedgerows, quite different from the 'outfield' on the greensand. Between 1086 and 1346, six square miles of woodland in the parish of Rotherfield (Sx) were cleared and partitioned. The twenty-four tenants of the eleventh century had multiplied tenfold by the end of the period.

There were many variations of the system of infield and outfield. The infield, the best land, was cropped annually; the outfield was brought into cultivation periodically. The infield of Mersham, for example, was close to the court lodge. In contrast to much of England, the enclosure of the south-east was almost completed by the fourteenth century. The surviving common arable fields are notable precisely because of their comparative rarity. The enclosures of later centuries were mostly of common pasture land and the lords' demesne land. Even then, the enclosures were often opposed by the local population. An attempt to enclose the Common of Westwood on the borders of Kent and Surrey in the reign of James I was defeated after long and sometimes violent opposition by the parishioners led by their parish priest. The common remained open until the parliamentary enclosures of the early nineteenth century.

The remaining woods, commons and heaths were an essential part of the medieval equation. The woodland, by its ultimate scarcity, became as valuable as farmland. Even in the deer parks, the sale of timber was an important source of revenue. An increase of population caused an increased demand for timber, for building, for fuel, for fencing, for furnace. The last areas of Wealden forest were economically valuable. The pressure for more farmland was lessened, too, by the outbreaks of plague and the decline of population following the Black Death in 1348.

With the development of new settlements and new parishes in the Weald came a pattern of footpaths linking the outlying parts with the centre. On the heavy clay soils, such paths were often paved. Along the footpaths radiating from the churches at Bethersden and Staplehurst, for instance, you can find slabs of Bethersden marble buried under the pastures, tumbled into ditches or forming bridges up to two metres wide. The Horsham stone served a similar purpose in the wet areas of Surrey and Sussex. When we follow the rights-of-way today we are often following landscape features that are medieval in origin. They are as much ancient monuments as the churches and farms that they linked, one very good reason for maintaining them.

Longer trackways linked settlements with outlying pastures and to markets. Drove roads became primeways, the King's highway was known as the 'alta via regia' and the roads to market became 'communis strata'. The longer routeways were related to river crossings. The east–west course of many rivers was as much a barrier to movement into the heart of the Weald as the forest itself. Fording sites are recorded in many place-names but they were subject to seasonal flooding and were supplemented by bridges. A ford and a bridge stand side by side at Eynsford. The earliest bridges were of wood but many were rebuilt in stone in the Middle Ages and many survive especially on the upper reaches of the Medway, the Sussex Rother and the Wey in Surrey. Dating is difficult due to a lack of documentary evidence but the six bridges over the Wey between Guildford and Tilford are all of similar design, suggesting that they were constructed

24. *Medieval bridge on the Sussex Rother at Stopham.*

at about the same time, possibly after the great floods of 1233 that had swept earlier structures away. They are unusual in that their cutwaters on the downstream side are rounded. The two at Eashing, one crossing a millstream with only a wooden balustrade, are now National Trust property. A group of narrow stone bridges span the Rother between Pulborough and Pyrford near the Hampshire border, the most famous being at Stopham which was recorded in charters in 1347. Fittleworth, Woolbeding, Iping, Trotton and Pyrford are all in good condition, though several show evidence of widening and repair.

The Medway bridges are larger and more imposing. East Farleigh, a five-arched bridge of the fourteenth century, has been described as the finest medieval bridge in the south of England.* The most photographed is Aylesford, because of the backcloth of the village. Its central arch spanning the main channel of the navigable river is of a later date. Twyford, Laddingfold, Yalding and Teston all differ in detail but their pillars and cutwaters all have the solidity of local ragstone. The balustrades in some cases have been rebuilt with flint and brick. All of them have a characteristic width of nearly four metres with recesses above the cutwaters. There are other bridges that may be medieval in origin, such as the inconspicuous Stephen's bridge west of Headcorn, built entirely of Bethersden marble.

25. *Three panels from the Norman lead font at Brookland church in Romney Marsh depicting the autumn months.*

New settlements meant new churches. New conquerors meant new fashions. Many of the small Saxon churches were rebuilt and enlarged. New churches sprang up in the Norman style. The forests supplied the oak shingle roofs, the enormous timbers of roof and belfry, sometimes the whole belfry, as in the remarkable detached structure at Brookland in the marsh. The spate of church-building so enraged the Devil, according to Sussex folklore, that he started to dig the dyke through the Downs near Brighton to let in the sea and drown them all. Fortunately, an old lady confused him with a lighted candle which he thought was the rising sun. The dyke remains dry and the churches safe. One of the claims for Goudhurst church, first mentioned in 1117, is that fifty-nine other

* E. Jervoise, *The Ancient Bridges of the South of England* (Architectural Press, 1930).

churches are within eyeshot of its tower. This is as much a tribute to their hill-top sites as to the early travellers' eyesight.

There are more than a hundred Norman churches in Kent. Whilst pure Norman churches are scarce in Sussex, nearly every church seems to show Norman influence. Even Surrey, with about ninety-eight medieval churches, has at least forty-three with Norman work. In the Middle Ages, Surrey was the poorest of the three counties. Most of its Norman churches are small and plain

26. *Mural of the Last Judgement, c. A.D. 1200, on the west wall of Chaldon church, as recorded by P. M. Johnston in the 1920s.*

as at Farley, Tatsfield, Wisley and Pyrford. The last two, in close proximity, are beautiful examples and most refreshing in a county where the nineteenth-century 'improvers' swept away so much of the medieval past. Chaldon church has the best surviving murals in the region, the entire west wall being covered with devices showing mankind climbing the ladder to judgement and then being consigned to the company of angels or a particularly unpleasant end with the demons. The twelfth-century graphics were discovered during rebuilding operations in 1870. There are murals in many other churches such as Hardham (Sx), Brook, Challock and Lower Halstow, all in Kent, but none as evocative of the medieval mind.

The two finest Norman churches are close together in East Kent, not far from the Roman road that linked Dover with Canterbury, in the villages of Barfreston and Patrixbourne. Barfreston has no spire, no tower. It is inconspicuous both on the map and in the landscape. It is composed of a simple nave and chancel built primarily of local flint. But there the simplicity ends. All the corner work is of creamy-textured stone imported from Caen in Normandy. Anything that can be done with stone is done here. The local church guide sums it up as 'a wonderful prodigality of ornamentation'. The eight-sectioned east window is full of animals and angels, flowers and foliage but this is only a foretaste of the beauty of the south door. God in majesty sits at the centre of the tympanum, surrounded by every flight of Romanesque fancy, of heraldic beasts and a gallery of medieval characters such as the forester, the minstrel, the miller and the armourer. Yet another arc of carvings displays dancing and carousing, coursing and riding, the whole composition framed by intricate mouldings. There are similar compositions in the lead font at Brookland and the stone font at Newenden. Even the blocked north door on the dark, Devil's side of the church is carved, including the representation of two dancing women on a capital. A third door, the priest's door, would be notable in any other church. The interior is comparatively plain but the arch linking chancel with nave is delicately moulded. So are the recesses and the string-course that runs round the nave, carrying a medieval strip cartoon to instruct and entertain the congregation. There are fragments of early murals. The church bell is outside in a yew tree as at Bilsington.

The church at Patrixbourne, dating from 1170, may have been built by the same masons who worked at Barfreston and Rochester. The south doorway, capped with a triangular canopy, has carvings to rival those of Barfreston and, incidentally, has the largest collection of mass dials that I have seen in any church, scratched deeply into the Caen stone. Above the priest's door is a figure that might be a representation of St Thomas, whose martyrdom was contemporary with the building of the church. 'Climping for perfection' is a Sussex motto and it is only in comparison with Barfreston that the Norman work might seem plain. But the moulded Norman windows in the tower are as mannered as anything in England. The church is the brightest spot in a rather dull corner of the Sussex plain.

A very different setting for two fine Norman churches is the busy port of Shoreham. St Nicolas in Old Shoreham is small and perfect enough to match the village atmosphere of the old flint buildings in the oldest part of the town. The crossing of the nave contains four Romanesque arches that contrast with the surviving Saxon door in the north wall. The oak screen and the tie-beams in the nave are thirteenth-century woodwork. St Mary de Haura, a variant of 'havre', is even more embedded in the coastal town, an impressive centre-piece. Its size and ornamentation, its thick Norman columns and mouldings, reflect the great days of the medieval haven. The sense of space inside is heightened by the lack of clutter. The Norman font of Sussex marble is not unexpected but columns imbedded in the outer wall are. They are part of the original nave that spanned the present churchyard. The rebuilding of the twelfth and thirteenth centuries is of a quality to match the cathedrals of Chichester and Rochester.

There are dozens of smaller treasures tucked away in isolated places like Coates, in the woods near the Rother. The simplest of structures, its major adornment is the cedar in the churchyard but the building is almost entirely Norman. The north door gives access to the manor house, a typical medieval association that is felt even more strongly at nearby Stopham. The sense of the church being a personal adjunct to the manorial family is manifested by brasses, tombs and armorial glass bearing the names of the Stopham Bartelot family from the thirteenth to the present century. In many churches there is a side aisle or private chapel dedicated to the great family of the manor. At Stopham, the family dominates the whole building. Yet even Stopham is surpassed by the collegiate church of Cobham (K), where nineteen brasses of the family spanning the three centuries from the thirteenth to the sixteenth cover the floor of the chancel around the imposing tomb of the ninth Lord Cobham. The finest collection in Britain, they symbolize the power and wealth of the Cobhams who built the church and the collegiate buildings to the south. The fourteenth-century ragstone tower is typical of many that were added to Kentish churches at this time. In another large collegiate church, at Lingfield (Sy), the Cobhams of Starborough have their tombs and brasses and heraldry. The first Lord Cobham was a hero of Crecy. His great castle which once housed the noblest of French prisoners has gone. Part of the moat remains.

The great landowning families were builders and fashioners of landscape and their medieval role is usually reflected in the church. Their memorials are works of art. The Courthopes of Chevening, the Knatchbulls of Mersham, the Camoys of Trotton, the Culpeppers of Goudhurst, the Bullens of Hever, the Sidneys of Penshurst – these are the people whose alliances and changes of fortune led to the creation or disintegration of large estates. The parish church is the best starting-point for a journey into the past or present landscape. Fortunately there are detailed studies of the churches of the region readily available, quite apart from the local guide books, but images of pleasure received keep coming to mind. A dull winter's day was transformed when I walked into St Nicholas' at Great Bookham and found one of the finest Norman churches in Surrey. The nave was rebuilt in 1180, the chancel added by the Abbot of Chertsey in 1341. A twelfth-century font of marble and the tombs of the Slyfields all added to the sense of completeness the building gave. The thirteenth-century pews of Dunsfold and the lovely studding effect of the galletted walls are minor delights but all would be foresaken for Compton's St Nicholas. How often that dedication leads to a church of special interest! Stand in the nave and look towards the east. The Norman chancel arch frames another unexpected arch within the sanctuary. This supports a wooden screen, the timbers of which are Norman, and a second inner sanctuary, unique in Britain.

27. *Medieval lych-gate, Boughton Monchelsea.*

The impetus behind the Norman church-building reached its climax in the cathedrals of Canterbury, Rochester and Chichester. This was not the colonization of the frontier but the transformation of the base from which that movement took place. The cathedral churches were amongst the largest landowners of the medieval world and at Domesday about half the land of Kent, for example, was owned by them. They affected every part of the human landscape and the focus of administration was the cathedral. The spire of Chichester, eighty-four metres high, puts that statement into physical terms. From the shore, from the plain, from the Downs, the tall, slender spire beckons. Chichester inherited the earlier diocese of Selsey. The rest of the region was divided up between the mother church of Canterbury, which had jurisdiction far beyond Kent, including much of East Surrey and parts of Sussex, and the cathedral at Rochester. The diocese of Rochester covers most of West Kent. Most of Surrey was included in the diocese of Winchester.

Canterbury was rebuilt after a fire in 1067 but the martyrdom of Becket and yet another fire prompted another reconstruction after 1170 to make a shrine worthy of the centre of pilgrimage. The new building was the first example in England of the transition from Romanesque to Gothic architecture, the pointed arches replacing the familiar round arches. The central tower was not added until about 1500. Bishop Gandulf rebuilt Rochester between 1070 and 1108 on the site of a Saxon church. Chichester, 'the most typical English cathedral',* just grew for the best part of a century from 1091. Stone from Caen and from Quarr in the Isle of Wight were used as well as marble from Purbeck and Sussex. The most unusual feature of Chichester, its detached bell-tower, was not built until the 1420s.

The cathedrals impose and inspire. They hold the tombs of archbishops, bishops and princes. The overwhelming size and splendour of nave leading to choir and sanctuary prepares the mind stage by stage for the final sense of awe. Canterbury, with its stepped levels and special associations, does this most effectively. Yet it is in the smaller details that the religious sense is sometimes most strongly felt. The carvings of the capitals in the crypt at Canterbury, the bas-relief of the Raising of Lazarus in Chichester, the misericord seats, are on the human scale, the necessary marginalia to the central soaring aspiration of the pillars and arches. The surrounds are as lovely as the buildings. The tranquillity of the precincts, the green courts, the cloistered walks, the constantly changing vistas through ancient archways and worn steps, feed the spirit with a silence that is tangible. At its strongest on the north side of the Canterbury precinct, the same sense of enclosure and comfort leads to St Richard's Walk on the south side of Chichester.

The power of the medieval church found expression in a variety of other buildings, monastic houses, court houses, bishops' palaces, outlying granges and tithe barns. Granted land by Norman kings and temporal lords, the church flourished. There were more than sixty monastic houses in Sussex alone. But the

* I. Nairn and N. Pevsner, *Sussex. The Buildings of England* (Penguin, 1965).

effects of the Dissolution, first of the alien priories, then of the whole monastic system under Henry VIII, were so great that there is nothing in the region to compare with the extensive ruins of northern abbeys. The story of Merton Abbey is typical. An Augustinian foundation of about AD 1117, only a Norman arch remains in the precinct near the church and part of a river wall. The rest was pulled down and used as stone for Henry VIII's palace of Nonesuch six kilometres away, a palace to be without peer. The village of Cuddington was cleared in the process. In its turn, the palace was demolished and only marker stones remain in the public park that was once its grounds.

Many of the monastic houses clustered round the cathedral cities. In Canterbury, there is the Poor Priests' Hospital, once home of the Greyfriars, the Blackfriars and the Eastbridge Hospital by the Stour. In Chichester, the Greyfriars establishment survived as a guildhall and now as a museum in a park by the north wall. The Hospital of St Mary's in the same quarter of the city has been in continual use since the thirteenth century. The Gothic doorway in St Martin's Square leads to a medieval atmosphere as palpable as the cathedral itself. Almspeople still live in the old infirmary hall. Beyond the living area is a screened chapel, with exciting misericord seats. In Faversham, the Cluniac abbey colonized from Bermondsey has disappeared almost as completely as its mother foundation. Davington Priory to the west survives in part as a private house and a twelfth-century church. Further west, on the Roman road to London, substantial remains of a hospital, the Maison Dieu of Ospringe, are open to the public under the care of the Department of the Environment. Archaeological finds from the area are on show in the stone and timber undercrofts. The priory at Bermondsey lies under the warehouses of London's dockland but the priory church of St Mary Overy (literally 'over the river') is incorporated into the present cathedral of Southwark. Parts of the Bishop of Winchester's palace, including a rose window, have been uncovered and restored in recent redevelopment of the Surrey bankside.

There is a particularly good group of later medieval buildings on the east bank of the Medway at Maidstone. All Saint's church, rebuilt by Archbishop Courtenay in the last years of the fourteenth century, is the finest church in the Perpendicular style in Kent. The College and its gatehouse, the Palace and the tithe barn, also known as the Archbishop's stables, and an undercroft make a group as complete as anything in the region. The visual grouping, so effective from the west bank, is broken now by a main road. Of the other monastic houses in the vicinity of Maidstone, three are still in use. Malling Abbey with its fifteenth-century gatehouse is occupied by Benedictine nuns. The Carmelite order own Thomas Wyatt's thirteenth-century castle at Allington. Aylesford Priory to the north, on the river flats, witnessed the return of the Carmelites in 1949 after an interval of seven hundred years. The magnificent gatehouse leads to a church, hall, cloisters and courts, moat and fishponds refashioned from the ruins of the original monastery. Its pottery is famous.

Boxley, once a Cistercian abbey of the twelfth century, is incorporated into a private house, its ancient perimeter walls enclosing gardens and plantations. The tithe barn is one of the finest in the country. Stone built, 75 metres long, its scissor-beam roof is a marvel of woodcraft. There is evidence that the barn was also a guest house and a brewery. That barn symbolizes not only the fertility of the area but the vast quantities of produce the abbey could command. One of its outlying granges was on the North Downs, the name Grange Farm still existing. The words 'grange' and 'court' attached to a farm name are usually an indication that they were once in the possession of the church. There are other notable barns at Lenham (K), at Berwick (Sx) and at Buckland Court (Sy), the latter being an unusual towered barn. Objects of pleasure to us, these barns must have been viewed very differently by medieval peasants.

Lewes and Hastings both had priories. St Leonards is much in evidence as a name but little else. The Cluniac priory of St Pancras was one of the greatest in Britain until its dissolution by Thomas Cromwell. Founded in 1076 as a direct offshoot of a Norman abbey, it covered the lower ground between the walled town of Lewes and the River Ouse. Tumbled walls and arches stand in the present pleasure grounds, the railway cutting right through the site. More famous and much visited is the abbey at Battle, begun soon after the Conquest on the battlefield of Senlac. The best feature is the ornate fourteenth-century gatehouse that fronts the market-place. The rest is very difficult to interpret, scattered through the grounds and buildings of the present school. For the layman there is as much to be gained for the moment from a visit to the crowded but fascinating museum across the market-place, but with the recent sale of the estate, the abbey ruins and the site of the battle have come into the hands of the Department of the Environment.

A school also occupies the archiepiscopal palace at Croydon alongside St John the Baptist, the finest Perpendicular church in Surrey, rebuilt after a great fire in 1867. Stonework of ecclesiastical palaces can be found in many towns and villages, such as Bromley and Trottiscliffe, Mayfield and West Tarring. Amongst the most complete remains are those at Charing (K) by the path to the church and now doing service as a farm. Minster-in-Sheppey is really two churches side by side, the nuns' church to the north and the parish church to the south, making one very impressive building. Some of the stonework may date from the original seventh-century foundation as a nunnery. The fifteenth-century gatehouse now guards the local car-park. The church stands on the highest part of the island and its collection of tombs, especially those of the lords of Shurland, is notable. Minster-in-Thanet was once a grange of St Augustine's in Canterbury and put there as the administrative centre of the holdings in the island. Both church and abbey have some early stonework. The abbey has been the home of a community of Benedictine nuns since 1930.

28. *Gatehouse of the Premonstratensian abbey at Bayham.*

The medieval isolation of the Weald was as suited to monastic calm as the Pennine Dales. That very isolation may have helped to preserve Bayham from the stone plunderers. On the border of Kent and Sussex in the broad vale of the Teise, it is the most complete monastic ruin in the region. The Premonstratensian monks from Brockley in Kent and Otham in Sussex settled there in the thirteenth century. The walls of the nave and part of the cloisters stand nearly to their full height, but the decorated arches and carved corbels built in local stone have weathered severely. A fourteenth-century gatehouse, a delicate structure very different from the crenellated towers of other abbeys, stands by the ponded river. The setting is as sylvan as its origins. In the eighteenth century the ruins were used as the centre-piece of a romantic parkland for the Earls of Camden. The old mansion stands to the west of the abbey. The new nineteenth-century mansion, also called Bayham Abbey, stands on the slopes to the north of the river. One memorable touch is the beech tree planted on the west wall, focus of the long view along the nave. Now in the hands of the Department of the Environment, the excavations south of the cloisters are revealing much more of the conventual buildings.

The same order of monks established St Radegund's Abbey, another isolated site high on the chalk plateau to the west of Dover. The north wall of the tower forms the gateway to the present farmhouse. The farmhouse itself is the old refectory and the guest house became a barn. Much of the original Caen stone went to build Sandgate Castle for Henry VIII on the Kent coast. St Radegund is in private hands but two of the most interesting Sussex priories which became private secular residences are controlled by the Sussex Archaeological Trust and, as such, are open to the public. Wilmington was founded before the Conquest but what remains of its outbuildings are mostly thirteenth and fourteenth century. There is older work in the church which completes the priory precinct on the north side. But there is enough of the old hall, the undercroft and the courts to make a delightful setting for a museum of old agricultural implements, ironwork and other nostalgic echoes of the rural past. Wilmington stands on a low hill in view of the Downs and the Long Man of Wilmington. Michelham squats in the wet lowlands of the Wealden clay, a moated site in the forest, by the flood plain of the River Cuckmere. A Tudor mansion has evolved from frater, refectory and other parts of the south range of the Augustinian priory. The church is outlined in the lawn to the north. The gatehouse tower, dating from 1395, stands astride the moat and was built to protect the monks and their records against the peasantry, for the monastery had been one of the targets of the peasant uprising in 1381. Within the grounds are fish ponds, a dovecote, a water mill, old barns and a collection of farm waggons. The house contains a collection of Sussex brass rubbings, prints and paintings.

Occasionally a church by its sheer size and splendour gives the clue to its association with a priory. There are few as magnificent as Boxgrove on the Sussex plain, west of Chichester. Caen stone and Purbeck marble embellish the Norman work in the nave and the thirteenth-century choir. The most delicate work is used in the extraordinary church-within-a-church of the De La Warr chapel. Norman arches and walls stand to the north of the church. This churchyard, incidentally, was one of the first recorded sites of the game of cricket. At

Hardham (Sx) and Shulbrede near the Surrey border, priory ruins are part of existing farms.

The wilds of the Surrey heaths were suited to the monastic ideal but even less remains than in Sussex. Of the Carthusians at Sheen, once favourites of Henry VIII, nothing is left but a name near Richmond Park; of Waverley, first house of the Cistercians in England, only forlorn ruins in private ground on a meander of the River Wey remain, though ornate stonework and tiles are on view in Farnham museum. Chertsey, founded in the seventh century on an island site by the Thames and resettled by the Benedictines after Danish destruction, occupied the ground to the north of the present church. The site can just be deciphered in the gardens and walls of the private houses around Abbey Green and Abbey Cloister Garth. The tiles manufactured here were the finest in England. Specimens portraying events from the Arthurian romances can be seen in the British Museum. Further up the Wey, in a similar riverside setting, is Newark, established by the Austin canons on an older site known as Aldbury. Parts of the south transept and the choir make a lofty ruin that catches the eye from Pyrford churchyard. Tandridge Priory is hidden in a farm, Reigate in a school but the priory fields of Reigate are the town's park and playing ground.

The church was one side of the Norman face. The other was the castle. The mailed fist throws a longer shadow than the hands in prayer in most of the region. Outside the main entrance to Pevensey Castle is a plaque commemorating the landing of William and his Norman conquerors in 1066. The castle rises within the enclosing walls of the Roman fort. Within the inner bailey is a demi-culverin, a gun made in Sussex. On the outer walls are blockhouses and gun-emplacements built in 1940 and disguised by the clever use of old stone and new concrete to look part of the ancient structures to withstand the last invasion that never came. Two thousand years of defence of the south-east angle are summarized in stone. Three successful invasions – Roman, Saxon and Norman – and three unsuccessful ones – Spanish, French and German – are reflected in the historic development of the site. The small planned borough to the east of the castle was the work of Robert, William's half-brother, one of the small band who expressed their new mastery by the physical strength of their castle-building. Sussex, organized into five divisions called 'rapes', was subdued by five castles – Pevensey, Hastings, Bramber, Lewes and Arundel. Later, Chichester became the centre of a sixth rape. Hastings castle still glowers down upon the original centre of the town though much of it has fallen into the sea with the erosion of the sandstone cliffs. Bramber is a broken tower and an enclosing wall on a deeply moated hill overlooking the levels of the Adur and the old medieval haven. The

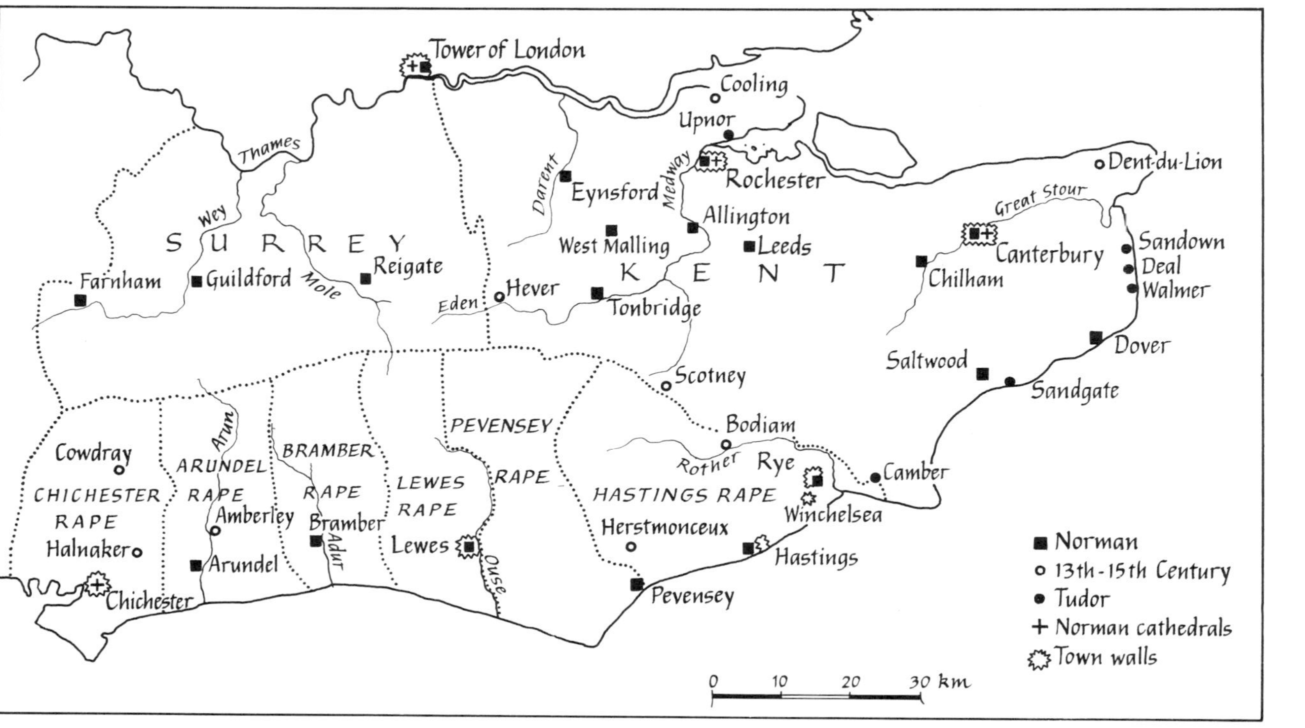

29. *Castles with substantial structural remains.*

site is in the hands of the National Trust. Arundel and Lewes both stand on strategic sites on the western banks of river gaps through the Downs.

Lewes still dominates the town as it was intended to do, from the time of its foundation by William de Warenne in about 1100. The fine barbican of the fourteenth century leads via the Norman gatehouse to a tightly enclosed precinct and the shell-keep perched on a motte. The view from the top is a topographer's delight. The barbican is the headquarters of the Sussex Archaeological Society. A second motte, a most unusual feature, and sections of the precinct walls complete the military presence. The setting of Arundel is even more impressive, at its most romantic when seen from the banks of the Arun, looming above the wooded river cliff, at its most formidable when seen from the south. But apart from the eleventh-century gatehouse and the shell-keep, the structure reveals the Victorian idea of a castle rather than the real thing. Still the family home of the Dukes of Norfolk, it is one of the most visited places in the county. Arundel was a newly established site, an older fortified burgh across the river at Burpham being left to oblivion. The embankments of the promontory fort are still clear.

The only remnant of Chichester's castle, destroyed in the thirteenth century, is a motte in Priory Park close to the city wall, very similar in position to the Dane John at Canterbury.

Dover was the key to the kingdom. On the west cliff overlooking the haven were the earthworks of an Iron Age fort and, possibly, a Saxon stronghold. On this same site, one of the greatest castles in Western Europe developed over a period of a hundred years, between 1154 and 1256. The great keep was the strongest in Britain. Around it two concentric circuits of walls and towers were constructed. The outer wall alone had twenty towers, the tops being lowered in the eighteenth century. Dover Castle is a town within a town. Its underground passages, storerooms and caverns seem to lock it into the solid chalk, like a tree rooting. A royal castle, it was occupied by the army until 1958 and only in recent years has it come into the guardianship of the Department of the Environment.

On the highway to London, both the cities of Canterbury and Rochester were fortified. Canterbury's keep, by the west walls of the city, is a rather forlorn ruin of flint and Caen stone, four-square and solid but neglected in a rather derelict part of the city, sharing little of the popularity of the cathedral. Rochester's keep, in contrast, overshadows the cathedral and looms over the important bridging point of the Medway. Its height of thirty-eight metres makes it the tallest in England. The curtain walls of Henry II's reign were built on the foundations of an earlier structure, dating from Bishop Gandulf. Bishops were as active as kings in castle-building to protect their interests and assert their status. Gandulf built another tower over at West Malling, a superb structure of ragstone, flint and tufa locked on a foundation of greensand. The tower seems to be part of the rock.

Another ecclesiastical castle was Saltwood, completely rebuilt with gatehouse and curtain walls by Archbishop Courtenay in the fourteenth century. The park-land to the south below the walls is hemmed in by the outskirts of Hythe. It is the home of a famous art historian and is open to the public. The Bishop of Winchester, too, was busy in his Surrey estates. His castle at Farnham is the best fortification in the county. The shell-keep on the motte commands a view of the curtain wall and of the great hall and other buildings now in private ownership. The keep is open to the public. Standing well to the north of the town, it guarded the route from Guildford to Winchester. An extensive deer park, now in part a public park, stretched to the north and west.

Most of the major river crossings had a defensive site near by and Guildford is no exception. The square keep, another of Henry II's time, stands high on the east bank of the Wey. Its inner bailey has been made into a public park with gardens and a bowling green. Flint work and Roman tiles are mixed with local stone in the typical herring-bone pattern of the stonework. One gateway remains in the surrounding wall, leading down to the river. Of the Clare's castle at Bletchingly and the Warenne's at Reigate, source of fierce feuding between the families, only the mounds remain. Other mounds can be seen at Abinger, Thunderfield, Walton-on-the-Hill and at Cranleigh. There are mottes dotted all over the North Downs between Maidstone and Sittingbourne but only Thurnham has a crumpled bit of flint walling hiding in scrubby woodland.

At Chilham, on the Stour, the twelfth-century octagonal keep is companion to the Jacobean mansion which still bears the name of castle. Eagles and falcons glide beneath its shade, much to the terrified delight of visitors. In the Darent Valley, nearer London, the curtain walls of Eynsford Castle, dating from 1100, show unknapped flint work as good as anything in the region. Newman, in fact, declared that there is no better example of a pre-keep castle in England.* The site may have been abandoned after the excommunication of William of Eynsford who was implicated in the death of Becket. After restoration by private owners in this century, the building came into the care of the Department of the Environment.

For sheer visual beauty there is no castle to compare with Leeds on the river

* J. Newman, *West Kent and the Weald. The Buildings of England* (Penguin, 1969).

Len, a tributary of the Medway. Its deer park was recorded in Domesday and the site on three islands in the broadest of moats is probably as old. It was the favourite castle of Edward I and was in royal possession for three centuries. The building has been modified by a succession of owners such as the Colepepers in the seventeenth century and the Wykeham-Martins in the nineteenth, but the bridge and the barbican, the gatehouse, the main building, the Maiden's tower and the ultimate gloriette spanning the islands combine to make a perfect whole. It looks from a distance like a grey ship afloat in the most romantic of seas, with exotic wildfowl flaunting their beauty in the still waters.

In the very heart of the Weald, a motte-and-bailey castle was built to protect the Medway crossing at Tonbridge, an ancient routeway linking London with the south coast. It was the centre of a large estate of the Fitzgilberts, the lowy of Tonbridge, a hunting area which became known as the north and south friths, names that are still current. A small area of the park still exists round the mansion of Somerhill. The shell-keep fell into ruin as its function was taken over by the fourteenth-century gatehouse. The castle was partially dismantled by the Cromwellians and eventually became a private residence. It now houses the local government offices with the bailey, moat and curtain walls doing service as a small park.

Castle-building continued throughout the medieval period but the main spate came in the second half of the fourteenth century with the French harrying the coast and the peasants rising in revolt, culminating in the march to Smithfield and the death of Wat Tyler in 1381. Many gatehouses were added at this time to existing castles and monastic houses. Three of the best examples of new military architecture are all moated sites. Cooling, 1381, stands on the edge of the marshes of the Hoo peninsula, in view of the Thames. Bodiam, 1386, is on the banks of the Rother where the Weald joins the southern marshland. Scotney is almost hidden in a tributary valley of the Teise. Bodiam is the archetype of the period, a square enclosing wall with a round tower at each corner and a square turret midway on each section of the curtain wall. Its simple perfection owes much to restoration by Lord Curzon in 1919. The simplicity is more apparent than real; other buildings once occupied the courtyard, such as the chapel, the hall, the kitchen and the stables. One of the square turrets formed the approach from a bridge across the moat, a gatehouse once fronted by a barbican.

Bodiam is perfection, Scotney a dream. Only one machicolated tower remains of the courtyard castle on an island on the River Bewl. Tudor and later additions were all fashioned in the early nineteenth century into an image of the picturesque, a scene as romantic and unreal as a theatrical set to be gazed upon

30. *Bodiam – fourteenth-century moated castle.*

from the new mansion on the hill. Between the two buildings is a quarry in the sandstone transformed into a rock garden. In the same military vein is Hever, which originated with Sir John Cobham's licence to crenellate his manor in 1384. Only slightly altered by its later owners, the Bullens, it is really a fortified house in a moat on the River Eden with a gatehouse as its strongest structure. It forms the centre-piece of an elaborate reconstruction of house, gardens and grounds by the Astors early in this century. Other mansions lay claim to the name castle, such as Chiddingstone near Hever and Lullingstone on the Darent, but this is more a reflection of eighteenth-century aspirations than medieval function.

Herstmonceux is the last of its genre. Moated, turreted, crenellated, as symmetrical as Bodiam, it looks like no other castle, being built entirely of brick. Crenellated in 1440, it was effectively dismantled by 1777 but restored again, like Bodiam, in the present century. Now the home of the Royal Observatory, seeking the purer air of Sussex after the pollution of Greenwich, only the grounds are open to the public. The domes covering the telescopes are as exciting visually as the castle itself on the edge of the Pevensey levels.

The major interest in the medieval architecture of the south-east lies not in its castles or cathedrals. They have their equals and perhaps their peers elsewhere in Britain, but no region can show a comparable number of timber-framed houses that have survived the ravages of fire, weather and time. Constructed mostly of oak and chestnut beams, these houses may be manors or court houses, homes of the wealthier tenant-farmers or humble cottages. Each one is a detective story needing an expert to unravel the history of its structure for 'virtually no medieval house survives in a clear-cut, unmutilated condition'.* The simple hall house grew by the addition of service rooms, solar and cross-passages to the Wealden house of the late medieval period with its characteristic wings and jettying upper storey. Timbers, being scarce, were used and re-used. Houses evolved by need. So we have the timbered splendour of Chiddingstone, providing the backcloth for historical films, an entire village street owned by the National Trust.

There are hundreds awaiting discovery behind later façades but several farmhouses such as Capon's Farm near Cowfold (Sx) and Clennell Brook Farm near Horsham have been dated to the thirteenth century. Cottages at Brenchley and Easole Street (K) both claim a similar age. These are in private ownership but there are enough timber-framed houses open to the public to give an idea of the richness available. The Clergy House at Alfriston, dating from 1380, was the

* R. T. Mason, *Framed Buildings of the Weald* (Coach Publishing House, Horsham, 1964).

first building to be purchased by the National Trust, in 1896. St Mary's at Bramber and the priest's house at West Hoathly both date from the fifteenth century. The Old Court Cottage at Limpsfield, once in the possession of Battle Abbey, can be seen from the roadside. Near by is the farmhouse of Stockenden, a stone and timber building of the fourteenth century. Stone has a greater chance of survival than wood but Old Soar Manor near Plaxtol (K), now owned by the

31. *Medieval priest's house at Alfriston, the first building to be possessed by the National Trust. The photograph was taken three years before its purchase in 1896.*

Department of the Environment, and Charleston Manor (Sx) are both remarkable. Charleston has been described as 'the perfect house in the perfect setting'.* Site of a music festival and periodically open to view, the oldest part has a small Norman window. Enormous barns, a dovecote and walled gardens complete the lovely enclosure in a wooded valley. Finest of all is Great Dixter near Northiam (Sx), a fifteenth-century house restored by Lutyens in the early years of this century. The house is complemented by a superb garden.

* Nairn and Pevsner, op. cit.

The best place to study the evolution of the timber-framed house is at the Open Air museum at Singleton in West Sussex. Amongst the exhibits there are two houses removed from Kent before the construction of the Bough Beech reservoir. Winkhurst (fourteenth century) and Bay Leaf (fifteenth century) have been rebuilt in what is believed to be their original form, all later modifications being excluded. They are an absolute wonder of tie beam, braces, studs, rafters, oarkins, arcades and sole plates, words which mean something when seen in the context of these medieval structures. They show carpenters' craft at its height. Most of the roofing material is thatch, though tiles and Horsham slates are also native to the region.

Many of the great houses such as Hever, Knole and Penshurst had their beginnings in this same period. The fourteenth-century hall at Penshurst is the finest in the region. Archbishop Bourchier's fifteenth-century work forms the nucleus of Knole but the development of these houses belongs to a later period. Of the lesser manors, Puttenden (Sy), now restored and open to the public, is a good example. Dating from 1250, it is one of the many moated sites on low-lying ground in the clay lowlands and the coastal plains. More than three hundred of such sites have been identified and most of them date from the thirteenth and fourteenth centuries. Most famous and most perfect is Ightham Mote (K). Fed from a small tributary stream, it is set in a wooded valley below the greensand ridge. Built on a ragstone foundation, the timbers of the later Tudor house look remarkably fresh. The inner courtyard contains the largest dog-kennel I have ever seen but its greater claim to fame is the stonework forming a Tudor rose. The small fourteenth-century hall is the heart of the site. Chapel, undercroft and solar, carved staircase and other rooms create the perfect medieval house. The white doves, the wildfowl and peacocks and the fat carp in the moat surround it with delight.

Moats served more than a defensive function. They acted as a drainage system, as a source of water for livestock and fire-fighting, and as a source of fish-farming. Many moated sites were deserted in later years, especially in the eighteenth century, in favour of higher, more healthy ground, as at Scotney. A few circular moats can be found, at Pagehurst and Castle Bank, for example, both in the parish of Staplehurst (K), and they may mark even earlier sites than the more typical square moat.

Around the castles and the greater manor houses, areas of the wilderness were enclosed, at first by ditches and palings and later by walls, for the raising and hunting of deer and other game. Deer hunting was a costly sport and on the twenty or so deer chases belonging to the Archbishops of Canterbury, for example, the breeding and sale of rabbits was an important source of revenue. Herons, hawks and swans were raised within the enclosures. A medieval heronry remains at Chilham (K). Extensive areas of common land, such as Ashdown Forest, became the private chase of a feudal overlord, in that particular case, John of Gaunt in about 1372, the forest becoming known as Lancaster Great Park. The Statute of Merton of 1235, a statute constantly quoted during the protracted attempts to save the remaining commons in the nineteenth century, established the legal ownership of the feudal lord and has been described as the first enclosure act.* Many such parks survive to give the region some of its finest open spaces today – Knole and Cobham, Arundel and Petworth, Richmond and Buxted, Leeds and Penshurst. Eight deer parks were recorded at Domesday, and by the sixteenth century, there were no less than fifty-five in Kent alone. Many can be traced by names such as Park Farm and Park Gate, by boundary ditches and old hedgerows. The outlines of Becket's two parks at Otford have been traced with the aid of hedgerow analysis and field names.

Greatest of the parks was the Royal Forest of Windsor Great Park. John Stowe spoke of 'the pleasure pastime arising out of the forest, chace and fourteen parks that wait upon it',† a pleasure that kings protected with severe laws. Of the fourteen parks comprising Windsor, several were in Surrey, including the heaths and commons to the north-west, stretching from the Thames right down to the Hog's Back at Guildford. Henry II wanted all of Surrey to be under forest law. Forest pleas relating to the Windsor Great Park were heard at Guildford in the thirteenth century. Charles I tried, in vain, to reassert this royal privilege. This reflected the poverty of large areas of Surrey soil and in turn may have contributed to the preservation of large areas of common and heathland today. The restriction of such claims was one of the privileges that the nobles contested at Runnymede on the Surrey side of the Thames. The Charter of the Forest was one of the lesser appendages of the Magna Carta but no less important on its impact on the landscape. The 4,400 hectares of Ashdown gave common grazing for as many as seven thousand pigs from the adjacent parishes. Grazing rights were exercised by distant priories such as Michelham. A rabbit warren covered more than 32 hectares. The disputes between local people maintaining complex traditional rights to furze cutting, bracken for litter, windfall wood and grazing against the bailiffs were legion.

The great estates had the resources to carry out large-scale reclamation schemes, organizing parks, 'ridding' the land of forest cover and reclaiming

* Lord Eversley, *Commons, Forests and Footpaths* (Cassell, 1910).
† *Stowe's Annals* (1631).

marshes. The reclamation of the Romney levels may have begun with the Romans and was recorded in eighth-century Saxon charters but the major period of drainage and dyke-building was in the twelfth and thirteenth centuries. Much of the activity was organized by the monastic houses. The 'innings' of the Walland Marsh, for example, are named after the contemporary archbishops of Canterbury, St Thomas, Baldwin, Boniface and Pecham. On the other side of the peninsula, the monks of Lessness Abbey were colonizing the marshes of Erith. Along the Wantsum channel, the earthworks that helped to hold back the sea and make Thanet part of the mainland still bear names such as the Abbot's Wall and the Monks' Wall, after the establishment at Minster. The marshes became famous for their sheep flocks, for their wool and the quality of their ewes' milk and cheese.

The marsh farms were amongst the greatest sufferers from the storms and floods of the thirteenth and fourteenth centuries. The monks of Christchurch lost nearly half of their ten thousand sheep in the 1320s. Other areas of land loss were along the Sussex coast, especially the Selsey peninsula.

With the storms and floods came a succession of bad harvests and, like another visitation of the medieval fates, the outbreak of plague. Many of the new settlements on marginal land found it difficult to survive. Some were eventually abandoned; others shrunk in size to mere farms or small hamlets. The figure of desertion, for Sussex, following the Black Death, has been put at 7 per cent of the total settlements, the greatest effect being on the clays and sandstones of the Weald.* But older settlements on the chalk country, as at Berwick and Alciston, were affected, too. The church at Lullington, near Alfriston, has only its chancel left, laying claim to be the smallest church in the country, last relic of a deserted village.

The same image of an empty or ruined church is found in the Romney marshes, such as Midley, one mile south of Old Romney. Dode Church on the North Downs of Kent was closed in 1349 and the parish combined with Paddlesworth. In the same vicinity are several shrunken sites, with farms bearing the old village names, such as Cossington and Tottington.

The pattern of settlement that had evolved by the close of the fifteenth century was no simple conquest over the last expanse of the great forest but the result of thousands of local adjustments to variations in soil, in climate, in social and economic conditions. With the dissolution of the monasteries and the centralization of power in the hands of the Tudors, the Weald was poised for its industrial age.

* P. Brandon, *The Sussex Landscape* (Hodder & Stoughton, 1974).

6

Iron Masters and Clothiers

Walking the quiet ways around West Hoathly through the deep green valleys and woodlands of the Sussex Weald, it is difficult to believe that this was one of England's earliest 'black countries', echoing to the roar of iron forges and mills. The village has a large thirteenth-century church, a well-preserved Priest's house, a large Tudor mansion, a medieval tithe barn transformed into a theatre, a straggle of cottages, an inn and an ornate village sign in wrought iron. One of its minor claims to fame are the bullet holes made by Cromwellian musketry in the church door. That door has another remarkable feature. Its thick oak timbers bear the date of 31 March 1626 formed with iron studs. Almost every building has its links with the iron industry that transformed the medieval outpost of the Cluniac monks of Lewes.

Early in the sixteenth century the monks gave up the Priest's house which had been their administrative centre and leased it as a farm to a local husbandman, John Browne. He continued as a tenant throughout the dissolution of the monasteries and a period of royal ownership when West Hoathly was one of the hundred manors granted by Henry VIII to Anne of Cleves. John Browne's son, Thomas, sought greater riches than a tenant-farmer could gain. He entered the business of mining local iron deposits, smelting it by local water power and local timber, and became wealthy enough to modernize the house and style himself 'yeoman'. He married into the Infield family, who had built the nearby mansion of Gravetye, moved into the dower house and transformed that building into a mansion. The status of the Infields is shown by two seventeenth-century iron tomb slabs on the floor of the church. The long pond that was dammed up to supply power to the furnaces and hammer mills is the centrepiece of the grounds of Gravetye, now a private hotel. The tracks leading to it are deeply worn by the heavy loads that were carted along them.

The threshold of the Priest's house is a 'bear', a large lump of unfused iron ore that was ejected from the furnace. Within the house is a collection of fire-backs, fire-dogs, cauldrons, trivets, tongs, hooks, pokers and other wares that were typical products of the industry that spread, in its heyday in the sixteenth and seventeenth centuries, throughout the Weald, from Abinger in Surrey to Ashburnham in East Sussex. Its products are scattered far and wide, in churches, mansions, cottages and local museums, but its impact on the landscape was far-reaching, not least in the great Tudor and Jacobean mansions that grew from its proceeds.

The extraction and working of iron was known before the Romans came. It was stimulated by the demands of the Roman fleet and legions. Cinder and slag from the primitive bloomeries were used to surface roads, as at Holtye. The bloomeries were small platforms cut into hillsides on which iron ore was smelted with charcoal. Dozens of such sites have been discovered, especially where the swift Wealden streams cut into the Wadhurst clay, main source of nodules and bands of iron. Other iron deposits were worked later in the sandstones of the region and in marl pits, marl being a mixture of clay and lime used to fertilize the fields. Water was all important, to wash the ore, to quench the fires and, later, to power the mills. The bloomeries have been identified from their small heaps of burnt waste materials. The image of an ironsmith at work appears on a Roman pottery vessel in Hastings Museum, but the earliest documentary evidence is in the Domesday record for East Grinstead of 'una ferraria'. By 1254, the Sussex ironmasters could cope with a royal demand for 30,000 horseshoes and 60,000 nails.

The industry was transformed in the late fifteenth century by the introduction of skilled workmen from the continent who brought new techniques of smelting and casting. Then the new hammer ponds first appeared, flooding the deep, narrow valleys as at Cowden, Worth, West Hoathly, Horsted Keynes, Horsmonden, Ashburnham, Thursley and Abinger. In many places, the dams, called 'bays', are still intact even where the ponds have been drained or silted up. The dams themselves and the ground below them are the best places to search for cinder, glassy slag and the 'bears'. One expedition at Horsmonden led me to a local cottage where 'bears' had been discovered under the floor of a barn. Bears have been used as stepping stones across the stream at Ashburnham and near the Forge Cottage on the same site are two round 'pigs' of iron. Larger lumps were called 'sows'. There are good examples at Hastings Museum and in the castle enclosure at Lewes. The sign of the Bear Inn at Burwash shows an Arctic animal but this, too, may have been a reference to iron, for the nearby mansion known as Bateman's, the home of Rudyard Kipling, was originally built by an ironmaster in 1634.

The iron industry was concerned with more than kitchen ware, church doors, tombs and firebacks. It made the weaponry of the Tudor and Stuart navies. A gun made at Robertsbridge stands in the inner bailey of Pevensey Castle. A falconet made in the Cowden Forge stands in the grounds of Crippenden Manor. By the entrance to Buxted Park in Sussex is a brick house with Dutch gabling, bearing the sign of a long-snouted hog. Here the first piece of English ordnance was cast. According to a famous jingle, 'Master Hogge and his man John, they did make the first cannon'. There are cannon balls in the church that stands just within the gates of the deer park. Wealden iron helped defeat the Spanish Armada, but a long-standing tradition of smuggling extended even to ordnance and Raleigh once complained that English ships were outgunned by foreign vessels equipped with English guns.

The earliest account of the iron industry was written in 1586 by William Camden in his *Brittania*, the first great survey of Britain. Of the Weald, he wrote, 'Full of iron it is in sundry places where for the making and fining where of there bee furnaces on every side and a huge deale of wood is yearly spent, to which purpose divers brookes in many places are brought to runne in one chanell and sundry medowes turned into pooles and waters, that they might bee of power sufficient to drive hammer milles which beating upon the iron resound all over the places adjoining.' On they pounded, supplying the Cromwellian and Stuart armies and navies. John Browne of Horsmonden was one of the most famous ironmasters. In an agreement signed by him with George Brown of Buckland (Sy) and Alexander Courthope, we read of 'all ordnances and gunnes, morter pieces, shott, barr iron, sowe iron, granadoes and all other commodities'. The wealthy landowners like the Courthopes and the Culpeppers worked together with the ironmasters for their mutual advancement.

The forest suffered. Richard Pedley's official survey in 1574 made for Elizabeth I reported 'great spoile and consumption of oakes and other woods' in his visit to seventy-seven ironworks. A thousand loads of 'great wood' were needed for the larger forges. Ashdown Forest lost much of its tree cover and became an open heathland. The Tudor monarchs attempted to control the cutting of timber within twenty miles of the coast, seeking priority for ship construction. But the trade went on and the complaints increased. The management of woodland by coppicing became widespread as a means of increasing the yield of timber from the same acreage. Trees became a crop. Birch, oak, hornbeam, chestnut, ash, hazel, maple, even plum trees were cut on a regular cycle to produce wood for charcoal. Of fifty-one furnaces recorded in 1574, only thirty-six remained in the next century. By 1717, only fourteen furnaces and ten forges were working.

In 1697, the young Duke of Gloucester, taking the waters at the new spa of Tunbridge Wells, visited the ironworks at Hoathly near Lamberhurst owned by the Filmer family. This royal accolade gave the mill its new name, the Gloucester furnace. Furnace Lane leads past the pond and the water leet to the forge site where 'bears' and other waste cap the embankment. Parts of the railings of St Paul's Cathedral that were cast here are on display in the museums of Hastings and Lewes. By 1784, this was the last working furnace in Kent. Ashburnham, in Sussex, lasted a little longer, making 173 tons of iron for the Napoleonic wars as late as 1796. By then, the iron industry had moved to the northern coalfields with the perfecting of coke as a fuel. The naval contracts had been lost to the Carron company in 1769. The final blow to the region's industrial pride was the installation of carronades, bearing the mark of the Carron Company, in the Martello towers ranged along the coast, to keep the French at bay.

The decline of the industry has been attributed to many causes – to the shortage of timber as fuel, to the importing of cheaper, better grade ore from Sweden, to persistent droughts in the Weald between 1737 and 1750 which meant that the mills had no power. There were odd survivals, such as a small mill on the Ravensbourne at the south end of the parish of Lewisham, where Ephraim How had a national reputation for his cutlery.

One of the most extraordinary products of iron is the south door of Staplehurst church. The hinges of the door are in the form of serpents. This device is not unusual but the rest of the door is embellished with fishes, eels, a cockerel and other images such as the wheel of life. The door and its unique metal work has been dated to about 1109. Other church doors with elaborate iron work are at Woking, Merton, Merstham, Crowhurst, Dunsfold, Charlwood, Alfold and Ockley. Alfold has other unusual examples of iron work inside the church such as a cockerel and a chandalier. Studded doors, such as West Hoathly, were not uncommon. The door of Wadhurst church, dated 1682, lies against a wall in Wilmington Priory (Sx). Wadhurst has by far the best collection of iron tomb slabs, no less than thirty in the church floor and in the graveyard. Dating between 1617 and 1707, the simplest have merely dates and initials standing proud from the surface. The most ornate have crests, heraldic shields and inscriptions. Some have dates and initials added later, inscribed in what was presumably a family tomb. There are others at Mayfield, Rotherfield, Cowden, Chiddingstone, East Grinstead, Maresfield and Hartfield. One of the earliest examples is thought to be the simple iron cross now inset in the chapel wall at Burwash. The finest example, as delicate as brasswork at its best, is in Crowhurst church (Sy). Anne Forster, related to the Gaynesford family of Crowhurst Place, rests in iron immortality complete with effigy and winding sheet.

32. *Fireback, 1636, showing Richard Lenard, ironmaster of Brede.*

Firebacks are found in nearly every manor house and mansion of note. Antique shops, 'Tudor cafés' and inns all have their quota protecting the stonework of the newly installed fireplaces from the heat of the open fires. The best collections are in Hastings Museum and in Anne of Cleves' House in Lewes. The earliest examples are broad slabs decorated simply with ropes, daggers and even the maker's hands pushed into the mould. Then came the heraldic devices, with figures and inscriptions, such as that of Richard Lenard, ironmaster of Brede. The later firebacks look like a gallery of classic art, emulating the continental examples that are found in the collection at Petworth House.

The small museum at Battle, like that of Haslemere (Sy), has useful models of the old iron sites and a collection of cinder, cannon balls and examples of pitty, foxes and twelve-foots. These last are all names for various types of iron-stone which were recorded, amongst others, by Arthur Young in his *General View of the Agriculture of the County of Sussex* in 1813. His comment then was that Sussex had ceased to be a manufacturing county. The most complete study of the Wealden iron industry was published by Straker in 1931. He identified at least 239 sites. His study has been the starting point for many researchers since. The Wealden Iron Research Group has a permanent display in Haxted Mill (Sy) with a map of known sites and examples of the many types of slag and cinder found. There is much still left for the explorer. Look for a hammer-pond, for a forge cottage or a Furnace Wood and start hunting. The last iron extraction site was in Snape Wood near Wadhurst, worked as recently as 1858. There are pits and hollows under the old woodland and the new plantations. But in parts of Surrey such exploration can lead to another old industry which competed with the iron works for fuel and power.

On the corner of the green at Chiddingfold, opposite the old thorn tree, is one of the best lych gates in the country, with a rare wooden slab for resting the coffin before entering the churchyard. The footpath of Sussex marble and Horsham slate leads to a church with an unusual memorial to another medieval industry. A small lancet window is made up of fragments of glass made locally. The names of the glassworkers are recorded – William le Francais, William Peyte and Laurence Vitrearius, the first of his craft who was making glass as early as 1226. The industry was still in existence four hundred years later. A similar window in Wisborough Green, dedicated in 1968, commemorates the Bungars and Caquerays from Normandy, the Hennezols and Thietrys from Lorraine. There are smaller fragments in the churches at Kirdford and Dunsfold, all in the same part of Surrey. In the churchyard at Alfold, a plaque in a block of Sussex marble marks the tomb of Jean Carré, the most famous of the glassworkers of the sixteenth century. Glass from this area was used in churches far and wide, such as St Stephens, Westminster. The industry was recorded in other areas such as Knole Park and Northiam (Sx) but the Surrey–Sussex border was the heartland. Timber for fuel, local white sands, water power, ash from burning bracken and beech, used as flux, were all locally available. There is little to be seen on the ground as compared with the iron industry but, with the aid of field names and local finds, at least forty furnace sites have been identified. Friends living in Wisborough Green showed me glass fragments and 'ropes' of glass that they had dug up in their garden. Similar samples can be seen, informatively arranged, in Haslemere Museum.

Many industries depended on skilled immigrants for their inception and their development. What was true of iron and glass was also the case with the most widespread manufacturing activity, the making of woollen cloth. Cottages bearing the name of the 'weavers' are even more prolific than 'forge' cottages. The cloth industry began in the reign of Edward III with the introduction of skilled workers from Flanders. Many of them settled in and around Cranbrook in the Weald of Kent. The prosperity of the trade was reflected in the building of a new church tower, typical of the many Kentish towers built between the fourteenth and sixteenth centuries. Many churches were enlarged at the same time, such as St Mary's at Goudhurst, known as 'the barn of Kent'. Canterbury was the main outlet for the broad cloth famous for its medley colours. One of the green lanes that the clothiers used to get their goods to the city has been restored recently near Upper Ruckinge by local volunteers.

The advantages of the Weald lay in its comparatively easy access to London and the continental markets, in the great sheep flocks of the Downs and the 'longwools' of the Romney marsh. Water power for driving the fulling mills came from the streams and fuller's earth was found locally. This is a clay deposit found in the Lower Greensand which was used to extract the grease from the wool. There are old pits at Leeds and Boxley and it is still worked in an enormous quarry at Nutfield in Surrey.

Turkey Mill, in Mote Park, Maidstone, is a long-established paper mill on the site of an earlier fulling mill, and there are many other examples. The timber of the Weald was important as a source of fuel for boiling the vats of dye, a source of many disputes with ironmasters who needed the same supplies. The decline of the woollen trade in the sixteenth century was the subject of royal intervention, 'for the trade of making and dyeing cloth has, for a long time, employed the poor people within twenty miles of Cranbrooke, as the greatest number of inhabitants thereabouts have lived thereupon'. The soils of the Weald could only support about half its inhabitants in farming according to a Bill of 1593.

A new influx of refugees in the late sixteenth century stimulated new specialist crafts such as silk at Canterbury, thread at Maidstone, bays, says and linsey wolsey coming from the large immigrant colony in Sandwich. Areas in the main towns became known as Petty France. Canterbury was confirmed as the staple market as late as 1616. When Elizabeth carried out her royal progress through Surrey, Sussex and Kent in 1573, she was touring an industrial region, seeing glass manufacture in Knole, iron at Bedgebury, cloth at Smarden and Cranbrook, ships on the Medway. Amongst her many pleasures at Sandwich was the sight of one hundred children lined up by the schoolhouse, spinning fine linen. The cloth trade was carried out in other centres such as Tonbridge and Sevenoaks (K) and at Guildford, Farnham and Wonersh (Sy). Some of the old cottages around the green at Wonersh claim to have had weaving looms in their upper storeys.

33. *Sixteenth-century hall house in the cloth town of Smarden, showing characteristic timber frame and jetties.*

Quite apart from the dozens of weavers' cottages, the most famous being on the banks of the Stour in Canterbury, there are many surviving timber-framed houses that were directly concerned with the industry. The cloth hall was the gathering place for material that was spun in the vicinity. One has been restored at Headcorn and others can be seen at Goudhurst, Biddenden and Smarden. There is another delightful reminder in a cottage at Staple on the Stour. Its thatched roof is capped with a spinster at her wheel. 'The houses of the Kentish clothiers,' writes R. T. Mason, 'were almost magnificent . . . they generally had a maximum of jettying and a lavish amount of moulded work.'* That magnifi-

* R. T. Mason, op. cit.

cence was also displayed in tombs of wool merchants such as that of Alexander Dance in Cranbrook. The Guildhall at Sandwich and the church of St Clement, where the immigrants were allowed to worship, were enlarged. Schools and almshouses were founded throughout the region, such as at Tonbridge, Sevenoaks, Guildford, East Grinstead, Godstone, Sutton Valance and Greenwich. Many of the woollen towns had new schools – Smarden, Tenterden, Biddenden, Cranbrook and Sandwich – all established in the sixteenth century. The free grammar school at Maidstone was endowed by a clothier, William Lambe, who also supported a school at Sutton Valance. The grammar school at Faversham was granted financial endowment from the revenues of the Abbey by Elizabeth. The old founders had been ecclesiastics, the new were merchants and financiers. A Lord Mayor founded Tonbridge School, another Sevenoaks, though this originated from an earlier period in 1432. An actor founded Dulwich College.

By 1724, Defoe reported that the woollen trade was quite decayed, 'scarce ten clothiers left in all the county' of Kent. The industry lingered on in the manufacture of cheap sacking, especially for hop-bags, both at Cranbrook and at Farnham. Silk was still made in Canterbury in this century and was revived by the Hart-Dykes, first at Leatherhead (Sy), then at Lullingstone (K), their product being used for royal coronation robes. The many ancient mulberry trees found in the gardens of mansions are a tribute to the enthusiasm of James I for the silk industry. One preserved at Charlton House lays dubious claim to be the first, being planted in the same year that the Scottish king brought the new sport of golf to neighbouring Blackheath.

A small metal industry was based on copperas, a sulphate of iron which occurred as nodules in the London clay. Gathered along the crumbling shores of Sheppey and Whitstable, it was smelted locally for a variety of purposes such as dyeing cloth and making ink. A street in Deptford by the tidal Ravensbourne, the major smelting centre, still bears the name. The finest bells were cast in this period, notably by the Hatch family of Ulcombe and John Parker of Canterbury, much to the delight of today's campanologists. The oldest bell, reputedly seven hundred years old, hung in the porch at Chaldon (Sy) until it was stolen recently.

The paper industry, in which Kent is the leading county, has its origins in Tudor times, a mill at Dartford being started by a German in 1588. The Eynsford Mill, further up the Darent, produced hand-made paper until 1952. Water power from the Medway, the Darent and other streams washed the pulp and supplied the power. London supplied the market. Rags, ropes and old sails from the Thames ports supplied the raw materials. A mill at Little

Chart makes an improbably named product for the newspaper industry called stereo-flong.

A rare item of industrial archaeology is preserved in a housing estate at Faversham, the Chart Mill, where gunpowder was made. The big wheel and the building date back to the early eighteenth century but the site is earlier. The Evelyn family made some of its fortune from the gunpowder industry and their major mills were near their Surrey estate of Albury on the Tillingbourne. The mill sites were the power houses of the early industrial era. There were nearly three hundred mills, almost certainly water mills, recorded in the region in the eleventh century. There were more than four hundred in the nineteenth century, a remarkable persistence. The early corn mills were adapted to later industrial purposes and then reverted back to flour-milling. The sites are easily identified and many wheels remain intact. Haxted Mill (Sy) on the river Eden is a working museum. Parts of the building are nearly three hundred years old. The eighteenth-century Woods Mill, near Henfield, is now the headquarters of the Sussex Naturalists Trust, another notable example put to good use. There is a great revival in interest in mill sites and others may be restored. Four other water mills are open to the public in Surrey, at Coltsford, Holstead, Grimshall and Shalford. After a thousand years of use, the water mill may not yet have outlived its purpose.

Some of the major markets for the Tudor industries were the newly founded Royal dockyards. Greenwich was the first, in 1513, followed by Woolwich and then Chatham. Sheerness developed after the Stuart restoration. Timber, iron, ordnance, ropes, cloth, gunpowder, glass, all went north to the estuary, though it was easier said than done. Defoe recalled that a cannon took two years on a journey from the Wealden forge to the docks. The manufacture of bricks and tiles was stimulated as much by the docks as by the rebuilding of country houses. While the docks have been overlain with the additions of later centuries, much of the evidence of the new housing remains. With the notable exception of such places as Great Tangley Manor, south of Guildford, built in 1584 in the traditional timber-framed style, the new wave of building used brick and tile and, to a lesser extent, stone, especially the Kentish ragstone and the Bargate Beds, both quarried in the Lower Greensand. Chimneys were added at gable ends or even inserted in the middle of houses; windows were enlarged, oriel windows bulged from upper storeys; jetties and bays were disguised with brick fronts; clay and wattle was replaced by brick-nogging. Black flint and red brick became the hallmark of coastal and Downland Sussex. Hall houses were divided up internally into smaller rooms, wings were added with service rooms and bedrooms. Barge boards were lavishly carved and decorated, as at Chiddingstone, and doors grew as wide as Tudor aspirations. The Englishman's home became his castle. The castle became a home. The lower orders aped their betters and, like the husbandman at West Hoathly, expressed their new status in brick and mortar.

The buildings that survive are, of course, of the 'polite' threshold, houses built to endure for families that intended to endure. The peasant dwelling was not likely to survive, although some of the smaller timber-framed houses were sub-divided and used for the lesser husbandmen. The region has the largest concentration of historic buildings in the country, a tribute to its wealth and its proximity to London. The country house was well within reach of the city merchants. The newly rich were willing and able to acquire old houses and lavish money and affection on them, a pattern that is as true today as it was then. The Crown led the way, gathering properties like apples.

'These all flourished with increase,' wrote Aubrey, the great historian, of the Surrey monasteries, 'till the ripeness of their fruit was so pleasing in sight and taste unto King Henry the Eighth, that in beating the boughs he brake downe body and all, ruinating those houses and seizing their rich possessions in to his own hands.' In Surrey, close by his palace at Hampton, Henry founded five more palaces at Guildford, Oatlands (near Weybridge), Woking, Nonesuch and Sheen. All, like Nonesuch, have foundered into the dust, pirated for their stone. The great parks of Richmond and Nonesuch serve as reminders of the royal love of the chase. The setting was as important as the house. Its courtyards, gardens, pleasure grounds, the park with trees and grassy rides, were as necessary to the new house as the style of the building itself. Time has been kinder to the Tudors in Kent, where they acquired a string of estates from Greenwich to the coast. The Palace of Placentia was built on the banks of the Thames. The excavation of the palace in 1970 proved its outline in the grounds of the Naval College and was then back-filled. The present assembly of royal buildings, amongst the finest architectural group in the world, the Queen's House, designed by Inigo Jones, and the Restoration splendours of the College, are the focal point of the Royal park. Whether seen from the top of the bluff looking down towards the palace and the river, or from the Isle of Dogs looking south, the buildings and the park are one composition. The formal layout of the park, its avenues and drives, was imposed on the Tudor deer enclosure in the 1660s.

To the south-east was Eltham with three deer enclosures. The Great Hall of the royal palace stands behind a medieval moat and bridge but the parks were ruined by the Commonwealth. Yet the pleasant openness of this part of London, its many playing fields and spaces, are related directly to the parks. Middle Park Avenue and Horn Park Lane recall two of them. The third, the Great Park, is now the Royal Blackheath golf course. The king snapped up Dartford Priory as a staging post and in the luxuriance of the Darent Valley and Holmesdale were two palaces of the Archbishops of Canterbury only three miles apart, at Otford and Knole. Recent building works at Otford revealed stone foundations so impressive in their size and structure that, together with the Tudor tower that stands by the church, they show a palace of truly regal proportions, another Hampton Court.

Otford, low-lying and damp, was not good for the king's health. He preferred Knole, 'for it standeth on a sound, wholesome and perfect ground' on the well-drained slopes of the greensand. Cranmer gave it to him. He had little option. Knole is perfection. Nowhere in the whole region, with the possible exception of Petworth, do I find such personal pleasure as in the 400-ha deer park enlarged and enclosed by Henry. The oaks and beeches, the chestnut avenues, are nearly as old as the Tudors. The mansion, one of the largest private houses in Britain, is comparatively modest in its superb setting. The Dutch gabling and rampant leopards on the west front are the result of rebuilding by the Sackvilles in the early seventeenth century when they received the estate from Elizabeth but within the Green Court is an older, fourteenth-century, building with great hall, staircases and sumptuous rooms from the time of the archbishops. Henry stayed seldom, visited infrequently. The house and much of the park are owned by the National Trust and some of the most famous furnishings such as the king's bed are undergoing a lengthy restoration.

Westenhanger is a very different story. Henry destroyed many a village to create his chase and the castle which included Fair Rosamund's tower. Now sheep wander in and out of medieval barns, and the castle, or what remains of it, is lost in a farm behind Folkestone race-course, almost as inglorious as his tower at Otford which became a hop-pickers' haven. The barns are worth preserving as well as the towers and tumbled curtain wall.

Henry was concerned with more than his personal acquisition of estates, parks and palaces. He had an eye on the needs of the nation and continued the castle-building tradition that, together with the royal docks, was intended to defend the south-east angle. The castles of Deal, Walmer and Sandown protected the anchorage, confusingly known as the Downs. They were castles with a difference; they were really massive gun-emplacements of revolutionary design with low circular turrets and bastions as functional as the concrete emplacements of the 1940s. They were still manned in the present century. Two others were built

34. *Knole House and park in 1830, drawn by T. M. Baynes.*

in the same style at Sandgate and at Camber on the shingle ridges near Rye. Sandgate, like Sandown, has been eroded by the sea, but a part remains in private occupation. The cannons, culverins, sakers and minions that stood ready to rake the invaders, were all products of the Wealden iron industry. The only sieges they ever withstood were the royalist uprisings of 1648. In the course of

35. *Camber Castle – Tudor gun emplacement on shingle ridges. Behind the shingle is rich farmland on reclaimed marshes.*

time the dramatic simplicity of the bastions was softened by later domesticity, Walmer, for example, becoming the official residence of the Lords Warden of the Cinque Ports. It was the main base for the fleet and the fireships that harried the Armada. Amongst its famous tenants was William Pitt, the Duke of Wellington and Lady Hester Stanhope. In their time new gardens were laid out. Walmer is open to the public but Deal is the best of the bunch in preserving its original form. In interest, Deal is almost eclipsed by Upnor, a unique Elizabethan castle, built on the left bank of the Medway to guard Chatham. The upper windows and gun bastions are reminiscent of Berwick's fortifications, due to the influence of Sir Richard Lee, the engineer. Evidence of the moat remains and the cannon threaten a maritime scene of yachts, barges, docks, wildfowl and power station.

Where the Crown led, others followed. Courtiers, favourites, merchants moved into the manors. Some of the landed gentry managed to ride the political and religious storms and hold on to their ancestral estates, particularly in Sussex, further removed from the immediate impact of change. Sutton Place makes a suitable symbol of the age. The brick and terracotta façade of the mansion built in 1521 by Sir Richard Weston, a protégé of the king, bears his initials on many of the bricks. The north wing has gone, but the courtyard can be admired on the occasions when the gardens are open to the public. The house was, until recently, the home of the richest man in the world. Situated in a meander of the River Wey, it is one of a number of outstanding houses, like Great Tangley, within easy reach of Guildford. In the same area is Loseley, built in 1561 using stone from Waverley Abbey. The internal decoration, furnishings, ceilings and fireplaces are superlative examples of Tudor architecture. Baynards, built near Cranleigh by the same family, the Mores, suffered a major Victorian modernization. Great Fosters, in contrast, near Egham, home of a sequence of judges, remains what it always was, a simple but imposing brick building of 1598, showing the influence of Dutch styles that we saw at Knole.

Slyfield, near Stoke d'Abernon, built after 1625, is another old hall house embellished with Dutch façade and gabling so prevalent in Surrey at the time. The classic example is Kew Palace, otherwise known as the Dutch House, built in 1631 by a London merchant of Dutch descent, using Flemish bond in the brickwork. The lodges of Ham House repeat the motifs. The immigrants brought more than their industrial skill and their gardening. They brought new styles of architecture, based on brick, which affected the whole region.

This Dutchness of the buildings was allied to a new fashion for formal gardens. John Evelyn's taste for arboriculture, for formal avenues, walled gardens and hedges, derived from a lengthy grand tour of Europe, was influential at all levels. With his brother he fashioned the grounds on the family estate at Wotton (Sy). He made his Deptford estate a delight of exotica, always seeking new ideas. His advice was used directly at Groombridge (K), where the Packers rebuilt the moated mansion on the same site, a lovely place loud with peacocks that remains almost untouched since that time. Formality, devised by Le Nôtre of Versailles fame, transformed the royal park at Greenwich, one of the few spaces to preserve the grand design into the present. The Dutch style is

36. *Decorated Tudor brickwork of Sir Richard Weston's house at Sutton Place.*

everywhere. Godinton, a miniature Knole, extended in 1628, set in a large park, has exquisite panelling and staircases carved by Huguenot workmen. The Dutch House at Sandwich, the church at Smallhythe, Broome Park (K), one of the chain of mansions and parks that line the Nailbourne in East Kent, all show the same influence. Squerryes Court at Westerham was built for the Wardes in the late seventeenth century and is still occupied by the same family. The house was made famous by its association with the young James Wolfe, victor of Quebec, whose statue dominates the Greenwich skyline.

With the fashion came the man. The professional architect emerged, men like Inigo Jones who gave the wealthy and influential what they wanted, new styles to match their pretensions. Many houses are attributed to Jones but the most certain are the Queen's House at Greenwich, Lees Court (K) and Chevening. Now the home of the Prince of Wales, Chevening was the estate of the Stanhopes who destroyed the village and cut the ancient Pilgrims' Way to empark their land. The original brickwork and pilasters have been restored with the removal of later rather dull façades. The house faces north to its sloping parkland and a key-hole cut through the woodland on the hill. Formal gardens and a lake lie to the south of the house behind high walls, dating from 1719. Lord Chatham thought it a visual feast to compare with the Alps and early prints show a formal layout of the highest order of landscape achievement.

Seventeenth-century brickwork stands cheek-by-jowl with Tudor flint and stone chequerwork at Hall Place, Bexley, another possession of the Archbishops bought by a London merchant. The mansion is a municipal museum and library. The gardens, truncated by a major road, are being restored most imaginatively as a series of Tudor gardens – herb, rose, water, rock, sunken – all enclosed with topiary work. The ingredients of Renaissance hall, formal garden, avenue, deer park and great wood, all on the grandest scale, can be seen at Cobham (K), albeit with a faded glory. As in most estates, the love of the formal was overtaken by a later fashioning of romantic English landscapes, the 'improvements' on Nature that were to be the hallmark of professional landscape artists such as Launcelot Brown and, as at Cobham, the Reptons. One battered avenue of lime trees is all that is left of the series that radiated from the great house. Repton swept the rest away.

Kent, always the most fertile and wealthiest of the three counties, is full of fine country houses of its industrial age. A lovely group range along the fertile slopes of the ragstone ridge south of Maidstone, from Boughton Monchelsea and Boughton Malherbe to Mersham-le-Hatch. Another group in the High Weald, in the iron and cloth country, includes Glassenbury, still in its moat.

Bedgebury and Scotney were both extended and then rebuilt on higher ground. The Tudor gatehouse at Sissinghurst and the tall tower must be much as they were when Elizabeth knighted John Baker in 1573. Penshurst has two faces. Seen from the west across the parkland and the ha-ha ditch, the house is massively Tudor, built in stone for the Sidney family whose tombs fill the nearby church. From the gardens to the east, it is a fourteenth-century hall house built for a London draper, four times Lord Mayor of London, Sir John de Pulteney. The estate was wealthy enough to support two deer parks. The South Park remains only in name. The North Park, much reduced by plough and planting, has some fine avenues on its perimeter ride and the stumps of ancient oaks.

In Sussex, the great rebuilding is seen at its best in a line of mansions and parks that range along the foot of the South Downs, mostly on the greensand outcrop, well-drained, undulating country so suited to the emparking fashion. Here are the finest houses in the county – Cowdray, Petworth, Parham, Wiston, Danny, Plumpton Place, Glynde and Firle. Cowdray, though ruined, is 'the epitome of Tudor architecture at its most sober'.* The great towers and arches rise from the flat land east of Midhurst and the motte of an earlier fortified site. One tower is open as a museum, a good viewpoint for the surrounding landscape.

A Percy castle and a Tudor house enfolded in a seventeenth-century mansion of the sixth Duke of Somerset, such is Petworth. Few houses can boast such a setting as the focus of a magnificent park. The upper and lower parks make one of the loveliest compositions in the region. They inspired Turner to interpret them in paint. Parham, once an outlying grange of Westminster Abbey, is even more authentic, a Tudor house in a Tudor setting, annexing the parish church as a private chapel, a familiar story. The medieval settlement stood by the church. The well-wooded park has one of the best-maintained herds of fallow deer in the entire region, culled regularly for venison. The deer are remarkable for the darkness of their coats, being almost black rather than dappled. The estate lies within the limited breeding range of the hobby, a small bird of prey regularly sighted there.

Plumpton Place was the home of Leonard Mascall, who reputedly introduced the carp and pippins into England for the first time in 1514, the former to stock his moat and the other to improve his orchards. One of Lutyens' many twentieth-century restorations, Plumpton is now a college. Quite different in its setting, almost on the cap of the West Sussex downland, is Uppark, a National Trust property. Much altered in the eighteenth century with Repton's work being apparent in both the house and the park, the present house was built between

* Nairn and Pevsner, op. cit.

1685 and 1690 on older foundations. 'Its parentage is Dutch,' writes Nairn, who calls it 'a copybook example of the Wren-type country house'.* In the Tudor period, the deer park was let to a London merchant as a commercial proposition, a nice reflection of the transition from medieval to modern England.

A glance through the official list of antiquities compiled by the Surrey County Council shows just how many houses, great and small, survive from the sixteenth and seventeenth centuries. There are nineteen around Wonersh, nine at Oxted, more than twenty at Shere and nine more in the vicinity of Dunsfold.

Another idea of the number and extent of the great houses can be gained from the early county maps that appeared at this time. Phil Symonson's New Description of Kent in 1596, John Speed's series in the 1610s and Blaeu's delineations in 1648 all depict the parks, usually with symbolic palings enclosing them. Apart from rivers and settlements, they are the main feature of the maps. Yet when tracing the broad movements in the changing human landscape, I am only too aware of the places, just as rewarding, left unmentioned, the smaller manor houses, for example, charted by Viscountess Wolseley in one limited area of Sussex. 'Those who inhabited these lesser manor-farms may, perhaps, have only helped on some humble craft, may have merely lived the daily life of the farm; yet we know that England owes her great undaunted fighting spirit to that legacy of health and vitality which these stalwart yeomen or ironfounders transmitted to their successors.'†

The ironmasters, the clothiers and the glassworkers flourished and made their contribution to the landscape. The great forest was subdued, cut over, colonized, settled. The quiet retreat of the deer became the roaring vale of iron. The ancestral home became the financier's speculation. The wealth of the monasteries, even to their enduring stone, was pilfered and redistributed. Then the mills fell silent. The industrial age of the Weald was gone. The yeoman, renowned for his wealth and independence, and the poorer farmers come back to the centre of the stage in the drama of the evolving landscape.

* Ibid.

† Viscountess Wolseley, *Some of the Smaller Manor Houses in Sussex* (Medici Society, 1925).

7

The Garden of England

A flock of sheep graze in an orchard white with blossom. The conical cowl of an oast rises amongst the farm buildings in the background. The scene is familiar, gracing many a book jacket and country calendar. Yet the ingredients of that visual cliché became parts of the rural landscape at very different times. The round oast was not in regular use until the nineteenth century. The commercial orchard originated with the introduction of new fruit stock in the reign of Henry VIII. Sheep flocks have grazed the pastures since Domesday and before but the present fat breeds would not have been recognized by medieval man, for they are the result of selective breeding in the eighteenth century.

The picture tells another story of change, for it is already an historic document. Few of the oasts are used for drying hops today. The sheep flocks have declined. The tall standard fruit trees are being grubbed up and replaced by orchards more suited to the economics of modern farming. All is change in the countryside. But the south-east still deserves its reputation as the garden of England. More than half the hop hectarage and a quarter of the country's fruit is grown in Kent alone.

'England is a fruitful and plenteous region,' said John Coke in 1549, debating with the heralds of France, 'so that we have seen fruites whereof you have fewe, as wardeines, quynces, peches, medlars, chestnutts and other delicious fruytes serving for all seasons of the yere.' Perry and cider were exported to France when he made his proud boast. Yet the fruitfulness of the region was only just beginning, due largely to the efforts of Richard Harrys, fruiterer to Henry VIII. Just north of Teynham, in the fruit belt of North Kent, there is an old wall in a new housing estate which bears a commemorative plaque to Harrys. It was there, at Newgardens, that he planted the 'sweet Cherry, the temperate Pipyn and the golden Renate' and other fruits that he had brought from Flanders in 1533. They were to be the parent orchards of all the cherries and apples that had spread to thirty parishes by the end of the century.

Turkey, carp, hops, pickerel and beer
came into England all in one year

ran the rhyme with some approximation to the truth. We have seen the introduction of carp, together with the pippin, already claimed by Leonard Mascalls of Plumpton in Sussex. Innovation was in the air. The exact origins are difficult to establish. The small village of West Bere in East Kent lays claim to the first hop garden. It has a manor within its bounds called Hoplands. There is documentary evidence of the first cultivated hop around 1524. The word 'oast' is Flemish in origin, suggesting a similar origin to Harrys' new fruits. In less than a century, hop cultivation had spread as far as Goudhurst in the Weald. Orchards and gardens were established in the areas that are recognizable today, the North Kent plain, the Stour Valley east of Canterbury and the ragstone ridge south of Maidstone. The soils of the greensand on either side of the Medway are more varied and more fertile than the same geological outcrop in Surrey. Hop gardens, orchards, small fruits and cob plantations sprawl over the fair land. They reach down even to the clay vales of the Weald where parishes like Smarden have more than half their area under hops and fruit, an area still signposted in Maytime as the 'blossom route'. Luscious names like Cox's Orange Pippin, Laxton Superb, Worcester Pearmain and Bramley Seedling give the orchards an individual distinction, the results of long experimentation by gifted horticulturists.

Kent maintains about half the total acreage of apples in England, two-thirds of the pears and more than three-quarters of the cherries. The East Malling Research Centre, set up in 1913 as an offshoot of the Agricultural College at Wye, encouraged new ideas, a difficult matter where traditional patterns were long established. 'They did nearly everything wrong in the light of modern knowledge,' wrote one research worker, a strange comment to make to men who had been in the fruit-growing business for generations. An orchard cannot be changed year by year like a corn crop. But change is being forced by competition from the continent. New varieties, like Golden Delicious, are establishing themselves at the cost of the old favourites. The standard trees, up to forty years old, are unsuited to easy picking. As a boy, I spent many a late summer's day perched on top of a ladder in a Sussex orchard, trying to pick quickly enough to earn money yet not so carelessly as to bruise the fruit. Those days are gone. New grafts, smaller trees as low as a bush, pruned and trained to put growth into the fruit rather than the tree, the Dutch spindle system, are all being introduced. Yet there is no visual evidence that the orchards are declining in popularity. Dozens of new plantations are appearing along the Thames shores, right down to the edge of the marshes. New freezing plants and packing stations bring the factory atmosphere to the villages such as Paddock Wood and Horsmonden, but I have seen freighter lorries bringing continental apples into a Kent village where the local fruit is lying rotting in the ditches because of the expense of picking.

The boom in fruit-growing came with the growth of London and the railway system. The line across the Weald from Tonbridge to Ashford was opened up by 1842. Cheap sugar from the Empire added to the stimulus for jam-making, especially using soft fruits, which were subject to damage in long, slow cart haulage. The small fruits were concentrated initially in North West Kent on the fringes of the urban areas. Plumstead had the finest cherries; woodlands around Eynsford were felled to make way for strawberries and other fruit. The Cray Valley was 'a series of gardens, cherries or pears or plums above and gooseberries, currants, raspberries or filberts beneath'.* As London grew, the gardens were built over. There are still strawberry fields close to town, on the slopes of the Surrey hills near Addington or at Keston in Kent where Londoners are invited to go and pick their own. The abundant labour needed for fruit-picking no longer exists and the 'pick-your-own' signs appear by the roadsides as far away as the Romney Marsh and the outskirts of Worthing.

Small fruits are more adaptable to changing market conditions than orchard fruits. They can be grown in artificial climates created by glasshouses and the new nylon covers that curl across the fields like white sausages. The ideal is to get crops maturing when prices are high, before or after the periods of glut. The cost of equipment and heating is high, and it would be so much easier if it could all be left to the natural warmth of the sun and the nourishment of soil and rain. But farming methods increasingly amend the natural cycle of the seasons. I regret the passing of the great picking forays, the happy days when a farmer at Ticehurst told me I could eat as many raspberries as I liked so long as I kept filling the panniers. Facing raspberry pie in the evening, after a full day's eating, I soon realized why he was so benevolent. The next day was all picking and no eating. Only a change to loganberries restored my youthful appe-

* William Cobbett.

tite. Now machines are being invented to replace the small hungry boys. At Matfield, there is even a blackcurrant-picking machine munching its way through the canes.

Hops remain the most distinctive crop of the region. They formed the basis of the brewing industry from the sixteenth century but they reached their maximum extent in the nineteenth century. By 1878, Kent had 65 per cent of the national area. Hops flourished around Farnham in Surrey, in the narrow, fertile vale of the Wey and helped an area that was suffering from a decline in the woollen industry. William Marshall recorded in 1791 that 'the passion for hop grounds having there risen to a degree of rage', wool was used with dung to fertilize the fields. 'A thing of perfect hazard,' commented Cobbett, having seen hops climbing everywhere from Dover to the Hampshire border. 'A lottery,' said Arthur Young. Hops were vulnerable to variations of the weather. The wind could blow them to the ground. Yet many a small farmer was saved by his hop sales to the factors in the Borough Market in London. 'I always consider that it was these hops that really started me in life,' wrote Samuel Marshall, a farmer at Puttenham near the Hog's Back, in 1902.*

The 'rage' for hops led to the introduction of new drying plant. The round oast was used by John Read in 1835, though I have seen one example at Brook (K) that claims to date from about 1815. The abolition of the heavy duty on hops in 1862 stimulated the final boom. Oasts appeared in groups of two, three and four, attached to barns, witnesses of the proverbial affluence of the hop farmer. Most were built of brick, though some were solid structures of local stone. Single oasts were erected by small farmers, the sort that have found a ready use in recent times as private houses. The early hop grounds were usually about half a hectare in size, though the largest extended over four hectares. The protection of the precious vines was one reason for small hedged fields appearing in contrast to the older forest clearings surrounded by woodland shaws. The enclosure hedgerow is not the typical field boundary of the south-east so it is surprising to find that, in William Marshall's opinion, the yeomen of Kent were 'amongst the first and best hedge makers in the Kingdom'.†

In special areas such as the Medway Valley west of Maidstone, the pressure for hops was increased by landowners raising rents so that tenant-farmers could not cover their costs with any less profitable crop. 1,840 hectares were under hops and the special ritual of hop-stringing and hop-picking was established. The shoddy and rags of London and the northern industrial towns were laid on the

* S. Marshall, *The Life of a Successful Farmer in Surrey* (1902).
† W. Marshall, *The Rural Economy of the Southern Counties* (1798).

fields to rot, a practice which can still be seen in a few places with a most pungent result. Thousands of Londoners came to pick the crop and many an East End school was emptied of its children for an autumn fortnight. It was the annual holiday for many families; the money bought the winter clothes. The carnival atmosphere that was perpetuated into the 1950s was as traditional as the crop. 'The hop-picking is a sort of jubilee, during which a licence of speech, and relaxation of manners, are authorized by custom; anything may be said and many

37. *Oast house near Sissinghurst.*

things done which would not pass uncensured at another season.'* The last time I saw that colourful scene was in 1970 at Beltring near Paddock Wood, under the largest cluster of oasts in the region, but machines, first used in the 1920s, have finally ousted the crowds. Hand labour is used only to separate the hops from the foliage on moving belts in the collecting sheds. Rows of small brick huts stand empty in the corners of fields, a poignant part of the landscape of rural architecture where the families once camped out. But not all the romance is gone. Watching a stringer at work, building the 'hills' of string, up and down,

* Ibid.

up and down, with a long bamboo pole, one thousand hills in a back-breaking April day, is to see a country craft at its finest. The early stringers worked by hand, walking on stilts. Most local museums, from Battle to Farnham, have collections of hop-tokens, first introduced by Toke of Godinton about 1767. A specialized form of payment to pickers, the tokens varied locally, being made of lead, brass, wood, copper and even cardboard. There is a collection in the Ypres Tower at Rye where Jeremiah Smith, seven times mayor of the town, was a hop-grower as well as a flockmaster, and some hop grounds still survive in the vicinity of Winchelsea near by.

The demand for hop-poles was another stimulus to the coppicing of woodland, especially of chestnut and ash, to supply the supporting poles. There are four thousand poles to an acre and, on average, four hundred need replacing every year, but new experiments with wire may reduce the number of poles needed. At the moment, the timbers are cut on an eighteen-year cycle so as to produce the height needed for machines to move unencumbered through the grounds. After the slump in hops of 1878, many grounds were grubbed up and replaced with orchards. Hops, like apples, are under pressure with demands for new seedless varieties to replace the Fuggles of Horsmonden and the Golding of Malling. A sign of the times is the new hop-powder plant at Rainham, built with the blessing of the Hop Marketing Board.

My favourite crop is the filbert or cob. Whenever I visit the plantations around Plaxtol, I have visions of reclining like a Greek under his olives waiting for the wind to blow the nuts into my lap. It is not quite as easy as that. The trees are subjected to the usual routine of herbicide and pesticide and the trees that were planted as an undercrop, under plums, for example, suffer from lack of sunlight. There are only about 280 hectares left, mostly of the filbert variety introduced by Lambert of Goudhurst in 1830. The nuts were once important as a source of vitamins for sailors on long sea voyages. Most of the cobs are within easy reach of the Medway, along the ragstone ridge from Plaxtol to Sutton, though there are isolated plantations of great age in gardens such as Sissinghurst.

Even more limited in extent than the cobs but of greater current interest is the vine. There are at least six commercial vineyards in the region, ranging from under a hectare at Brede to three hectares on the south-facing slopes below Hambledon Hill. Four ha have been planted at Biddenden in Kent, replacing grubbed-up orchards. There are other small yards at Newick and Slaynes Hill, both in Sussex. Horam is not only the site of two small vineyards but the centre of active wine-production, producing wines good enough to export to the continent. There is nothing new about vines in the south-east. Vineyards were recorded at Chart Sutton, Leeds and Chislet in the Domesday survey of the Kent manors and a vinedresser was mentioned at Wandsworth in Surrey. The Brooklands font depicts October as the month of the vintage but this may reflect the imported Norman image rather than a local scene. Many field names, such as the Vine, show that the yards were once widespread, probably due to monastic influence. The future of English vineyards is as uncertain as their origins. Much depends on the agricultural policies of our European partners. But many private owners are planting a hectare or two, mostly on the Wealden hills such as Penshurst.

A wide variety of vegetables was known to the Romans. Their gardening skills were maintained in monasteries and kitchen gardens together with herbs and flowers but market gardening as a commercial venture was introduced by the same Flemings who changed the industrial scene in the sixteenth century. The low-lying land around Sandwich suited the cabbages and carrots and other seeds that the immigrants had grown in their homeland. Such was the demand for their produce that growers migrated to the London area, establishing gardens on the flood plain of the Thames at Lambeth, Battersea, Wandsworth and Bermondsey. By the eighteenth century there were two thousand hectares of market gardens in Surrey alone, all within sixteen kilometres of Covent Garden and the Borough Market. The fame of Mortlake for its asparagus, of Battersea for cauliflowers, Deptford for onions and exotic fruits at Lambeth lasted until late in the nineteenth century. Even as late as the 1920s, Black's Guide Book to Surrey could still aver that 'Mitcham is to some degree the herb-garden of England, and many acres of fragrant lavender are grown and distilled in the vicinity'.* The house-owners of Mitcham would hardly recognize the description today. Even as the lavender grew, the London County Council had bought land 'for the purpose of a gigantic housing estate'.

At Lambeth, in grounds owned by the Dean and Chapter of Canterbury, John Tradescant, horticulturist extraordinary, finally settled in 1625, having moved from Meopham in Kent. His travels in search of new fruits and flowers had taken him all over the world, even to Barbary and Muscovy, and brought him such fame that he was appointed Keeper of His Majesty's Gardens, Vines and Silkworms at Oatlands, one of the many royal palaces in Surrey. His collection of exotica, maintained by his son, eventually formed part of the Ashmolean

* J. E. Morris, *Black's Guide to Surrey* (A. & C. Black, 1926).

collection. He is credited, amongst other achievements, with the introduction of the common larch, now one of the most popular conifers.

Lorries laden with market garden produce still rumble up the roads to London, especially from the low chalk plateaux of Hoo, Cliffe and Thanet. In recent years, I have noticed more potatoes, vegetables and tulips growing on the marshes around Appledore, too, invading the last pastoral domain. Some of the most fertile, level ground, blessed by nearly 2,000 hours of sunshine, the highest in Britain, is on the coastal plain of Sussex, around Angmering. The glasshouses, first introduced in about 1860, glint in the sunlight, though the bird's-eye view from Highdown Hill shows the inexorable spread of Worthing and its suburbs over the fertile farmland. There are few roads in the area that do not have their quota of farm-gate shops and nurseries selling everything from mushrooms to young trees. Judging by the trade, Candide's injunction to cultivate our gardens has not fallen on deaf ears. Yet the fruits, hops and market gardens occupy only a limited part of the farming scene.

Nearly two-thirds of the land surface of the region is under the plough and another quarter is under permanent pasture. When the leading farmers were making their reports to the Board of Agriculture in the 1790s, corn was king. Grain for London was the most important produce of Surrey farms and, of Kent, John Boys wrote that 'the chief part of the agricultural commerce of the county is that of exporting corn to the London markets'. That extensive ploughland only reverted to pasture after the long period of agricultural depression from the latter half of the nineteenth century until the Second World War. Cheap imported food from the far-flung Empire and Commonwealth drove the home farmers to seek some sort of salvation in dairy farming, but the process is now being reversed.

Agricultural innovation came early to the region. Sir Richard Weston of Sutton Place in Surrey published a tract on crop improvements for stock feed in 1645 when, as a Catholic royalist, he might have been expected to have all his attention focused on survival during the Civil War. He was just as concerned with the effect of the great clover and ideas on turnip husbandry that he had seen in Flanders. How much the south-east owes to its close contact with the continent! One of the grasses Weston introduced was called Nonesuch, presumably after the royal palace. Like all good innovators, he turned his mind to a variety of projects and canalized the River Wey for fourteen miles, one of the first canals in England. He used it, too, for watering the low-lying meadows on his estate.

Another pioneering tract on *The Inrichment of the Weald*, written by Gervase

Markham in 1649, emphasized the importance of marl as a fertilizer. Five hundred cartloads were needed on every acre and cartage was difficult, so literally hundreds of marl-pits were dug. The necessary mixture of clay and lime was found in almost every field in the Low Weald. The same pits often yielded slabs of Bethersden marble which could be broken up for fertilizer as well as used for paving and decorative stone work. Marl was dug in deeper pits in the clay-with-fling deposits on the North Downs. Lime, lumps of chalk, pigeon dung, straw ash, all were led to the fields and mixed with dung to enrich the pastures and ploughlands, doubling the amount of livestock that could be maintained.

The basic field pattern had been established in the medieval period, densely settled with comparatively small, enclosed parcels of land, especially in the piecemeal colonization of the forested areas. The purchase of adjacent fields enabled farmers to make larger holdings. 'The enlarging of fields, within the Weald especially, has been a continuing process up to the present day,' writes Baker.* There was some division of demesne land, with the planting of new hedgerows. Similarly, some of the parks and deer chases were divided up as at Westwell, Aldington and the friths of Tonbridge. There were a few surviving areas of open arable fields at the foot of the Downs, on Thanet and at Cliffe. Three hundred acres remained unenclosed, for example, at Clandon and four hundred and fifty acres at Bookham in Surrey. Most were divided up during the period of parliamentary enclosure acts in the eighteenth and nineteenth centuries, a process that was to reach its climax with an attack on the commons, as at Lewisham in Kent, Birdham in Surrey and Selsey in Sussex.

The rapid growth of tillage was given by John Evelyn as one of the main reasons, together with iron-working, glass-making and ship-building, for the 'impolitick diminution of our Timber'.†

The period of late enclosures coincided with the agricultural surveys and the general spirit of 'improvement' that swept the entire country. Arthur Young, surveying Sussex, was most impressed with the work of the large landowners. His pages are filled with references to the Earl of Egremont at Petworth, the Duke of Richmond at Goodwood and to the estates of the Earls of Chichester and Lord Sheffield. They experimented with fertilizers, introduced new drainage systems, planted new hedgerows, especially at Goodwood, and cultivated new fodder crops. 'Turn your fallow to crops that shall feed the cattle,' advised Lord Sheffield, echoing Sir Richard Weston more than a century earlier. Wheat, barley, pease, tares, oats, coleseed and turnips all took their place in new rota-

* A. R. H. Baker, 'Field Patterns in Seventeenth Century Kent', *Geography*, January 1965.
† John Evelyn, *Sylva* (1662).

tions. Yet it was a small farmer, a Mr May of Battle, who first grew potatoes as a fodder crop in the 1790s. The essential pattern was known as up-and-down farming, by which pasture could be rotated with ploughland. Arable was the primary use, followed by fruit and hops, then fat sheep and cattle in order of importance. In Sussex, around Chichester, arable farming reached perfection. 'It is impossible for corn land and for agriculture to be finer,' said Cobbett, who knew good farmland when he saw it.

38. *Shearing Kent sheep in the Weald at Bethersden.*

The Downlands, the marshes and the High Weald remained as strongholds of the pastoral tradition, though the ubiquitous pigs of Domesday were less in evidence than sheep and cattle. Three famous breeds of livestock originated in the region, the Southdown sheep, the Romney or Kent breed and the Sussex red cattle. The improvement of livestock by selective breeding was largely the work of John Ellman of Glynde (Sx). His flock of five hundred Southdown ewes gained a national fame. Fed on a combination of close folding and rich downland grass, they formed the basis of a progeny that spread across the country. George III and Coke of Holkham were amongst the purchasers. 'It is the herbage of the Downs which renders the flavour of the mutton so exquisitely fine, the flesh so firm, the wool so excellent,' said Arthur Young. Others attributed the special flavour of the meat to the tiny snails that infested the grassland. Travellers in Sussex ever since have enthused about the half million sheep that roamed the Downs right up until the 1930s. That splendour has not survived the plough-up policy of world war and peace-time subsidy. There is a twelve-kilometre stretch of arable land on the Downs north of Brighton without a hedgerow or

39. *Shepherd's cott near Birling.*

shelter belt and scarce a sheep in sight. Near Birling Gap stands one shepherd's cott, a single-roomed house of flint and brick, the last of its kind and now protected as a listed building, a monument to a rural landscape and a way of life that had passed. But not quite. The traditional sheep fair of Findon continues to be held on the green at Nepcote, just below Cissbury Ring. The famous grasslands remain in patches, in nature reserves and on steep valley sides, difficult to plough. The sheep numbers on the Downs have declined to about 140,000.

Recently I saw twelve ewes drinking from a dew pond near Ditchling Beacon, a scene remarkable for its rarity. Most of the dew ponds have joined the rest of the pastoral landscape into oblivion. The memory lives on in the opulent springs that gush from the foot of the Downs where the huge flocks used to be watered. Pub names like the Shepherd and Dog, and tracks like Sheep Lane stand witness to the old days.

The Southdown sheep are used as breeding stock for crossing with other breeds such as the Romney, a large, long-woolled sheep that thrives on the marshes. The Romney forms a large proportion of the half million sheep that graze in Kent, a county that has twice the number of sheep per ha as the national average. It has the longest lineage of any English sheep breed, recorded at least as early as the thirteenth century. 'The sun never sets on the Romney sheep' which, like the Southdown, was exported all over the world. In view of the intensive sheep grazing, the lack of settlement in the marshes is at first surprising but the flocks were traditionally herded by 'lookers' attached to distant farms. The outwintering of young stock on inland farms is still carried out.

Cattle are found throughout the region, the proximity to London making dairying an economic proposition from the late nineteenth century. Albert Wadman of Firle was the first farmer to send milk to the capital by train. There are some outstanding dairy herds of Friesians and Shorthorns, as at Ide Hill near Sevenoaks and the Loseley herd in Surrey, but on a national scale the region is not of major importance. An older tradition of beef cattle raising is maintained by many pedigree herds of the Sussex Red, magnificent brutes the colour of deep mahogany. An ancient breed native to the Weald, it was famed for its strength as a draught animal and as a plough team. It was shown at the first Smithfield Show in 1799. Its capacity for fattening on a minimum diet, its hardiness and suitability to crossing with Shorthorns and other cattle for good quality beef have led to a revival of interest in its breeding. The pastures on the Wealden clay soils, which can be so poor that only Sussex Reds can find nourishment in them, have had one surprising product. The area south of Ashford, around Bethersden, produces the finest wild white clover seed in the country. The clover benefits from heavy grazing in early summer by sheep and will continue to give good grazing cover for many years, especially when planted with local perennial rye-grass. The seed, harvested in August, is exported all over the world.

Farming is changing as rapidly now as at any time in its long history. Some of the physical controls remain. The Wealden clays are still cement in summer, soup in winter. I was staying on a Sussex smallholding during the dry summer of 1975, a summer of near disaster for many local farmers dependent on a small dairy herd, which was to be followed by the even drier summer of 1976. Only wealthier farmers with capital to invest on complex irrigation systems could maintain bulk milk production. The heathlands, too, remain as 'a barren sand, soft, deaf and duffy' as Stevenson described them in 1809. But it is the demands of the market, the proximity of London and the continent, that effect most change. In the last decade, for example, I have seen maize grown for green fodder gain in popularity until it can be seen on every soil type from the chalk slopes of North Kent to the sandstone ridges of Sussex and the alluvial flats of Romney. Many a crop of cobs has proved a bonus, sold at the farmyard gate. On the North Downs above Boxley, I have seen a monastic grange of small intakes in woodland develop into one enormous field, two miles without a hedgerow. The flint rubble after ploughing looks like the skeleton of the earth laid bare. In Holmesdale there is an 800-hectare farm run by three men, every building new and strictly functional. The milking parlour for the Friesian herd is as up-to-date as a car factory. The malting barley goes from field to factory without being touched by hand. New pressures, new crops, new landscapes. This year's farming is next year's museum piece.

Wye College collects farm tools and ploughs and houses them in a great barn at Brook. At Wilmington Priory, the walls are ranged with scythes, oxen yokes, spring guns, sack settlers, breast ploughs, muck cromes, cradle churns, sheep shears, cow muzzles, drenching horns, shepherd's crooks, milkmaids' churns, whimbles, dibbers, costrels, dock diggers, bull poles and manger blocks. There are a number of carts at Michelham Priory and a variety of tools at the Open Air Museum at Singleton, including a fully equipped smithy. One of the most evocative symbols of the heyday of farming is the hulk of a plough that stands alongside the Plough Inn at Trottiscliffe. If ever an implement deserved a place of honour it is this, the Kentish turn-wrist plough. It gained its name from the fact that the position of the mould board could be altered to turn the furrows in either direction. That is the only flexible thing about it. Its central beam of oak is fully 3 metres long. The cross beams and handles and iron-sheathed share are all on the monumental scale. Two wheels rolled in front of the plough and the whole device needed a team of eight oxen to drag it through the soil. Arthur Young called it 'clumsy and unmechanical' but agreed that the Sussex farmers declared it to be the best of its kind. Marshall declared that there was enough material in it to make a Highland cart. Its very weight enabled it to work the heavy clays of the Weald. It was recorded in 1523 and was still in use in the present century. Without it, the Weald could not have been won. The very shapes of the small, square intakes may be attributed to it.

The living museum of the new farming remains in the farm houses and steadings. As we have seen in previous chapters, a remarkable number of buildings survive from the earliest period of vernacular architecture based on timber. Many existing farm buildings are medieval structures modified and extended in later years. Big timbers were scarce by the seventeenth century and were needed for the inner frames of house, church and barn, especially in roofing. The new vernacular had to express itself in new materials such as the bricks and tiles

40. *Sussex oxen and a turn-wrist plough on the Sussex Downs early in the 1900s.*

made from local clay deposits. Used in conjunction with flints, the results can be seen to perfection in Sussex, in a broad belt along the Downs, overlapping the lower ground on either side. Hard bands of chalk clunch were pressed into service, notably between Harting and Duncton in West Sussex but also in parts of the North Downs along the Hog's Back and around Boxley (K). Elsewhere sandstone became the dominant material and many sturdy farmhouses of the eighteenth century would not be out of place in a northern dale. The walls were softened in appearance by the use of tile-hanging and weather-boarding, using imported softwoods, such as Norway cedar, from the seventeenth century onwards. The earliest weather-boards or clap-boards were made of local oak. The tiles cladding the walls were made in a variety of shapes giving a decorative effect most striking in groups of houses. Barns and cattle sheds or 'hovels' became standardized by the eighteenth century. Usually made of plank timber on a foundation of squared stone blocks, they were constructed on a system of aisles, with timbers dividing each aisle. Eight-aisled barns are not uncommon, often leaning precariously with the passage of time. The date that the barn was built can sometimes be seen carved on one of the aisle timbers. Timber barns as lengthy as the largest stone tithe barns can be seen at Lenham and Alciston.

41. *Staddle barn at Cowdray.*

The barns and cattle sheds are characteristically grouped with the farmhouse in a loose courtyard arrangement. Perhaps the most perfect survival is at Peper Harow in Surrey. The centre-piece is a staddle barn, a small, single-roomed structure with sloping roof, standing on mushroom-shaped stones, designed to keep the rats out and the air circulating. Staddle barns were in use by the sixteenth century but most of the existing examples date from a later period. The word 'staddle' is almost identical with the small 'stadl' or hay-barns that exist in Scandinavia and the Alps. There are dozens surviving. I have seen them in East Kent, at Coldred, for example, in Sussex, at Cowdray, and in Surrey. The vast number of staddle stones that embellish lawns and drives show just how many such barns have been demolished. A fine staddle barn has been erected at Singleton, and the Open Air Museum is the best place to study the construction of barns. In one example, every timber is given its correct name, such as rafter, ridge, collar-beam, brace, corbel, tie-beam, purlin, strut, sole plate and king post, the private vocabulary of the carpenters' mystery.

Even more dramatic reminders of the great days of corn are the windmills perched on many a hilltop. There are several restoration groups at work throughout the region, though it is perilously late. At the turn of this century there were still 134 windmills working in Kent alone, but only 15 working by the time of Coles Finch's comprehensive survey in the 1930s. Symonson's map of Kent surveyed in 1597 shows mills all round the coasts and along the high ridges. They look like post-mills, small structures turning on a central 'tree'. The oldest mill in the region is of this type. Standing twelve metres high and built in 1665, it dominates the skyline at Outwood Common (Sy), a great attraction lovingly preserved. A similar type of mill on Keston Common dates from 1716 but is in poor condition. The post-mill at Rolvenden was featured in a recent Italian film about the Canterbury Tales, though it was built four centuries after the pilgrims passed that way. Another stands at Nutley on the edge of Ashdown Forest, restored by local enthusiasts. The splendid isolation of such mills is shown to perfection by Chillenden Mill in the rolling ploughlands of East Kent.

Jack and Jill stand together on the Sussex Downs above the village of Clayton. Jill is a post-mill of 1821. Jack is a tower mill of 1876. The tower mills are taller, sturdier structures better able to withstand gale-force winds. But the tower mill at Polegate, restored by the Eastbourne and District Preservation Trust, lost one of its sails in the autumn gales of 1974. Other tower mills stand at Shirley (Sy) and at Halnaker, the oldest of its type, built in 1740 to grind corn for the poor of the parish. Many such mills have been converted to private use, the tell-tale stubs looking like small lighthouses.

The most common survivors are the smock mills, named after the traditional rural dress. The fantails which turned the sails into the wind are, like the interior workings, models of engineering achievement, as much part of the industrial as of the agrarian heritage. The finest example, still in working order, is the Union Mill at Cranbrook (K), twenty metres high, built in 1814. Another stands on Chailey Common, the traditional centre of Sussex. Others stand at West Kingsdown and Meopham on the chalklands of Kent, at Reigate Heath (Sy) and at

42. *Outwood Mill built in 1665 and still in working order.*

Woodchurch on the edge of Walland Marsh. There are even survivors on Wimbledon Common and in Lambeth, far from the nearest cornfield. The road from Tunbridge Wells to Eastbourne curls along the high ridges of the Weald and passes several mills, one at Cross-in-Hand still in working order. One of the last smock mills to work commercially in 1971 is at Stelling Minnis in East Kent.

The King's Mill at Shipley (Sx), built in 1879, once the home of Hilaire Belloc, has been restored by the West Sussex County Council. In all about sixteen mills are now open to the public.

The landowners who were enthused with the improvement of their crops, stock and general farm management turned their attention to their own mansions and surrounds. 'There are few counties which can vie with Surrey in the number and elegance of the gentlemen's seats,' wrote William Stevenson in his survey of the county in the late eighteenth century. The 'round-frocked farmers' were loathe to abandon their well-tried ways. The gentry had no such qualms, transforming old manors and deer parks into new mansions and romantic parklands. John Evelyn had led the way in his Surrey estates. His work at Albury called forth two enthusiastic pages in Cobbett's journal, but the formal park was already out of fashion when Cobbett rode by. Eighteenth-century taste was for the naturalistic scene, a return to wilder visions, albeit carefully controlled, such as Petworth where 'the park is very fine and consists of a parcel of those hills and dells which Nature formed here when she was in one of her most sportive modes'.* Nature had given the background but Capability Brown completed the work. Two broad basins, the upper and lower park, were studded with trees, clumps of beech and pine, single oaks and chestnuts punctuating the pastures. Sussex Red cattle, sheep and deer roam the greensward. On the highest point stands the Belvedere tower commanding a panoramic view north to Leith Hill, south to Chanctonbury. The focal point of the whole composition is the house at the end of a serpentine lake. 'Percy to the core,' said Walpole, referring to the owners, the Dukes of Northumberland. Petworth retains the perfection that the landscape gardeners sought for their patrons.

A transformation was carried out at Goodwood under the third Duke of Richmond. The house was redesigned and enlarged. The most elegant stable-block and kennels in the region were designed by Sir William Chambers and James Wyatt. The park was enlarged and planted with exotic trees, including one thousand Cedars of Lebanon. No effort or expense was spared to improve on Nature. The Duke moved the Petworth road to improve his prospect from the house. Moving a highway was not an unusual proceeding. The owners of Chevening and Chilham had enclosed parts of the Pilgrims' Way and aligned new roads round the perimeter of their parks. Pitt himself had changed the line of the London road and annexed part of Keston Common to extend his grounds at Holwood. He and William Wilberforce enjoyed themselves with billhooks and

* William Cobbett.

scythes, cutting through underwood to make new paths, with the advice of Humphrey Repton, one of the exponents of the new landscape art. The Reptons, father and son, would turn their hands to anything, from interior designing to lodge cottages, from pleasure grounds to broad vistas of wood and park. The best example of their work in the south-east is at Cobham (K). Luxuriant gardens, grottoes and follies cloak the hill slope north of the Hall, a visual link between the house and the parkland to the east. The house is now a school, the park part farm and part golf-course. The woods have been sold off, though the original concept is still visible, culminating in a superb but derelict mausoleum designed by Wyatt in 1783, set on a rise in the woods. Repton worked at Uppark, too, high on the Sussex Downs. Many of the trees and the gardens have gone but the rustic dairy and a folly tower remain.

Repton's advice was sought but not taken by the Earls of Camden at Bayham. The earl persisted in his own design with a new house alongside the ruined abbey, an ideal counterpoint for the Gothic imagination. Landowners fresh from the Grand Tour of Europe, full of classical memories, indulged their personal whims. Mad Jack Fuller built a tall cone just to win a bet that he could see Dallington church steeple from his house. Temple, observatory, obelisk and rotunda rose on his estate at Brightling (Sx) and he ended up in his own monumental pyramid in Brightling churchyard, wearing a top hat and holding a glass of claret. He was an M.P. and an early admirer of W. J. Turner's paintings, so presumably he was not entirely mad. He also saved Bodiam Castle from destruction. In a calmer vein, Alexander Courthope of Sprivers at Horsmonden kept a personal diary in which he recorded every tree he planted, the avenues he fashioned, the new farm buildings, the fish ponds he dug and the bell he put on to his new house to frighten off house-breakers. There were many of his ilk creating new landscapes in the Weald.

Transforming streams into ornamental lakes and winding streams as a central feature of a prospect such at Petworth was one of the hallmarks of the work of Launcelot 'Capability' Brown. At least nine parks in the south-east bear his handiwork, from the rhododendron dell at Kew to Ashburnham Park near Battle. The five lakes of Sheffield Park (Sx) were made for James Baker Holroyd, Earl of Sheffield and President of the Board of Agriculture. The exotic shrubs and trees are not in keeping with his more open style though they are lovely in their own right. They were planted by A. G. Soames in this century. Brown was content to use trees, including the new evergreens or 'greens' as he called them, to punctuate a landscape, as at Danson Park near Bexley (K). The older moated manor house was drowned beneath a new lake and a new house built on higher, healthier ground. He favoured the ring-belt of trees that acted as a screen round the park and adopted the ha-ha, the sunken ditch that kept cattle and deer away from inner gardens yet left the view from the house unhindered. He fashioned the terraces and lake at Chilham (K) and worked at Claremont (Sy) and at Roehampton. Some of the greenery around the All England Tennis Club is a survivor of his planting at Wimbledon.

One of the most complete landscapes is at Mereworth (K). The present road to Maidstone seems like a private drive dividing the lodges, stables and walled gardens from the domed Palladian villa to the south. The Vane family called in Colin Campbell in the 1720s to plan the setting. The old village and church were destroyed and rebuilt to the west of the park. The new church would not be out of place in a London square, an urbane Queen Anne building that includes some of the tombs and ornaments from the original church. A triumphal arch, reminiscent of Rome, stands guard on the southern perimeter of the park.

Another venture in the Palladian style was carried out by a Venetian, Giacomo Leoni, for the Onslow family at Clandon Park (Sy). The magnificence of the house and its setting is best realized in one of the paintings inside the house but the marble entrance hall is sufficient in itself, a reception room of grandeur, to sum up the period. Some of the garden is intact, complete with grotto, but the parkland is now farmed. Polesdon Lacey, like Clandon, is now owned by the National Trust, one of its most important possessions in Surrey. The present building is a restored Regency house designed by Thomas Cubitt in the 1820s but many of the garden features, such as the superlative Long Walk, were begun in the 1760s, and developed by Richard Brinsley Sheridan, the dramatist. Its setting is the finest attribute of the house with Box Hill and Ranmore Common within its visual compass.

A seminal moment in the evolution of parklands was Charles Hamilton's fashioning of Pain's Hill (Sy). New housing and the widening of the A3 trunk road have damaged the view but a group of enthusiasts are trying to preserve what is left of this predecessor of Brown and Repton.

More fortunate in its destiny is Scotney, the most delicate of early Victorian essays. The young Edward Hussey and William Sawrey Gilpin did the usual thing in forsaking the damp, moated castle site for a new house on the hill. But everything else was unusual. The castle was moulded into a romantic ruin; the quarry that supplied stone for the new house was made into a luxuriant garden and exotic trees planted, all balanced as carefully as a painting. From the balustrade by the house, the view focuses down through the gardens to the last machicolated tower of the old castle. Beyond, in the pastures, is one cedar, a perfect foil to the tower. Scotney is now the local headquarters of the National Trust.

One of the more functional structures in the grounds is the thatched ice-house, dug into the wooded hillside. Ice-houses dating from the eighteenth and nineteenth centuries can be seen in many parks, such as Knole and Albury, Hatchlands and Ham House, where ice was stacked with straw for summer use. Just as ubiquitous were the belvedere and folly towers, mock temples, Gothic ruins and crazy cottages. Even Knole's Tudor calm was augmented by castle ruins

43. *Scotney – nineteenth-century exercise in the picturesque.*

brought from nearby Otford and a Bird House designed as a 'cottage orné'. Lodge cottages were designed with rustic façades and narrow gothic windows, designed to look at rather than live in. Towers aspired to the sky, the most famous being Richard Hull's achievement built in 1766 on Leith Hill, the top of the tower reaching the magic one thousand feet above sea level. The Gibraltar Tower at Heathfield, partly commemorative, was also used as an observatory to witness the owner's home-coming. The Waterloo Tower at Quex is even more remarkable, rising from the East Kent skyline like a miniature Eiffel Tower.

Belvederes commanding a view of the estate were especially popular where the great house was built on lower ground. Waldershare's is the finest from the point of view of its architecture, a three-storey structure of brick and Portland stone built in 1725 for Sir Henry Furnese. There are others at Caterham and Claremont and Squerryes at Westerham. May's Folly at Hadlow (K) began as the 170-foot tower of a nineteenth-century 'castle', built so well with brick and cement that it outlasted the castle and rises conspicuously amongst the orchards and gardens of the Kentish plain. Just as conspicuous is the Vandalian Tower on the estate of Uppark built in 1774 to commemorate a new colony of settlers in the Americas. The idea was to see and be seen.

Follies are often pompous and usually funny, a laugh in the landscape. A great flint arch on the hill above Slindon leads to nothing in particular. At Reigate, the authentic castle enclosure is entered from a mock castle gate built in 1777. At Eynsford there is a lovely brick and flint bridge that only a cat could cross, being composed of a single balustrade.

Surrey has maintained its special tradition as a centre of the gardening art, pioneered by the Flemish immigrants. Augusta, Dowager Princess of Wales, started a botanical garden at Kew in 1759. Under her son, George III, aided by Sir Joseph Banks, it became famous. Taken over by the nation in 1841, it developed into one of the foremost scientific collections in the world, with Sir William Hooker as its first official director. Very much a public pleasure ground, its prime concern is still with the identification of species, their distribution, and the training of botanists. In 1924, the Royal Botanical Gardens took control of an estate at Bedgebury in Kent and built up a collection of more than two hundred species of conifers from the temperate zone from seedlings specially raised at Kew. Glades and avenues lead through 40 hectares of undulating sandstone country to create vistas of Western Canada, of the Himalayas and the East. Swamp cypresses hand their elegant branches over a lake that was once the site of a moated manor. A chequer-board of forest plots enables the botanist to study the growth rate of various trees and their adaptation to the rigours of a Wealden climate. The occasional tall oak reminds us that this is still England. The National Pinetum is now controlled by the Forestry Commission. Meanwhile, Kew has found another annexe free from the congestion and pollution of London. In 1963, Wakehurst Place, its gardens and tree collection, was bequeathed to the National Trust, which leased it, in turn, to the Royal Botanical Gardens. The dry, sandy soils make a contrasting habitat to the flood plain of the Thames. It now contains one of the finest tree collections in Britain, noted for its exotica such as the Davidia, the 'handkerchief' tree from China.

There is an unmatched collection of famous gardens in the same vicinity. Wisley, close to the A3 trunk road, is the headquarters of the Royal Horticultural Society. Four other sites, all National Trust properties, are at Winkhurst, Claremont near Esher, Nymans near Cross-in-Hand, and Sheffield Park, making the Surrey–Sussex borderland a gardener's paradise. The arboretum at Winkworth was the life's work of Wilfred Fox, who planted a steep hillside with more than sixty-five species of tree. The woodlands and lake are the habitat for nearly a hundred different species of bird. At Nymans, the barren sandstone has been transformed into a series of specialized gardens – heather, rose, herb, rock and water – all grouped round and unified by a ruined mansion. It shows the influence of William Robinson who also fashioned the grounds at Gravetye, over the border in Sussex. Robinson was a prolific author and editor of gardening magazines, advocating a return to the informal cottage garden. He loathed the forced formality of such schemes as Paxton's at Crystal Palace which he dismissed as 'costly rubbish'.*

One of Robinson's opponents was Sir Reginald Blomfield, who was responsible for a revival of the formal gardens at many places, such as Godinton, Knowlton and Waldershare, all in Kent. The two attitudes were combined with the most exquisite results at Sissinghurst. Victoria Sackville-West and Harold Nicolson took over the derelict Tudor pile and made its moat and courtyards the setting for one of England's loveliest gardening achievements. 'The strictest formality of design, with the maximum informality in planting' was the key to the pattern. A sequence of gardens, enclosed with clipped hedges, cob plantation, orchard, walls and moat, contribute to an annual cycle of colour and fragrance. In the Tudor tower is Victoria Sackville-West's study and the press that printed T. S. Eliot's *Waste Land*, a felicitous irony. Although the gardens are now maintained by the National Trust, visitors walk quietly here, with a sense of intrusion into a private dream.

Many neglected castles and mansions were purchased in the late nineteenth and early twentieth centuries by men of wealth who restored the buildings and recreated their parklands and gardens. Most dramatic was Hever, medieval home of the Bullen family. The Waldorf Astors, with the aid of more than a thousand labourers, restored the moated castle, made Elizabethan gardens, a lake, grottoes, waterfalls and a mock Tudor village for the estate workers. The main road was annexed as the private drive and a new road aligned round the perimeter of the park, a surprising echo of the power of the embarking landowners

* William Robinson, *The English Flower Garden* (1883).

two centuries before. The Italian garden laid out between the house and the lake is one of the most exciting of outdoor museums, containing objects d'art from Italy, Greece and the East, pottery, statuary, sarcophagi and sculpture, the family collection assembled during many years' residence in the classic world. The same spirit animated the first essayists in the gardening arts.

So, over a period of four centuries, the garden was fashioned. The variety of soils, the kindness of the climate and the comparative wealth of its inhabitants has given the rural landscape of the south-east its unique character. From hop-ground to nursery, from Goodwood to the shepherd's cott, from Kew to the cottage garden, the scene has evolved in its minutiae as the result of man's patient quest for the control of the natural environment. The Surrey heaths show as pretty a face as the Medway orchards. When Tennyson sought his retreat on the wilds of Blackdown, the land was already tamed.

Turner and Constable, Shepherd and Samuel Prout had shown man the image of his own creation and it looked fine. It reached perfection in the paintings and sketches of Samuel Palmer, living at Shoreham in the Darent Valley, where even William Blake could find a temporary peace for his restless spirit. As I write, I am looking at a water colour by Palmer. A shepherd surrounded by his woolly flock sits under an arch of leafy branches. Beyond is a tree laden with fruit and the outline of a church spire. In the background are gently swelling hills with the corn cut and stooked, ready for the gathering. A landscape reflecting human aspiration. The garden of England.

8

Boroughs and Market Towns

It was bad enough for a gun cast in the Weald to take two years to reach its destination on the Medway. Enemies may have come and gone but the gun, at least, was usable. For corn, fruit, vegetables and other produce to take as long would be disastrous. London, the coastal ports and dockyards were growing rapidly in the eighteenth and nineteenth centuries and demanding ever greater food supplies. The hoys and barges were plying the watery highways and short sections of canals reached towards the interior but the new commercial agriculture needed more than water passage. New markets needed new roads. The market town was not only the natural focus of the agricultural activity of a district; it was one more step on the way to London.

Most of the inland towns grew up on natural highways. They were staging posts. The coaching inns were as famous for their hospitality then as they are for their architecture now. They are remarkably persistent in site, usually near the market-place, and still functioning as inns, retaining some of the warmth and character of their origins. Some of them, like the Kentish Drover, recall the old ways of getting livestock to market. The first thing we learn from Chaucer is the pleasure of travel and the delights of the Tabard and the Bell. The inn-signs of the south-east are as evocative of the rural past as the museums of rural life.

Chaucer's road from London to Canterbury was turnpiked by 1750, though the sea highway as far as Gravesend was often preferred. The stretch from Gravesend to Rochester was the first to be improved as early as 1711, with its extension to Canterbury following in the 1730s. The road beyond Canterbury, linking with Dover, was not turnpiked until after 1780, a section which is still, incidentally, one of the worst roads in the region for the traffic it bears. Queen

Elizabeth had insisted on improvements to the Wealden roads after her progress in 1573 had shown them to be worse, in her opinion, than those in the Peak District, an improvement that was more apparent than real, judging by Defoe's comments more than a century later. The roads on Sheppey were singled out in her reign, due to the naval interest. But the turnpike age of better surfaced roads began effectively in 1696 on the route from Reigate in Surrey to Crawley in Sussex. Sevenoaks and Tunbridge Wells were linked by 1709, much to the relief of the gentry taking the waters at the new spa. In the same decade, Surrey was made more accessible by the turnpike from Southwark to Kingston, extended to Petersfield, across the border in Hampshire, by 1749. The spokes of the wheel were being forged piecemeal around the metropolitan hub. Then came the cross-links tying the spokes together. The process took more than a hundred years.

By the 1750s, Guildford was part of the web, linked with Farnham and Leatherhead, but Horsham was still comparatively isolated until the 1820s, when it was joined with Pulborough to the south and Leatherhead to the north. It seems scarcely credible that travellers from Horsham were often recommended to go to London by way of Canterbury for 'the cross roads are in all probability the very worst that are to be met with in any part of the island'.*

The highways have been widened, straightened and resurfaced since, but the main network of the turnpike age endures. So does a collection of road signs, mile-posts and mounting-blocks from the age of the horse, cart and coach. Finest of the mile-posts are on the road from Eastbourne to East Grinstead skirting the western edge of Ashdown Forest, bearing the sign of the Pelham buckle, insignia of a great Sussex family. The later generation of signs, prolific in Surrey around Haslemere, for example, are of cast iron and of more uniform design than the earlier stone signs.

Mounting-blocks are found by roadsides, usually at the brow of a hill, by stables, by churchyard gates and by the porticoes of mansions. Some are carved simply out of huge slabs of sandstone, as in the village centre at Marden (K), or of two or three blocks. One example stuck in the bank by the churchyard at Boughton Monchelsea bears the date 1707 on the upper block. One even survives on Shooters Hill on a narrow part of the Dover road now within London's boundary. A very minor addition to the landscape they may be but they are a tangible link with the journeys of Defoe and Cobbett and the visitations of Jane Austen to her relatives in the region.

* A. Young, *General View of the Agriculture of the County of Sussex* (1813).

The turnpikes were opposed on the grounds that they 'imported London manners and depopulated the country'. Cobbett scorned them for bringing the dwellers of the Wen into the country and taking labourers from their useful work in the fields. He regarded the turnpike from Reigate to Brighton as an improvement merely to benefit the stock-jobbers who could 'skip backward and forward in the coaches' from city to coast, though he did admire the sandstone fragments that made such a good surface. During his rides he kept manfully to the older lanes, deep in mud though they may have been. He liked the shade of the bank-side trees.

The sequence of road development is seen to perfection in the Chevening estate near Sevenoaks. An old track from Knockholt Pound cuts down through the chalk escarpment to Chipstead, a direct and precipitous alignment known locally as Breakneck Corner. It was the old fish road to Rye, in use before the Stanhopes enclosed the park. The 'new' road, now called the Old London road, lies to the east, taking a much gentler gradient. Further east again is its successor, cutting through the bare chalk at Poll Hill. There, too, is the most recent piece of highway engineering, the dual-carriageway by-pass cutting a broad swathe past Sevenoaks.

The problems for early travellers were a reflection of the varied terrain and the rugged slopes that still surprise many visitors with mental pictures of soft southern landscapes. The Duke of Wellington turned down the offer of Uppark on the Sussex Downs mostly because of the effect it would have on his horses, a typically pragmatic decision for the great man. When Mad Jack Fuller left his estate at Brightling for the parliament at Westminster, he went equipped as for an expedition, complete with guns. The hill-climbs over heathlands like Hindhead were notorious not just for their inclines. The gibbet on the hill was a reminder of other perils of the road. One of the advantages of the sea-route to Gravesend was that it avoided troubles even so close to London as Blackheath, Shooters' Hill and Dartford. Gradually the new roads ousted the footpad and the highwayman. The market towns entered a new era of growth, reflected in their architecture. The Georgian period had an even greater impact on the visual landscape of the towns than it did in the country areas.

The first towns of importance were on the earliest highways – Chichester on Stane Street, Canterbury and Rochester on Watling Street. The walls of Romans, the castle and the cathedrals of the Middle Ages, symbolize their continuing importance through the early stages of town development. The visual focus of all three cities is a medieval one, spire and tower. But the centre of activity is the market. Just in front of the Christchurch Gate in Canterbury is a small, irregular space, the Buttermarket. To one side, Mercery Lane, Guildhall, High Street and Longmarket, the buying and selling, the bustle of the crowd. On the other, the cathedral precinct. The transition from one world to the other is difficult, the contrast too great. The spirit needs a sort of limbo, a waiting area like the loggia of a medieval town. Yet the two are part of the same pattern, for the market grew under the protection of the cathedral.

44. *The cathedral and precinct at Canterbury in the south-east quadrant of the walled city. The congested streets to the left of the picture were the main market area; the foreground shows post-war rebuilding.*

In Chichester, the contrast is not so great, for the detached bell tower of the cathedral dominates West Street. In Canterbury, the cathedral is withdrawn. In Chichester, it is part of the main street scene, though houses stood in front of it until the nineteenth century. Even more pertinent, Bishop Story built a market cross in 1501, at the very centre of the city's crossroads, an elaborate edifice symbolizing the conjunction of church and commerce. From John Norden's map of the city in 1595 until the present Ordnance Surveys, the market cross occupies the central position. On George Loader's plan of 1812, a new building appears just to the north of the Cross, called the New Market House. Built by Nash in 1807, and still in use, it epitomizes the new age of commerce, the new affluence and elegance of the market town, an elegance reflected in every quarter and almost every street.

Chichester has a magnificent simplicity of structure. It is shaped like a shield, quartered by four main streets, North, South, East and West, each leading to the site of a city gate. Each quarter, like a heraldic shield, has its special device. To the south-west, the cathedral precinct; to the south-east, the Pallant, derived from the word 'palatine'; to the north-east, the park and the priory, St Martin's Square and the medieval hospital; to the north-west lies an area that remained open until the eighteenth century. The shops line the main streets. The livestock market is within earshot, just outside the walls to the east, close by the house where John Keats wrote the *Eve of St Agnes*. The green fields reach right to the city walls in the south-west, though a new ring road and a light industrial estate break the continuity. Nineteenth-century housing clusters round the railway station and the old haven to the south. Yet within the walls it is the eighteenth century that dominates. 'North Street is the perfect street for an English county town,'* writes Nairn, yet even that is rivalled by the lovely red-brick houses with Baroque façades in the Pallant. Four lanes quarter the Pallant in a repetition of the main pattern of the city.

The north-west quadrant has suffered most change. New administrative offices, new library, new flats, all impressive in their own way, dark-red brick and Cumbrian slate, have introduced an element quite out of keeping with the city's earlier style. The modernity of the new Festival Theatre is more acceptable, being set in a park to the north of the city near St Richard's Hospital. The small suburbs that have developed along the routes from the city gates have a mixture of old and new housing that in no way swamps the identity of the centre. One of the most surprising aspects of the city is its halo of gravel workings. From the hills to the north, it looks like an island site.

Canterbury has many more scars to hide. War-time bombing destroyed part of the old city. Bus station, multi-storey car-park and a modern shopping precinct make a bizarre frontispiece for the cathedral. The view from the Dane John mound is an illustration of what not to do in reconstructing a medieval city. Some of the back streets, too, behind Castle Street, for example, are tatty if not derelict, making the castle keep and the Poor Priests' Hospital in Stour Street unexpected bonuses. But the cheek-by-jowl appearance of Victorian brick warehouse and medieval stone gives variety, at least, to the work-a-day place. The best of the city lies between Westgate and the High Street with a goodly survival

* Nairn and Pevsner, op. cit.

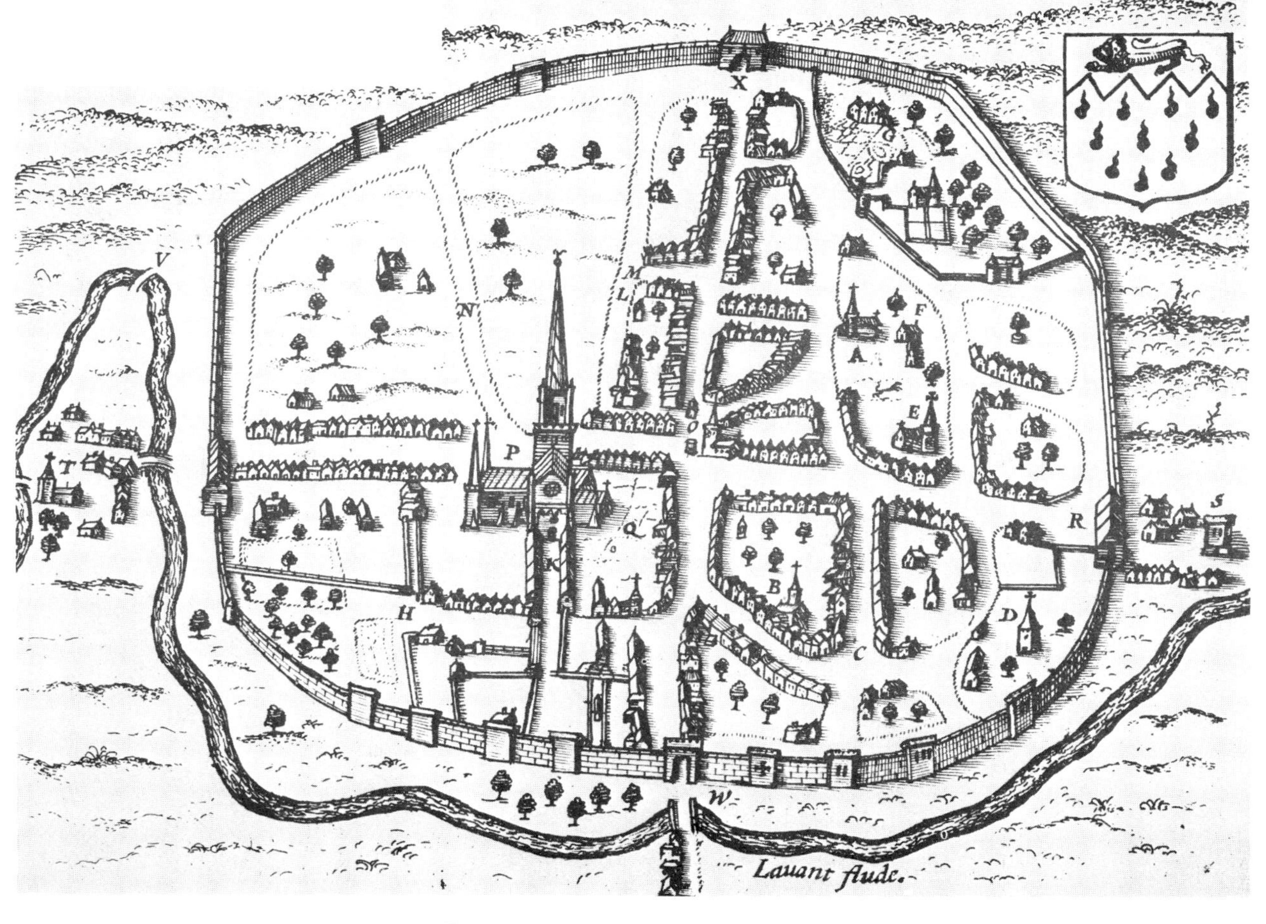

45. *John Speed's map of Chichester, 1610.*

of medieval buildings. The only eighteenth-century building comparable with Chichester's abundance is grouped around the Dane John, a space given to the public by an alderman in 1790, complete with landscaped mound and monument. Some of the best buildings are occupied by municipal offices.

Canterbury has a more complex development beyond its walls than Chichester, in keeping with its greater population, 32,000 as compared with Chichester's 21,000. To the south-east are the spaces and places associated with St Augustine's Abbey and the park that used to stretch as far as Fordwich. To the north and west is the railway area, the cattle market, Victorian terraces and industry. On the northern hills overlooking the city, on the site of Hales Park, are the clean-cut lines of the new University of Kent. The city lacks the precision of Chichester; the nineteenth century invades the old core. The River Stour makes a visual divide. The area between the river and the Westgate is a no-man's-land, perhaps due to the destruction of the walls in this sector, though the old alignment can be followed by Westgate Gardens, Pound Lane and St Raigund's Street.

Rochester beats them both with a population of 56,000 but the figure is meaningless for the city is inseparable from the rest of the conurbation that embraces Chatham, Gillingham, Strood and a quarter of a million people. The medieval city was barely the size of one of Chichester's quarters. Rochester is the bridge. It was so important that parishes as far away as the central Weald had to contribute to its upkeep. Historic plaques on the present bridge tell the story of the crossing of the Medway. Bridge Street and the High Street form the main axis. To the south are the precincts of castle and cathedral on either side of the moat where Dickens wished to be buried. To the north is the dockside area on what was once a marshy bend of the river. The traffic along the present one-way system of the High Street obscures a handful of fine buildings, the Guildhall of 1687, the Corn Exchange of 1706, complete with ship motifs on the roof tops. Most memorable is La Providence, a courtyard of almshouses built for French Protestants in 1718 and recently restored with the utmost delicacy. There are two old coaching inns, one with a fourteenth-century undercroft. Maps of the seventeenth century show the market-place in the middle of the High Street, which must have rivalled today's traffic congestion.

So much for Rome and the first breed of planned towns that time and changing fortunes have weathered into more haphazard patterns. Two of them stand at opposite extremities of the region, each the natural centre of a large rural area, West Sussex and East Kent.

. . . . .

'Gaps, towns and castles,' wrote R. S. R. Fitter,* putting a long historic process into a neat nutshell. After the Norman Conquest, new roads linked the coastal ports with London, the towns growing like oases in the green desert of the Weald. The roads from the south sought the gaps in the hills that ran in ridges from east to west. The Norman castles commanded the routes. The towns grew in the shelter of the castles. Town and castle were synonymous in the early feudal period. 'In the middle ages, what is a town? It is a castle that has prospered.'† The towns of the south-east were 'planted' as centres of administration, defence and commerce. Yet it is diversity rather than uniformity that is a feature of the sites. Guildford on the steep eastern slope of the Wey gap is quite different from Arundel on a chalk bluff overlooking the broad Arun levels. Reigate and Bletchingley, strongholds of the feuding Warennes and Clares, have only a loose connection with the high, dry pass from Croydon. In the Mole Gap there is Dorking and Leatherhead at either end but no castle. In the Darent Valley there is a Norman castle at Eynsford but no town. A failed castle? Each site is unique, yet there is a deal of truth in Fitter's simple equation, and nowhere is it more fitting than in the most Norman of counties, Sussex – six rapes, six Norman centres. Two of them, Hastings and Pevensey were ports. Chichester came from the sub-division of the most westerly rape, Arundel. Between them are three river gaps, three Norman castles, three towns.

Lewes, situated on a chalk promontory, with the broad water meadows of the Cuckmere to north and south, has the most striking strategic site and grew to become the administrative centre of the entire county. The High Street runs east-west, linking the two gateways, continuing as School Hill down to the river crossing. To the north is the castle precinct. To the south, the parallel lanes or 'twittens' running down to the town wall and the Winterbourne Valley divide the old town up into blocks. Each block has its frontages on the high street and its burgage strips behind it, a typically Norman planned system. A few medieval timber-framed town houses survive, proudly displaying their dates, but most of them have been replaced by solid brick Georgian frontages, the sort of property that Cobbett considered a 'model of solidity and neatness'. The 1799 plan of the town shows the old market site immediately beside the castle gate. The High Street is still the main shopping centre but the cattle market is in the valley to the south by the railway station. The apparently simple structure of the walled town is complicated by an extension along North Street to the church of St John-sub-Castro, which incorporates a Saxon door from an older church

* R. S. R. Fitter, *The Home Counties* (Collins, 1951).
† Fr Funck Brentano, *Le Moyen Age* (Hachette, 1951).

on the site. This, together with the fact that the town had two mints in the time of Athelstan, raises the unusual possibility of Lewes being already a substantial town under Saxon kings. The extent of the town ditch and wall can be compared with the deserted Saxon township of Burpham on the east side of the Arun Gap.

The persistence of the town's importance is shown by the nineteenth-century county prison, complete with Victorian machicolations. Outside the town are two suburbs, Southover and Cliffe. Opposite the timbered front of Anne of Cleves' Museum is a small terrace of late-Georgian houses. Behind them were the priory grounds, the ruins sliced through by the railway. Cliffe huddles dangerously under an eroded chalk slope across the river. The top of the slope gives the best view of the place, which has had its share of accolades from travellers, such as Defoe's 'full of gentlemen of good families'. It is now full of 14,000 people.

Lewes' castle is a noble ruin. Arundel's is the home of the Dukes of Norfolk. The castle is so dominant that the town seems a mere appendage beneath its walls, one street curling from the lime-lined river walk and the Maison Dieu past the triangular market-place up to the nineteenth-century church of St Philip Neri. The spires of the catholic church surmount the view of the town from the south, giving a quite different impression from the view from the river. Three parallel streets lead out of the high street and they contain a pleasant collection of eighteenth- and nineteenth-century housing, Tarrant Street, Arun Street and, especially, Maltravers Street. Lewes lives easily with its medieval past; Arundel is overwhelmed. Steyning has thrown it off to such effect that it is scarcely recognizable as a town. But it had a Saxon mint, borough status and the Norman castle of Bramber protecting its inland haven on the River Ouse. Its Norman church, 'certainly the best in Sussex', according to Nairn, enriched with Saxon fragments, is big and grand enough to give credence to its early status. Its curving High Street, once the site of a famous horse fair, is hardly wide enough to cope with the traffic thundering down to Shoreham harbour, yet, at the centre, tucked in between shopfronts and Georgian houses, is a small Market Hall with tile-hung front and small clock turret. A late-Victorian town hall, built in 1886, stands along the road.

Steyning has many surprises. Church Street stands comparison with the best of any town. There is hardly a building out of key, hardly a false note in the gradual unfolding from busy High Street to sequestered church. Timber-frames, tile-hanging, Horsham slate roofs, knapped flints and river cobbles, all that makes Sussex building good is used in subtle variations with bricks, pausing at a small green space with a fine town house before the final approach to St Andrew's where the path to the porch continues the unravelling line the street began. The modern infilling to the south of the church is spacious and much less obtrusive than usual. Beyond the church the fields begin. They lap the southern side of the town, too, with Dog Lane and Sheep Lane leading to the downland and a fifteenth-century Poor House in Mouse Lane. Steyning gives an idea of what towns were like before the present era of urban growth. Even in 1900, a Sussex guide book could say that 'apart from the watering places there are only five towns where the population reaches 4,000'.* Of the five towns – Lewes, Chichester, Horsham, East Grinstead and Burgess Hill – four have now grown to more than 20,000 inhabitants. Steyning has just over 3,000. Like Arundel, it remains on the small scale.

The rhythms of history bring places to fame and then to oblivion. Outside Chichester, the only surviving market cross in Sussex, for example, is at Alfriston, the main settlement in the Cuckmere Gap. The simple stone cross stands in a small triangular market-place with a few shops, the centre of a rather self-consciously pretty village with impressive inns and well-tended cottages. The church, known as the Cathedral of the Downs because of its size, stands on an isolated knoll by the river. Looking back to the village, the tall houses have the look of quayside buildings, as if to remind the visitor that this was once a small haven.

'The market towns are usually members of the village series, places where the local roads converge to pass northwards and southwards through the water gaps in the ranges. Of these gap towns, Maidstone, Guildford and Lewes have obtained an added importance as seats of county administration,' wrote Mackinder.† Guildford was one of the only two Surrey settlements recorded in the Domesday survey as 'boroughs'. The other was Southwark, on the south side of London Bridge, which still maintains the Borough Market, some hop-factors' houses and a fragment of the Bishop of Winchester's palace, a slender link with Surrey's past. But Guildford has retained its own vigorous independence as a market town and, spasmodically, as the county town, for it is only in the last decade that the administrative offices have moved from Kingston-upon-Thames.

Guildford is on the line of the ancient east-west ridgeway as it descends from the Hog's Back, once known as Guildendown, to cross the River Wey. One interpretation of the name is the ford over the Wey. Another, more adventurous, is the ford where the golden flowers grow, marsh marigolds, perhaps. The Saxon

* F. G. Brabant, *Sussex. Methuen Little Guides* (1900).
† H. J. Mackinder, *Britain and the British Seas* (Oxford, 1906).

46. *The market cross at Alfriston.*

tower of St Mary's is the earliest visible evidence of the town, a royal estate since the reign of Alfred. The street pattern is reminiscent of Lewes, a High Street running down-slope to the river with narrow lanes such as Jeffries Passage and Swan Lane dividing the road frontage up into blocks. Two roughly parallel roads run north and south of the High Street, named on early maps as Lower Back Side

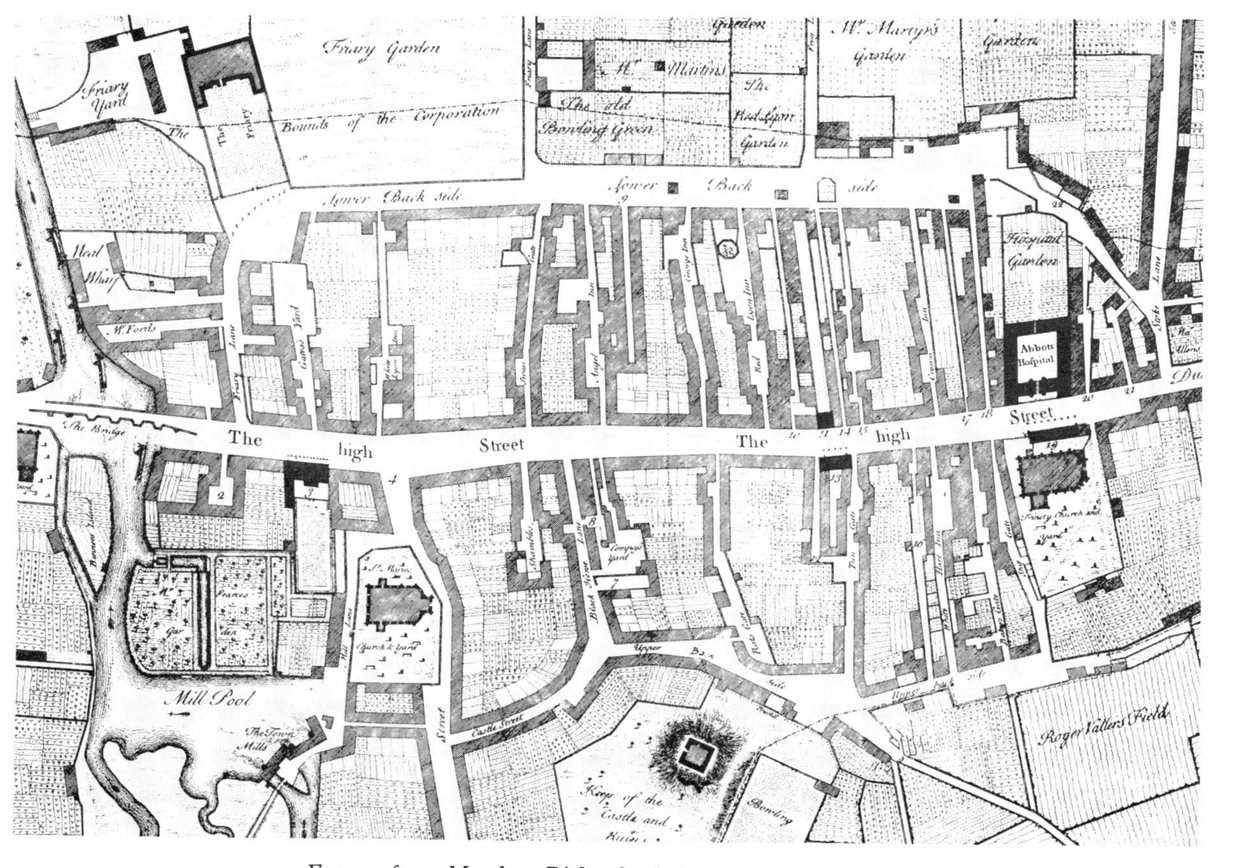

47. *Extract from Matthew Richardson's 'Ground Plan of Guldeford', 1739.*

and Upper Back Side. They marked the limit of the burgage strips, a pattern common to many medieval planned towns.

The power which planned the town is represented by the castle motte and bailey to the south, with a massive keep of Burgate stone, flint and chalk. The new Guildford, shopping precincts, offices, theatre, has developed on the low ground by the river, a difficult, restricted site. Even the glossiest of the new buildings needs sandbags to keep the water out when the river rises after winter rains, as in 1974. But this use of the low ground has had the advantage of leaving the older part of the town comparatively unchanged. Eric Parker described the High Street as 'the model of what the High Street of an English town should be'.* In gratitude, the town has erected a plaque to Parker in the same street. The deceptive slope of the street makes its visual impact unwind like a film, the climax being the Guild Hall of 1683 with its clock tower. Jetty houses, barge boards, coaching inns and the Hospital of the Blessed Trinity of 1619 line a street that was thriving long before the turnpikes brought new traffic and new prosperity. But there are Georgian frontages in abundance and especially in Castle Street.

On such a site, the town had to grow either uphill or across the river. Victorian villas sprawl above the town on to the airy foothills of the downs. The red-brick cathedral, first envisaged in the sixteenth century, finally begun in 1936 and finished in 1966, was built on Stag Hill to the west, later joined by the new university complex, a town in itself. The commercial and industrial part of the town is squeezed into the valley between, alongside the railway and the Wey Navigation, which now does service as a linear park. The new by-pass cuts across the western downland, dragging new estates with it, Onslow and Park Barn. With a population in excess of 60,000, Guildford has developed its own halo of suburbs, its northern extent creeping dangerously close to Woking and the urban belt that stretches unbroken to London. For the moment, unlike so many Surrey towns, it remains a distinct and identifiable place with a thriving livestock market to maintain the country air.

By the thirteenth century there were four Surrey boroughs, each sending two members to Parliament. Joining Southwark and Guildford were Bletchingley and Reigate. The last two are only five kilometres apart on the greensand ridge. Only another three kilometres on is Gatton, which also had two parliamentary representatives by the fifteenth century. Three boroughs and six M.P.s within ten kilometres! Borough status reflected the power of the manorial lord as much

* E. Parker, *Surrey. The County Books* (Hale, 1947).

as the size of the place. Gatton is literally a house and a park, now partially occupied by a school. But it has the most extraordinary town hall in the country. A tiny classic building of 1765, about the size of a summer house, it was built by Sir Roger Copley by his own front door, a short walk to vote for two members of parliament. One of its Latin inscriptions reads 'Let the well-being of the people

48. *Eighteenth-century Town Hall in Gatton Park.*

be the supreme law.' This was no symbol of the people's power but of the rotten boroughs which made Cobbett rage as he passed through on his way home to Farnham. Bletchingley, at least, has one long broad thoroughfare, wide as a market-place, a church and a castle mound to recall the great days of the Clares who had thirty-eight manors in Surrey and more elsewhere. It was disfranchized, with Gatton, by the 1832 Reform Bill. Bletchingley is now a conservation area and outside the immediate confines of the village are several exceptionally fine houses, such as the seventeenth-century Pendell Court and the medieval Place Farm.

Of the three medieval boroughs only Reigate flourished, perhaps because of its proximity to the Croydon road coming south through the wind gap in the Downs at Merstham. Together with Redhill on the Brighton railway line, it now has a population as big as Guildford. Despite an inner ring road nearly as strangulating as that of Ashford, the old main street and market area with a brick town hall of 1728 just survives, tucked in between the castle precinct to the north and the priory area to the south. Reigate, like Redhill, was overtaken by the growth following the railway's arrival in 1841 and it became 'a perfect repository for common or garden architecture of the last hundred years'.* A few Georgian survivors, even fewer Tudor; for the rest it is a respectable residential town, a juxtaposition of open common and Victorian expansion so typical of many Surrey towns.

Kingston-upon-Thames and Farnham did not appear on the early list of boroughs, largely because they wanted to avoid the expense of being represented. But both had early importance. Farnham is visually the most exciting town in Surrey. Its castle, the finest fortified structure in the county, lies on high ground north of the town in what was once an extensive deer chase belonging to the Bishops of Winchester. As late as James I's reign, it was used as a hunting centre within the bailiwick of Windsor Forest. Castle Street descends the hill to join the main axis of East Street and West Street at a point called the Borough. The main street is part of the ancient highway that links the well-defined route of the North Downs ridge with the chalk plateau to the west and the direct route following the upper reaches of the River Wey towards Winchester. The gap it commands is that remarkable one where it seems the River Wey ought to flow north into the Blackwater Valley but makes a dog-leg to the south. In the Borough stands the Town Hall built in the 1930s, one of the least attractive buildings in a town rich in good architecture that reflects the prosperity of many periods, the medieval bishops, the woollen industry, the corn and hops of the eighteenth century and the markets of the nineteenth. It remains one of the most important corn markets in England. This is Georgian England to perfection. This is Cobbett's England, both metaphorically and in reality, for Farnham was his birthplace. He was a local innkeeper's son. His memorial is in the churchyard.

The eighteenth-century buildings, with a combination of solidity and elegance, stand in an almost unbroken line along the main streets, apart from East Street

* I. Nairn and N. Pevsner, *Surrey. The Buildings of England* (Penguin, 1971).

which is the poorer end of town. The expert's eagle eye will see several recent copies of the earlier styles but they do not offend my layman's eye. Two of the best houses are together in West Street, Willmer House, 1718, and Sandford House, 1757. Willmer House is now the town museum with an impressive collection of materials from the past, including tiles and stonework from Waverley Abbey. Apart from William Cobbett, who figures largely in the collection, another notable resident was John Henry Knight, who invented the first English motor-car, a silent trench-mortar and a brick-laying machine! Some of the lanes and footpaths in the vicinity of St Andrew's church are paved entirely with dark brown carstone, durable and attractive. 'Railway Farnham' lies across the river to the south, covering a bigger area than the old market town.

'The streets are wide and open,' wrote the *Gentleman's Magazine* of eighteenth-century Dorking, 'and from its natural situation the town is remarkably clean.' Clean and open, its setting is Dorking's greatest asset. The High Street lies on a gently curving hill crest which gives the shoppers a permanent view of the open spaces all about the town. An early Anglo-Saxon settlement on the Roman Stane Street as it aimed for the Mole Gap, the town acquired fame for its coaching inns, like the White Horse, for its cricketers, its poultry, cherry wine and snails. Older books on Dorking sound like good food guides. The large parish church is Victorian, its spire of more than sixty metres being completed in 1874 as a memorial to Bishop Wilberforce. As with Leatherhead, its counterpart to the north of the Mole Gap, there are few buildings of major interest. Leatherhead can claim two famous coaching inns and a fine medieval church and the timber-framed town houses have been discovered behind the façades of some old shops in the High Street but on the whole the towns have achieved a twentieth-century anonymity.

Dorking, though bearing an obvious relationship to routeways using gaps in the chalk hills, is itself situated on the greensand ridge that fronts the chalk escarpment. This situation occurs time and time again on the eastward extension of the greensand into Kent – Westerham, Sevenoaks, West Malling, Maidstone and, finally, Ashford. In most cases, the main streets of the towns follow an east-west alignment, suggesting that the cross-country route was as important in the early formation of the settlements as the north-south routes through the gaps. Westerham is on the minor scale, another of those places like Steyning that fits uncomfortably into the category of town or village. Yet a royal grant of 1619 renewed an ancient right to a market. The open triangular green by the church is dominated by a statue of Sir Winston Churchill to add to the memories of Wolfe, Pitt and other great empire-builders who were associated with the area.

Befittingly, the place has many good buildings of that same period. The finest of all, the manorial residence of Squerryes, to the west of the place, dates from the seventeenth century.

Sevenoaks, with 18,000 inhabitants, is a much more substantial place sprawling down the slope of the sandstone. Yet the core of the old town, the shambles, the parish church and the sixteenth-century grammar school grouped on the hill by the entrance to Knole Park, is limited. The substantial town houses of the seventeenth and eighteenth centuries are in the same area but much of the town is later growth down towards the railway station and the livestock market in the valley. 'Remarkable for the many good houses and the respectability of the inhabitants,'* is a description in 1800 which sounds very much like that of Lewes quoted earlier and would do service for most of the market towns of the period. Terminus for regular train services to London, Sevenoaks is a commuter town but one that has retained two of the finest open spaces, the park of Knole and the Vine cricket ground. Sevenoaks was a comparatively late arrival on the town scene. So was Maidstone, not receiving its charter of incorporation until 1549.

The view of Maidstone from the west bank of the Medway is as good a townscape as one could wish for. Even without the visual power of a castle keep, it rivals Rochester. Its church is the largest built in the Perpendicular style as befitting a collegiate church rebuilt by the fourteenth-century Archbishop Courtenay. Close by is the College of 1396, the palace, a priest's house and an enormous barn known as the Archbishop's stables. The town was virtually the creation of the archbishop, though the site on the Medway crossing was of earlier importance, traditional midway point of the county, dividing the diocesan lands of Rochester from those of Canterbury. A Roman road from Rochester south to the Wealden iron workings crosses the River Len, a line followed by the present-day Stone Street, St Gabriels, Week Street and Sandling Road by the County Jail. The new industrial and commercial activity of the Tudor period brought Maidstone into focus as the centre of the county. The Medway was its highway, but the small tributary of the Len supplied the power to a series of mills, some of which are still in action as paper mills.

The market centre of the town grew up at the junction of the Roman highway and the Medway crossing. There is the usual group of mid-row buildings disguising the earlier more extensive market space, the Town Hall of 1762, somewhat overshadowed by the County Hall, Sessions House and County Jail, which

* G. A. Cooke, *Topographical Description of the County of Kent* (1800).

announce that this is more than just another market town. While a few old shop-fronts and townhouses survive, especially in the area of the church, there is the usual air of redevelopment, of old buildings tumbling and new façades gleaming. Three railway stations have pulled the Victorian growth to the north and west of the old town together with the livestock and new retail market on the low ground. There is a healthy survival of breweries, like paper-making one of the long-established industries of the town. Larger than Guildford, with 72,000 people, the town has reached the halo of outlying villages such as Bearsted, Willington, Loose, Barming and Allington but, mercifully, in doing so it has preserved the fine open space of Mote Park with its eighteenth-century mansion, pavilion, trees and, incidentally, the county cricket ground. The simple structure of the town is confused inevitably by the one-way road system which regrettably cuts the tithe barn off from the rest of the medieval core but at least leaves room for a healthy heartbeat.

Ashford's system, in contrast, is so tight that it is like a noose round what is left of the old town. Its surgery has been so drastic that one wonders if the patient can survive. Inevitably, a shopping precinct and new office complexes make a shining new example but, at the time of my last visit, the destruction of the old was more evident than the promise of the new. Ashford still has hopes of being one of the growth areas of the south-east with a population surpassing that of Maidstone or Canterbury and the new town centre will reflect its new status as a regional centre but, meanwhile, somewhere inside the ring road is the relics of a small market street with a church, its yard and some surprisingly good buildings, linked together by narrow lanes. The livestock market, the largest in the county of Kent, has moved to a more spacious site. In the 1850s a new town was laid out by Samuel Beazley, mostly for the workers in the new locomotive workshops of the Southern Railway. The industrial area along the Stour is the most important feature of the town and many more modern factories have joined the railway workshops in extending the industrial zone. Five railway routes meet here at the southern end of the Stour Gap where the Weald becomes a broader, more featureless plain than elsewhere. Ashford has easy links with Canterbury, Maidstone and the coast at Folkestone. The A20 trunk road which utilizes the gault clay vale is doomed for upgrading to motorway status throughout much of its length, which can only increase the attraction of the town for industry and commerce.

There are not many towns like Ashford in the Weald. The traditional site for Wealden settlements is on the sandstone ridges, avoiding the heavy clay lowlands. Some of the forest clearances, the hursts and dens, emerged as natural centres and achieved a temporary status as sites of markets and fairs. Annual livestock fairs are still held at Biddenden, Horsmonden, Northiam, Ham Street, Tenterden and Heathfield, mostly for sheep sales. Weekly markets continue at Hailsham, Haywards Heath and Wadhurst, usually in close proximity to railway stations, though lorry transport is more significant now than rail. The urbanity of some of the smaller centres was also due to the passing prosperity of the iron and cloth industries. Tenterden, Cranbrook, Wonersh and Goldalming, Chiddingfold and Wisborough Green combined their craft industries with their roles as centres of small rural areas.

In the days of the horse and cart, markets were closer and more numerous, dealing with a limited area. The smaller markets were between 8 and 10 kilometres apart, a distance that still forms a significant part of the network of towns. 'Most towns,' writes Chalklin of Kent, 'were centres not of industry but of commerce and their distinctive feature was the market. By 1700 they were probably held in all the towns with over 500 inhabitants.'* Lambarde recorded twenty markets in Kent in the sixteenth century. The catchment of the markets was changed, first by the turnpike roads and then by the railways with a consequent decline of the smaller centres. Market day is now synonymous with a retail market. The livestock markets are now found in only fourteen towns in the three counties.

These small towns, representing a secondary development after the Norman planned towns, are the service centres of the Weald. In the west, for example, Midhurst, Petworth, Billingshurst, Pulborough, Henfield, Cuckfield, Cranleigh and Haslemere all have their banks and their businesses, their professional men, their local administrative offices. Some of them have even developed small shopping precincts, such as Billingshurst, or even modern shopping parades as at Cranleigh, as if to determine their status. All the more remarkable to see the name Village Hall trapped within Cranleigh's modernity. The distinction between town and village is blurred in such places.

Petworth, for example, is in essence a mansion and a park, ancestral home of the Percies and then the Wyndham family. The town, as in Arundel, clings to its skirts. The place has urban pretensions, with a market-place and a town hall built in the classic mode in 1793 by the Earl of Egremont whom Arthur Young admired so much. Amongst the warren of small streets, Lombard Street, Pound Street, Saddlers Row, Angel Street, there is a High Street, but it is unlike any other high street, quiet and domestic. Coming from the confined cobbled delight

* C. W. Chalklin, 'A Seventeenth-century Market Town: Tonbridge', *Archaeologia Cantiana*, LXXVI (1961).

of Lombard Street, the Town Hall looks somewhat pretentious, especially for little more than 2,000 citizens.

Midhurst, situated like Petworth on the greensand ridge, bears much the same relationship to the Cowdray estate as Petworth does to its big house. But a Norman motte stands to the east of the church, the site of the castle until the imposing Tudor house was built down by the river. The entry from the south crosses a ponded river and is immediately confronted with a mid-row of houses, including a sixteenth-century timbered Market House. The market-place itself is merely a space in front of the church. In an endless fascination of old street names like Sheep Lane, Wool Lane, Knockhundred Row, the sixteenth century rubs shoulders with the eighteenth in an easy calm, undisturbed by the traffic filtering up the main shopping area of North Street and South Street. It is on a Saturday that places like Midhurst really show their town face, when the car-parks are full and the shops busy, when friends are met, a meal taken and the car laden with stores for the coming week, the weekly focus of the surrounding rural area.

One of the consolations of becoming a comparative backwater is the survival of the architecture of the earlier affluence. The smaller towns of the Weald are nearly all visually rewarding.

The larger towns in the Weald grew up on the major highways, on the clay vales surrounding the High Weald. Tonbridge on the crossing of the upper Medway is just midway between London and the coastal ports of Hastings and Rye. The Norman town lies to the north of the castle precinct, delimited by Bordyke and a remnant of the town ditch that cut an arc to the north of the river. The area contains the oldest buildings in the town, some in current danger of demolition, the market-place and the coaching inns. The market has been in existence since the fourteenth century. The cloth and iron industries added to the population in the sixteenth century, a time when the famous grammar school was founded by the Skinners Company in 1553. As with Cranbrook, nearly half the population became paupers with the decline of these industries. The castle was sold to a merchant in 1627 and by the end of the eighteenth century much of the stone had been used in other buildings. Revival came with the Medway Navigation after 1740 but the present townscape is Victorian rather than Georgian. Its role as an inland port was hampered by the number of locks between the town and Chatham and it was the railway in 1842 that really brought the impetus for new growth. The railway town of more than a thousand houses grew up on the south side of the river on the priory site, similar to Lewes, with the resulting development of a distinct industrial area by river and rail. Boats, mostly of fibre-glass and other modern materials, are still made here but one of the most famous industries is the manufacture of cricket bats and balls. Victorian building, including many fine detached properties, spread over the ancient hunting friths of the Norman lords, giving Tonbridge a residential air it has never lost. More than a tenth of its inhabitants commute daily to work in London.

Horsham, 'capital of the Western Weald', stands at the junction of clay lowland and the sandstone hills of St Leonards Forest. At the northernmost extent of the Rape of Bramber, the town is first recorded as a borough in 1236, though never incorporated by a charter. Like Gatton and Reigate, it supplied two members to Parliament and also had a grant of two annual fairs from the Archbishops of Canterbury. The 'Hang Fair' coincided with the Assizes. The centre of town is the Carfax, the crossroads of North, East and West street. The fourth arm is the Causeway leading down to St Mary's church and the river, quite the finest collection of buildings in the town. A tree-lined cul-de-sac, lined with eighteenth- and nineteenth-century buildings, it also houses the best timber-framed house, now the town museum.

At the centre of the town is the Victorian town hall, the Corn Exchange and, surprisingly, a band-stand. The focus of the town is moving north with municipal offices in Horsham Park, and the headquarters of banks, insurance companies and commercial houses mustering along North Street. The old common to the north-west has been built over. For years the undisputed centre of the Sussex Weald, the town now finds a precocious competitor in the presence of the new town of Crawley only 9 km away, with three times the population of the older town.

Haslemere and East Grinstead, like Sevenoaks, were both late-comers to town status and both, like Sevenoaks, are dominated by one broad rising High Street, end-stopped by good houses. Both have a strongly Georgian atmosphere and even the chain-stores in Haslemere conform to the subdued elegance of the place. Haslemere was enfranchized in 1584, granted rights of market and fair. Its importance on the highway to Portsmouth was emphasized by eleven inns, of which only two remain. Everything of note, hotel, museum, shops, is in the one street but its halo of expensive houses each withdrawn into its own private grounds makes the break between town and country difficult to define. East Grinstead keeps an even finer collection of timbered houses to vary the eighteenth-century frontages, and the almshouses of Sackville College built in 1617 are as good an example as any. The town kept its livestock market until the 1950s.

A ring of old market towns stands within a radius of about ten miles from the centre of London – Kingston-upon-Thames, Croydon, Bromley. Their populations make them the biggest towns in the region, Croydon and Bromley both having more than a quarter of a million people. But the figures mean little, for the towns are all within the continuous built-up area of London and within the new administrative county of Greater London. Each is a centre of commerce in its own right and Croydon, especially, appears as a minor version of the City of London, its skyline dominated by towering office blocks and cooling towers, the new symbols of power. But the supreme function of each is that of a residential area feeding London, focus of suburban life. The earlier symbols of power are ecclesiastical, the Bishop of Rochester's palace at Bromley and the Archbishop's palace at Croydon. Even in 1900, Eric Parker felt that Croydon's palace was 'unhonoured, unhappy and ignored'.* The medieval core of the town, represented by the church, the largest Victorian edifice in the county rebuilt by Sir Gilbert Scott in 1870, the palace and Archbishop Whitgift's Hospital of 1596, still has a neglected air as compared with the new Croydon, the most overwhelming centre in the region. Between the main railway stations, East and West, is an area of glass and concrete which points its importance to the sky, outbidding every church spire. With car-stackers and fly-overs, Croydon shows the realization of municipal ambition. It is only just on the human scale. Yet Croydon has another face. From the Wandle Park, the skyline is of industrial chimneys, gas works, gas conversion plants and power stations.

Bromley is more dominantly residential and its aspirations not quite so inflated. Its new Churchill Theatre does not quite compare with Croydon's Fairfield Halls. Its shopping precincts are not on the scale of the Whitgift Centre. Its old market-place banished the stalls to a backstreet many years ago but its shopping attracts people from miles around, including large areas of north-west Kent, much to the concern of market towns such as Sevenoaks. Neither Bromley nor Croydon has more than a handful of buildings to catch the antiquarian eye but Bromley's slopes are full of Victorian residential comfort and a halo of golf-courses developed on the erstwhile great parks of gentry such as Sundridge and Langley, both Repton landscapes, and Beckenham Place, the home of John Cator, on visiting terms with Samuel Johnson and Carl Linnaeus. Johnson's wife is buried in Bromley church, which was badly damaged during the 1939–45 war. Both towns were submerged beneath the tide of twentieth-century speculative building yet both jealously guard their independence, symbolized by their town halls, Croydon's of 1892, Bromley's of 1906.

Kingston-upon-Thames is isolated from London by the wide open spaces of Wimbledon and Richmond but its links with Surrey have been cut since the

* E. Parker, op. cit.

reorganization of local government in 1974. For years it housed the county administrative offices. By its Guildhall stands a squat, square sarsen stone, the King's Stone, the Coronation stone of seven Saxon kings in the tenth century. Narrow lanes like Harrow Passage and the Apple Market lead to the market-place, a square lined with buildings of every age from medieval to modern, though some of the most striking timber-framed jetty houses are twentieth-century rather than sixteenth. The stalls and the market hall of 1706 give this precinct the sense of a real market-place, something missing from most of the other large towns. This essential Kingston is easily missed by travellers heading for the bridge over the Thames, for the newer shops line the main road north of the market-place.

Kingston is the first of a line of towns along the Surrey bank of the Thames, which includes Molesey, Walton, Weybridge, Chertsey and Egham. The 'ey' termination indicates an island site on the flood plain gravels of the river. Surrey now includes part of the north bank as far as Heathrow airport, a strange, confused world of industry, reservoirs, residential estates and some surprisingly lovely survivals such as the village of Thorpe and the meadows of Runnymede. The administrative centre of the new district is Walton-on-Thames but the most interesting town by far is Chertsey. Chertsey, like Farnham, had avoided the worst features of twentieth-century commercialism in the high street. The approach from the east crosses the Thames by an eighteenth-century bridge designed by James Paine, who was also responsible for Richmond's fine bridge. Bridge Road leads to the town centre along the broad London Road to the junction with Guildford Street, the natural centre where the church, the library and the old Town Hall of 1851, now a museum, group together. The eighteenth century 'urbanity of big trees and smooth brickwork'* is present throughout the town but especially in Windsor Street, the extension of the London Road to the west. The abbey precinct lay between the town and the low-lying meads to the north. The lanes in this area follow the alignment of abbey buildings, though little more than fragments of walls remain incorporated into existing housing. There is a section of the nave floor and some pillars in a private garden and some arches and decorated stone in the land leading to the river.

At Chertsey we are on Thames water. The extensive reservoirs, the cacophony of gulls, the gathering of wildfowl bring more than a hint of the sea. Small craft ply downstream to Richmond and the tidal Thames, linking with the water highways. The south-east region is a peninsula and it is on the coasts that the most exciting of its townscapes evolved.

* Nairn and Pevsner, *Surrey*.

9

Ports and Resorts

Looking through the family photograph album I came across a picture of myself aged five, flanked by my two elder brothers. We all look very severe. I am dressed in an overcoat, a scarf and, most improbably, a bowler hat. Arms crossed I look quite Napoleonic. The occasion, as far as I remember it, was the annual family holiday on the Thanet shore. Holidays for me are memories of ruining new shoes on cliffs and the mud flats of Pegwell Bay, of long walks along piers and the inevitable bliss of an ice-cream cornet. But there were also overcoats and biting on-shore winds driving us into the promenade shelters. This was not so much a comment on the rigours of the south-east coast as on the fact that we took our holidays in what is known in the trade as off-season. All the statistics prove that the south-east is sunnier and warmer and drier than most other parts of Britain but I can remember snowflakes quite as common as sunbeams.

The memories flooded back on a recent Easter Monday at Margate with a force eight wind blowing down the North Sea and the temperature perilously close to zero. But the lads from London playing football on the sands by Dreamland were stripped to the waist. They were determined to enjoy themselves. Even in a recent September, I have seen families huddled up in blankets and overcoats in the lee-side of groynes in a resort that shall remain nameless as it advertises itself on its brochure as sunshine even in winter. And yet we all want to be beside the seaside. Ever since Dr Russell assured us of the beneficial effects of sea-bathing at Brighton and Benjamin Beale invented the bathing machine at Margate, the annual exodus has gone on to the point where thousands choose not only to visit but to live on the coast and the untouched areas are mere fragments of shingle and cliff.

There is an almost continuous belt of buildings from the Thames dockside right round to the Selsey Peninsula. What gives the coast its character is not the smell of the sea and castles in the sand but the extraordinary variety of human landscapes. A Roman fort rubs shoulders with a caravan site. Bathing huts cower under a Martello Tower. Hovercraft hurtle alongside in-shore fishing craft and frighten migrating birds. Ice-cream stands and bingo halls flaunt themselves in front of elegant Georgian terraces. A medieval town, almost intact, slumbers under the pall of a giant power station. And still the sea erodes the cliffs and deposits the shingle and goes about its eternal business of changing the coastline. Man repairs the paintwork and builds the sea-walls and dredges the harbours in the never-ending contest.

The coast is also the front-line of defence against invasion and the ports that welcome trade and passengers are enlivened by the forts that protected them. It is only in the last two centuries that the pattern has been obscured by the mushroom growth of resorts, filling up the spaces. When I pottered as a child through the vast excitements of Pegwell Bay I did not realize that I was treading on England's most strategic corner. There is hardly a good natural deep-water harbour from the Solent to the Thames Estuary. When Romans invaded, when Saxons and saints followed, they all aimed with unerring choice to the comparative shelter of Pegwell, protected by the shifting sandbanks off-shore. The Tudor navy could ride in safety in the Downs, protected by the gun-batteries of Deal, Walmer and Sandown castles. The story begins, as so many stories do, with the Romans. They established their small harbours and their protective forts at Richborough and Reculver, at Dover and Lympne, with roads running like spokes of a wheel to the hub of Roman life at Canterbury. Of the four places, only Dover continues to function as a port, though Port Richborough has grown effectively into an industrial area with small shipyards since its adaptation as a war-time supply base in the last war. The Roman quay at Dover lies inland close to what was the deeper mouth of the Dour. Changes in the coast have destroyed them, Reculver by erosion, the others by silting of the channels. Small craft may have reached up the Stour even as far as Canterbury but the limit of tidal water is Fordwich, two miles downstream. Fordwich was the medieval outport of Canterbury, incorporated as a town in Henry II's reign and keeping its status, with its own mayor, until 1883. Alongside its church and quayside stands its tiny town hall, of timber and brick, with courtroom, storeroom and prison, but the port was already in decline before that town hall was built in the sixteenth century.

Larger ships and increasingly difficult navigation drove trade to the river mouth at Sandwich, one of the best medieval towns in the country. Like the nearby Roman port it, too, faced decline and fall as the channel between the Isle of Thanet and the mainland silted up due to changes in sea-level and to the reclamation of the marshes by the monks of Minster. It was a thriving Saxon port in the seventh century and by the eleventh century was paying, amongst

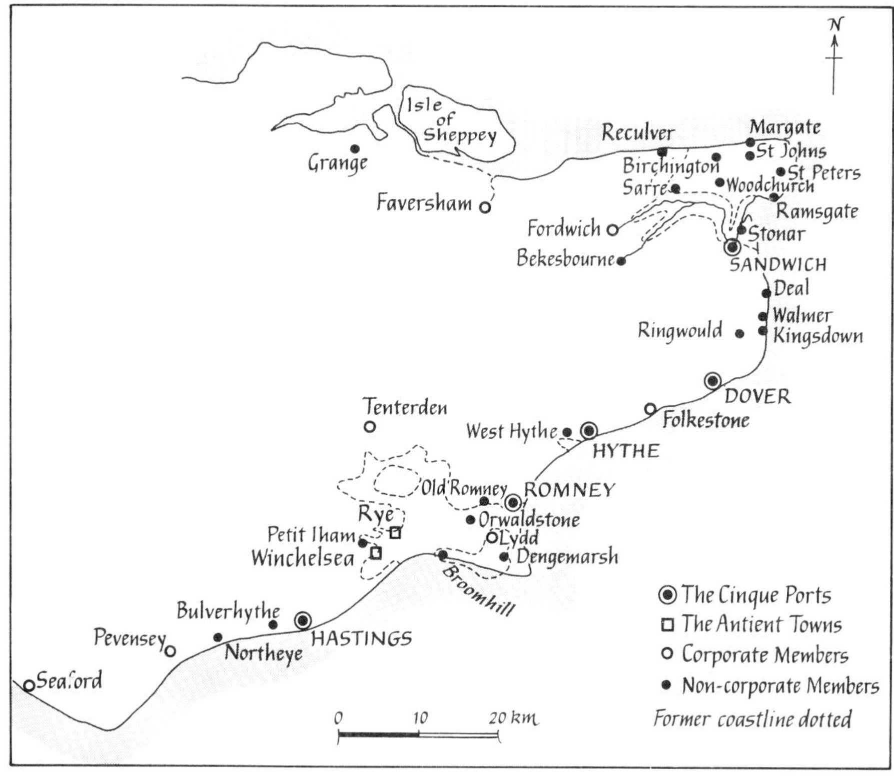

49. *The confederation of the cinque ports (based on M. Burrows,* Cinque Ports *(1895)).*

other things, an annual rental of 40,000 herrings to Christ Church, Canterbury. It had 383 houses and was the seventh town in England in size. Kings and prelates sailed from Sandwich – Becket, Richard Lionheart, Edward III. The fishing fleet formed the nucleus of the Navy, giving ship service to the Crown for the defence of the realm in return for its privileges. The last charter to confirm those privileges was granted by Charles II, who landed at Kingsgate in Thanet on his return from exile. Sandwich was one of the original Cinque Ports confederation that developed from ship service to the Saxon crown. The other four were Dover, Hythe, New Romney and Hastings. Such was the power and privilege that they gained that they created small empires, gathering other smaller havens under their wing, as corporate or non-corporate members of the federation depending on their status, but more simply known as 'limbs'. Sandwich, as we have seen, had Fordwich as a corporate member and non-corporate members at Deal, Walmer, Ramsgate, Stonar, Sarre and Brightlingsea, while Dover controlled Folkestone, Faversham, Margate and seven other havens mostly on Thanet. Pevensey and Seaford were limbs of Hastings, as was Bekesbourne, now a small village well inland near Canterbury. Rye and Winchelsea, originally appendages of Hastings, grew to new status to become the Two Antient Towns, equal partners with the Head Ports. Some of the jig-saw of the confederation makes no sense until we try to reconstruct the old coastline and trace the older, deeper havens before the sea smoothed the outline, eroding the cliffs and destroying some older harbours such as the port area of Brighton and filling in the river mouths. Take the geological map and let the sea reclaim the areas of alluvium. The arms of the sea point deeply inland as far even as Smallhythe near Tenterden. Even the castle at Bodiam could be reached by small craft with shallow draught.

The fierce rivalries and self-interest of the Cinque Ports needed an overriding administration. By the twelfth century, the Court of Shepway was formed, meeting traditionally near Lympne, the old Roman site, with a Royal Officer, the Warden of the Cinque Ports. They became more aware of their privileges than their duties. Piracy and smuggling and occasional forays against the French led to the inevitable retaliation and demand for help when the French replied so effectively, especially in the fourteenth century. But it was the sea's activities and the development of the new larger ports that defeated them. By 1619 only one ship from the Confederation traded overseas, to Malaga and Bordeaux. Many of the ship-owners had gone to the port of London. But the pride of the great days lives on in the heraldry of the towns and in the office of Lord Warden who has his official residence in Walmer Castle. Sir Winston Churchill and Sir Robert Menzies are the two most recent occupants of the office. Even more significant is the relict landscape of that medieval power in the present urban scene, for Sandwich is not alone in its historic splendour.

The churches of Sandwich still bear the scars of French attack. Even with the welcome influence of industry brought by the Flemish weavers and Huguenot craftsmen, the town's illustrious days were numbered. That very decline has meant that the town survives as an historic jewel with narrow lanes lined with timber-framed medieval houses and red-brick houses in the Dutch style. Earth ramparts and watery ditches surround it and one gate, the Fisher Gate, remains from the fourteenth century, though rebuilt in the sixteenth. Its most famous riverside building is the Barbican, built in 1539, controlling the river crossing, at first a ferry point, then a drawbridge. The present swingbridge, at which tolls are still paid, was built in the nineteenth century. The three churches, St Mary's, St Peter's and St Clement's, each dominate a sector of the town, St Mary's reputedly on a Saxon foundation. Street names like Upper End of the Chain, Strand Street and Butchery Street are as fascinating as the old buildings, the Weavers in Strand Street, the Dutch solidity of Roger Manwood's house that Queen Elizabeth I visited. The brick Guildhall by the market-place has been restored but the whole town needs to be traced and retraced for it can lay claim to be one of the most complete medieval towns in England, which will be further preserved by the construction of the new by-pass north of the town.

Schemes were put forward for the improvement of the haven even up until the eighteenth century but the site for a new harbour was finally chosen at Ramsgate, in 1755. Yet all the marine documentation for harbours such as Ramsgate, Margate and Broadstairs had to be obtained from Sandwich, the only one recognized as an official port by the Customs Commissioners. Ramsgate at this time was already the busiest of the Thanet ports, with trade in coal, timber and naval stores. Its new harbour, quay and lighthouse were a source of great pride and appeared in the topographical sketches of artists like George Shepherd alongside the more usual castles, abbeys and great mansions. It is a busy harbour, importing foreign cars, and advertises itself as a gateway to the continent. Central feature of the harbour is an obelisk thanking George IV for using the port on his way to Hanover in 1821 in English and Latin. Royal accolade was as important to the ports as to the resorts. Victoria visited Ramsgate as a girl, so the Royal Crescent and the Royal Esplanade are doubly supported. The names point to the period of transition from port to resort. Nelson Crescent, 1798, the Paragon, 1816. The wealthy English travellers were deprived by the Napoleonic adventure from doing the Grand Tour of Europe, so it was holidays at home. Ramsgate was one of the many 'watering places' to benefit from the new fashion. Its pattern, too, is typical. A High Street leads to the port crossed by another main axis, in this case King Street and Queen Street, running parallel with the shore. Ramsgate shows a sign of the new times that is repeated in many a seaside town that is not sure of its role. A major chain store is opening on a prime site on the harbour side. Some towns have almost turned their backs on the sea, so tumbledown are the 'fronts', but not Ramsgate. All the roads lead naturally to the harbour and the obelisk, to gear, tackle and the smell of boats.

Under local government reorganization, Thanet is now one administrative district, but the towns keep their own special flavour. Every place had its own special reputation, its own clientele. Londoners were very careful to announce their holiday plans. By their choice you knew them. Margate was jollity and Dreamland; Birchington gently relaxing and slightly superior; Broadstairs select and ideal for yachting caps. One common factor of the Thanet towns is that each has its older village core, stone church, flint cottages, about a mile inland, villages that were once more important than their seaward expansions: St Lawrence for Ramsgate, St Peter's for Broadstairs, St John's at Margate, All Saint's at Birchington. St Peter's is effectively joined to Broadstairs, alias Bradstow, by subsequent development around the railway station. Broadstairs, a discreet, trim little bay and harbour once sent its fishing craft to the hazardous Greenland cod fisheries. It preserves one of the rare medieval gateways, York Gate, to protect the narrow street that climbs steeply from the harbour. Behind it is a cluster of flint houses in lanes and courtyards like Union Square. Dickensian Broadstairs is of a later vintage, many of the houses, such as Bleak House, advertising their connection with his novels. St Mary's and St Peter's both appear in early records as 'limbs' of the Cinque Port of Dover. Ramsgate, although adjacent, was a limb of Hastings.

Margate, too, was a limb of Dover but its church of St John the Baptist on the hill top is virtually the only medieval survival. Originally a chapetry of Minster, the church was made parochial in 1290. Margate's final emergence to fame was as a pioneer of seabathing in the 1750s due to the invention of a bathing machine by a local Quaker, Benjamin Beale. Its attractions were mirrored in Georgian architecture such as Cecil Square and Hawley Square, in the Theatre Royal and the Royal Sea Bathing Hospital. King Street links the old part of the town with the Parade and the harbour. Rennie's pier of 1810 was of importance when Margate was a packet station for Ostend and a key link with the Low Countries during the Napoleonic wars.

The poet, Thomas Gray, described Margate in 1766 as 'Bartholomew Fair by the sea-side'. The image is still appropriate for that stretch of the front from the Clock Tower along the sands to Dreamland. The day-trippers are not just a fond memory. They roll out of cars and coaches and trains on every bank holiday, ready for football on the sands in any weather, with the typical determination of Londoners in pursuit of pleasure. The new residential districts which developed at Cliftonville and Westgate from the 1870s onwards are favourite areas for retirement.

Dover is still the key to the kingdom. Like the other Cinque Ports, it has had its problems but, unlike the others, it has maintained its position as a major port with nearly three million gross tonnes of shipping using the docks, mostly passengers and freight lorries bound for the short sea crossing to Calais, itself so long an English toe-hold on the continent. The valley of the Dour striking across the furthest extremity of the North Downs makes a natural route and haven at exactly the right strategic point, sheltered by the headlands of the South Foreland and Shakespeare Cliff; a natural gateway and a natural highway, the symbolic entrance to Britain.

To the west of the Dour, a river now mostly culverted, is the oldest part of Dover, the Market Square, St Mary's and the Biggin on the site of the Roman encampment, set there when the Dour was wider and the haven well inland. Wall fragments of the Roman town have been excavated during redevelopment, brick and flint bastions sticking like ribs through the debris above Market Street. A painted villa lies beneath the surface. East of the Dour, a later town of quite elegant nineteenth-century terraces and villas spreads up to Connaught Park under the shadow of the Roman pharos, Saxon church and Norman castle. The most interesting buildings within the town are grouped along Biggin Street and the High Street, leading from the harbour inland to Canterbury – St Mary's with its lovely west entrance, the medieval Maison Dieu (now museum and town hall) and the warm Dutch brickwork of Maison Dieu House, from the barrier between the shopping centre and the new town centre developing by the river. Dover is a place that most people, going or coming, pass through. It deserves more. But it is not a place to look at; it is a work-a-day town of 35,000 people that always seems to be probing further and further up the valleys to the west by the great redoubts and Priory Station. On any holiday the East Cliff forms a grandstand for crowds sitting hopefully in the sun gazing down at Sealink and hovercraft, the cargo vessels by the Inner Harbour and the Marine Station by the Admiralty Pier, the longest marine walk in the world, a sea-angler's paradise. The front between the west and east docks is striking a new pose. An impressive skyline of office towers and hotels lines Town Wall Street. The white sweep of Waterloo Crescent and the sands strike a more leisured note. Memorials of Matthew Webb, channel swimmer, Charles S. Rolls and Bleriot, aviators, recall other variants on the channel-crossing theme.

The broken church of St James, destroyed by enemy bombardment, is one with the castle and the mouldering gun-emplacements of later years to remind us that travellers can be invaders. Dover has borne the brunt. A muscular and enduring town. What began with the Roman Dubris, base of the Roman fleet, grew by way of sixteenth-century jetties and Victorian enlargements to become the busiest passenger port in the world, coping with five million people and a million vehicles every year.

Folkestone had its small haven at the mouth of a valley cutting through the greensand. Above it, the old town stood on a hill called the Bayle, a corruption of bailey and possibly the site of an early castle. Narrow streets with a slightly neglected air wind up towards the church of St Mary and St Eanswythe. The last named, a lady of royal blood, persuaded her father to build a nunnery within the castle precinct. A lead casket containing her relics is buried within a wall of the present church building. Folkestone has a Roman link, too. A large villa was found in the 1920s on the cliff top near Cope Point containing tiles bearing the Classis Brittania sign of the Channel fleet. Telford's harbour of 1807 went the way of many harbours, blocked by shingle, but Folkestone's present prosperity is largely the product of the South-Eastern Railway Company. They successfully restored the harbour and set up a steamship service in 1843. The nineteen-arched railway viaduct is as exciting as any other piece of architecture in the town. But Folkestone seems to be a bit impatient with its past and all the present energies are most apparent well away from the harbour and Bayle. The Guildhall in the old town has been replaced by a new civic centre in the west in Castle Hill Avenue where a grid pattern of streets was laid out between the station and the Leas. The Leas is the pride of Folkestone, a clifftop walk with gardens backed by a line of elegant hotels. Or it was. Although a conservation area, blocks of the hotels have given way to modern apartments of dazzling design and the red-brick rear-end of a supermarket complex. Folkestone is uncertain of itself. The port is still there, the resort air remains, the Victoria pier and the 1905 promenade survive. But Folkestone has grown larger than Dover and, with a less constricted site, has grown inland to the foot of the Downs by Sugarloaf Hill. Folkestone is now 'only', to use the words of the property advertisers, an hour and a half from London by electrified rail. To the west, it makes an effective conjunction with Sandgate, a small cliff-top settlement, one street and a Henry VIII castle. Then there is just time to see the open sea before the coast road curls into Hythe.

Hythe has a military air, barracks, shooting ranges, streets named after Sir John Moore and the terminus of the Royal Military Canal, 'Pitt's ditch' intended to make things difficult for Napoleon but now lynchpin of the drainage of Romney and Walland marshes. In the height of its Cinque Port glory, the town stretched west, according to ancient topographers, as far as West Hythe and Stutfall, the Roman Portus Lemanis. The fort is a ruin sliding down a slippery slope to a shoreline that has not seen the sea for five centuries. West Hythe is a deserted village. The changes in the course of the River Rother, once the Limen, finally left the havens high and dry. The present town has a regular pattern of streets, with a charter of incorporation from Elizabeth I. The eighteenth-century town hall is most imposing but there are older fragments such as the medieval St Bartholomew's Hospital. The church high on a hill to the north dominates the whole town. The room over its porch did service as the original meeting place of the town council. A plaque in the church also records one of its citizens, three times mayor, who had the right, traditional to the Cinque Ports, of bearing the canopy above the king at his coronation. He was also Bailiff of Yarmouth, which shows just how far afield the medieval tentacles stretched.

Later extensions of the town have covered the shingly space between the canal and the sea. The sea walk is impeded by firing ranges and barbed wire and peremptory notices, but we can hardly grumble. They are our equivalent of the Martello Towers and the Military Canal. But they do not look as romantic. Hythe's holiday industry was closely linked, in any case, with the military. It was the resort of invalids and claimed to be 'as genteel and more select' than other more famous watering places, 'and of late years much improved by the families of many military officers of rank, permanently or occasionally stationed in the vicinity'.* The presence of towers and guns and soldiery was an attraction rather than a disturbance to the early holidaymakers. They were people of rank and property. They enjoyed military display. It gave them a sense of security and well-being even when strolling along the promenade. After all, Napoleon and the French republicans were not far away.

The Royal Military Canal was built between 1804 and 1809, much of the work-force, the military supervision and the maintenance being based at Hythe. John Rennie came fresh from work on the East India Dock to supervise. Pitt gained the support of the local landowners by pointing out the advantages to them of good drainage, of water supply and cheap transport. There was even the vision of a canal link through the Weald of Kent to the Medway. The French never came and the transport never materialized. But the drainage was a boon and anglers enjoyed the carp, tench and perch that stocked it even in 1806. They still do. Lined with elms, now sadly decimated, the canal and its banks make a lovely linear park, so attractive that parts have been given to the National Trust.

* W. Teignmouth Shore, *Kent* (A. & C. Black, 1907).

Contemporary with the canal were the Martello Towers that made a fortune for the brick companies. Never fired on in anger, many were quarried for material, some fell into the sea but many survive to add a moment's variation to the sandcastle theme. Named after a tower at Capo Martella in Corsica which had resisted the British fleet, seventy-four of them were built as gun platforms along the Kent and Sussex coasts. Twenty-six are still standing and some sufficiently well preserved, as at Dymchurch, to be used as museums. One at Seaford became a café and several are private residences. The best of them is the Wish Tower at Eastbourne, housing a most imaginative exhibition of the defence of the coast. One map even shows the five lines of defence of London and the Medway ports, in the event of French invasion. In hindsight it would be easy to echo Cobbett's jibes about a waste of money, but these stark functional towers had a deadly purpose, to hold guns and ammunition and protect the weakest sections of the coast, the low, accessible shores. That same shore, so long amongst the wildest and emptiest in England, home of smuggling bands, has seen the caravan sites and holiday camps creeping precariously between high tide and marsh – Dymchurch, St Mary's Bay, Littlestone and Greatstone, Lydd – until the final punctuation mark of the power station at Dungeness.

Tucked away behind the summer façade, two kilometres from the sea, is New Romney yet another Cinque Port abandoned by the River Rother when it changed its course after a great storm in 1287. Before this time, ships tied up at the quayside near the church. The size of St Nicholas's church, the last of the three medieval churches, is in keeping with the great trading days, when the broad High Street was a famous sheep fair. The four streets in parallel, filling what was once an island site in the marsh, may have persisted since Saxon times, for Romney, like Lewes, was important enough to have a mint long before the Norman Conquest. Most of the buildings today date from the eighteenth and nineteenth centuries, but some medieval structures such as St John's Priory hide behind later façades. Nearby Lydd was another Saxon foundation, with an early prosperity based on fishing, trading and the great sheep flocks of the Marshes. It was a 'limb' of New Romney. The church contains Saxon stonework and possible evidence of a Roman foundation.

After many variations in its erratic course to the sea, the River Rother flowed along the western margins of the Walland Marsh by the island site of Rye. Rye spoils you forever. It makes every other place dull. Mermaid Street, cobbled, lined with timber-framed houses, must be one of the loveliest streets in England and the rest of the town is nearly as fine. Both in its inner structures and in its general setting it reaches an urban perfection. From the East Guldeford Level, it rises on a small conical hill straight out of the marsh, a jumble of rooftops crowned by the tower of St Mary the Virgin, so big and so impressive that it is called the Cathedral of East Sussex. On my most recent visit a storm was breaking over the coast; the violent play of light, holding an awareness of the sea, made a topographer's dreamscape. It had the same magnetic effect as the summit of a mountain. The approach heightens the tension as a fortified landgate bars the entry. Every good town should have a gate. Rye has little of that no-man's-land of semi-rural, semi-urban land-use that destroys distinctions.

50. *Watchbell Street, Rye.*

Within the gate and the encircling walls, the first effect is of a jumble of narrow lanes and changing slopes. But it falls into place gradually. A High Street makes the main axis from Land Gate to Strand Gate. East Street, West Street and Lion Street run uphill from it to the market-place, the town hall and the church enclosure. The whole is surrounded by a road on the flats following the line of the old walls, Fishmarket Road, South Undercliff, the Strand, Wish

Ward and Cinque Port Street. But the simple pattern always keeps the element of surprise. The straight High Street suddenly turns and dips down the Mint to the Strand. Watchbell Street and Church Square lead to two vantage points, the Green and Ypres Tower both linked to the quayside by steep flights of steps. The view down shows workshops and warehouses and small boats and the comforting realization that this is still a working town and not a historic museum. Of course, Rye is conscious of its fascination; the shops have that special gleam in their eye that beckons the tourist and potters and artists rub shoulders with fishermen from the harbour and cattlemen from the market. There is the house of Henry James as well as the Augustinian Priory. The Ypres Tower, older than the walls, is now a museum with an eccentric collection of local material, and some very revealing sidelights on the great days of sheep, iron, trading and smuggling. Incorporated as a town in 1289, Rye wears the dignity of its past with good humour. Like its near neighbour, Winchelsea, it began life doing ship-service with Hastings, but it grew in status to become one of the two Antient Towns (and insists on that special spelling of Antient), Winchelsea being the other, of equal status with the five Head Ports of the Confederation.

Winchelsea could not be more different. Old Winchelsea lies under the shingle somewhere near the sand dunes of Camber. Shattered by several storms in the thirteenth century, especially of 1287, the town was completely rebuilt on a flat hill-top on the manor of Iham, west of Rye. It was planned by Edward I on the same lines as his 'bastide' towns of Wales and France. A builder from Bordeaux helped in the planning. A strict grid of streets enclosed thirty-nine building plots like a modern American housing 'block'. The centre of the new town was the church standing in a large square. The church, like the town, was never completed and what was there was sacked by the French. Only eleven blocks are now built upon; the others lie under pastures and parkland, some of it is now in the possession of the National Trust. The main axis runs north-south from Pipewell Gate to the New Gate, which stands in isolation in the fields. The main cross axis runs from the Strand Gate to the site of St Leonards. The three gates, mostly of the fourteenth century, survive and many of the older houses in the vicinity of the church have medieval cellars (thirty have been recorded) that were filled with wine from Gascony. Yet with all that history, the appearance of the town is much more like a garden suburb than a medieval port, self-consciously superior. The magnificent Alard tombs in the church are one of the strongest echoes of the past, two of the Alards being Admiral and Warden of the Cinque Ports.

51. *Medieval town planning – the new port of Winchelsea built in the reign of Edward I. The twentieth-century resort of Winchelsea Beach lies beyond the reclaimed marsh in the background.*

Winchelsea has crept back stealthily towards the sea in a rash of bungalows and villas that crouch behind the sea wall at Winchelsea Beach. Across the Rother, the holiday camps and caravans defy an occasional dousing by wind-blown sand from the active dunes that line the shore.

The combination of Cinque Port, watering place and railway resort makes its most emphatic statement on the sturdy cliffs of Hastings. Though not specifically mentioned in the pages of Domesday, Hastings was an important Saxon town. Comparatively isolated on the extremity of a ridge of sandstone hills, it was the centre of a territory initially independent of Sussex and Kent. The cyclical ups and downs of its history are all reflected in the present townscape. There are two valleys, Priory Valley and the Bourne, divided by a high sandstone bluff on which the ruins of the Norman castle stand. There are distinct and different towns in each of the valleys. But the Old Town in the Bourne Valley is not, surprisingly, the earliest site. Hastings began in a deep protected haven, like Dover, at the mouth of the Priory Valley. Following the erosion of the White Rocks headland which protected it, that first haven became uninhabitable due to flooding and a new town was laid out in the twelfth century in the Bourne Valley, in essence two main streets, now known as High Street and All Saints Street, one on either side. Flooding was just as much a problem here as it had been in the western valley, so by the fourteenth century a sea wall was raised across the mouth of the Bourne and a stone wall against the French raiders. Some fragments remain behind new flats in Winding Street, with a plaque marking the site of the Sea Gate of 1385. Though many of the burgage strips were filled in with later, especially nineteenth-century, terraced housing, a number of early timbered houses survive. Hastings structure has been modified by the laying out of a third street along the course of the Bourne, pointing towards the old market-place. The Bourne Valley is still the fisherman's quarter and their gear, tackle and ships, and, most of all, their unique net houses on the shingles of the Stade under East Cliff are some of the outstanding attractions of the town. The tall many-storeyed timber structures have fascinated artists from Samuel Prout to the present day.

The new watering place had a ready-made site for expansion into the old Priory Valley but the first planned stages carried out by Joseph Kaye in the 1820s were close by the cliffs below the castle. He even cut away some of the cliff to accommodate the classical sweep of Pelham Crescent and its centre-piece, the church of St Mary in the Castle. But it was when the railway came into the Priory Valley in 1851 that the new Hastings was made. The rocks from the many tunnels and cuttings were used to create a new shoreline above high tide.

Although the old town hall had only been rebuilt on its old site in the High Street in 1828, the new one built in Queen's Road in 1880 signified the emergence of the Victorian town as the centre of Hastings life, the main shopping area, focusing on the Albert Memorial Clock Tower. The sea-front hotels are Victorian, the pier 1872, though the White Rock Pavilion dates from the 1920s.

52. *Wooden net houses on the Stade at Hastings.*

Hastings' 'west end' is unusually interesting, being another new town planned and built by a London builder, James Burton, and his architect son, Decimus. The plan for the new watering place in 1828 was influenced by Burton's work in Regent's Park. Crescents of elegant houses swept down a very steep cliff-slope around the centre-piece of St Leonard's Garden, once an old quarry, down to the esplanade which was lined with assembly rooms, hotels, marina and baths. By 1836 'a desert has become a thickly populated town',* an exclusive area causing no little jealousy in its older neighbour. A small bust of Burton stands in a very inconspicuous corner of the Subscription Gardens. He deserves greater fame. The villas flanking the park up Quarry Hill and Maze Hill are typical of the

* J. Manwaring Baines, *Burton's St Leonards* (Hastings Museum, 1956).

buildings Decimus was to build throughout the south-east as ideal homes for 'genteel folk'. The Esplanade was regarded by Parry as 'one of the finest in Europe'.* Inevitably he compared it with Brighton and although it was not as long, its 'close contiguity' to the sea gave it the advantage. Its flower beds and grass-plats were a 'happy addition'. Bathing, boats, bands, billiards, cards, medical advice, artistic instruction and a good inn were all there to distract and instruct, but for 'amusements' visitors were advised to 'resort to Hastings'. With such discrete charms, no wonder the resort received a royal visit in 1834 by the Duchess of Kent and Princess Victoria. The St Leonard's Hotel was suitably renamed the Royal Victoria Hotel, which it still is. Just beyond the west marina of St Leonard's is a small place called Bulverhythe of no obvious importance, yet this is a name that appeared in the early Cinque Port annals as a limb of Hastings.

The two most westerly corporate members of the Cinque Port Confederation, both limbs of Hastings, were Pevensey and Seaford. The Norman castle standing within a major Roman camp and the site of the first Norman landing are enough attractions for any site but Pevensey, in fact, has even more to offer in the form of two villages, one on either side of the castle precinct. Pevensey itself once had the status of a borough which it kept until 1886, and its tiny guildhall-cum-courthouse sports the oldest seal of any of the Cinque Ports. It is really only two short streets, a market-place and a church but it is full of old flint buildings. The West Ham is even smaller and its best remaining buildings are timber-framed, standing by yet another fine medieval church.

The Norman church of St Leonard's, though 'barbarously repaired' according to Parry, a big building of flint and ironstone conglomerate, is just about the last remnant of the glory that was Seaford, a medieval port that was powerful enough to become a rotten borough. Such was its decline through the now familiar combination of silting and French attacks that the citizens joined Jack Cade's rebellion. The changing course of the River Ouse finally created a better haven on the opposite side of the valley and there the new haven was built. Newhaven also had the benefit of nineteenth-century improvement, first the railway in 1847, then the straightening of the river mouth, the construction of breakwaters and a regular passenger service with Dieppe. It is no longer famous for its oysters but it is a working port with half a million tonnes of shipping each year.

Seaford, meanwhile, found a new function as a small select resort with a remarkable abundance of residential schools, using the sea and the open Downs

* J. D. Parry, *The Coast of Sussex* (1833).

behind the town as part of their educational function. The shingle is still a problem, recent winter storms hurling it over the promenade and emphasizing the visual sense of a no-man's-land between town and shore with the remaining sea-front buildings having a battered look. The vacant ground is now being tentatively filled in by new housing.

Beyond Newhaven, the coastal rash breaks out in full force. From Peacehaven to Bognor there is effectively forty kilometres of buildings and only a three-kilometre stretch of untouched coast just to the west of the Arun. No more room on the shore for all those who want to be right beside the seaside, so the new conurbation probes its speculative fingers up the valleys of the Downs more than eight kilometres inland from Worthing and Brighton, gobbling up hitherto individual villages into their maw. There are still active ports on the West Sussex coast, such as Shoreham and Littlehampton, but nothing comparable with the richness and variety of the Cinque Ports.

The urbanity of West Sussex is due not to the pursuit of maritime commerce but to the pursuit of pleasure. The transformation of a small, fading fishing port called Brighthelmstone into a royal resort outdid even Margate's spectacular growth. It was fairy story epitomized by the exoticism of the Royal Pavilion. Where Brighton led, others were to follow. Brighton was to be the peer of resorts. All others were compared with it. Yet its beginning was not promising.

Much of the old fishing area below the cliffs, similar to the Stade of Hastings, was swept away in a storm in 1705. The loss of more than a hundred houses led to fears that the town would become depopulated. But history smiled in the shape of Dr Russell, a Lewes practitioner, who published *A Dissertation Concerning the use of Sea Water in Diseases of the Glands* in 1750. Three years later he followed his own advice and moved to the town, building a house on the site of the present Royal Albion Hotel and enclosing a medicinal spring. The principal diversions from the severe business of bathing were then hunting and horse-racing but Brighton's 'second founder' soon extended that range.

People of rank like the Duke of Gloucester had been coming to Brighton since the 1760s but it was the Prince Regent's visit to his uncle, the Duke of Cumberland, in 1783 that gave the new resort its popularity and unique reputation. Brighton had always been a bit 'racy', a character that had led other resorts to copy unsuccessfully or to denigrate and seek cosy respectability. The Prince enjoyed his visit and leased a farmhouse on the west bank of Brighton's river, the Wellesbourne, which flowed through the Steyne. With the help of Henry Holland, John Nash and other architects and landscapers, the site was transformed by 1822 into the Royal Pavilion, adopting the current fashion for Oriental exotica. George IV never returned to his pleasure dome after its completion. Where princes went, others followed. The Royal Crescent, the first set of buildings to comfort the sea, was begun in 1798. A population of 7,000 at the beginning of the nineteenth century grew tenfold in the next fifty years and that was before the coming of the railway in 1841 – the first resort to be so linked – made it so accessible to London.

The Steyne is the heart of Brighton. Others have copied it, at Worthing and Bognor, but with no great success. In spite of traffic and the somewhat faded beauty of the older buildings, it retains its air of Regency promenade. Marlborough House, the best survivor, is now an information centre and Mrs Fitzherbert's house has been translated into a YMCA. The Dome, the Royal Riding School and stables, completing the Pavilion Precinct, now house a concert hall, museum and art gallery. The town centre round the Market Place is completed by the Corn Exchange and the old Town Hall of 1832. The Old Town of 'twittens', better known as the Lanes, lies west of the Pavilion, a warren of small shops, cafés and pubs, bounded by North Street, East Street and West Street.

The greatest contrast with the Old Town is the extensive area to the east, elegant crescents and gardens designed by two young architects, Amon Wilds and Charles Busby. The builder was Thomas Cubitt and the instigator and owner of the land, Thomas Kemp, one of the Lords of the Manor. Kemp Town was a speculative development on the grand scale, still largely intact though the houses of the wealthy have mostly been subdivided into apartments. Built in the 1820s, Kemp Town was well established before the railway opened up a new era of growth north and west of the Old Town and brought in a new clientele, the mass migration of Londoners that was to give the town its soubriquet of London-by-the-Sea. Cobbett had already written witheringly of the city men scurrying up and down the turnpikes from the Great Wen. The railway brought thousands where the coaches brought dozens to the smaller hotels, the terraced rows and the red-brick villas, the guest houses. Although the Royal Albion Hotel was built in 1828, the great sea-front hotels like the Grand and the Metropolitan date from the second half of the nineteenth century, the classic statement of 'sea-view'. Yet even Brighton seems unsure of itself. The most imposing architectural statement for the shoreline is now a major conference hall. Flats for sale and 'prestige offices' stand cheek by jowl with hotels and souvenir shops. By the Black Rocks a mammoth development of marina and a miniature sea-town are emerging.

Inland, the suburbs have curled round the Iron Age camp at Hollingbury and the race-course to engulf the quietude of Stanmer Park and produce a new

53. *Nineteenth-century town planning – the parades, squares and crescents of Kemp Town. The new suburbs of Brighton curl over the downland slopes to the north.*

university campus. The largest population centre in Sussex with 170,000 people, Brighton is all things to all men. And there are still a few fishing boats slouched on the shingle. In spite of two piers with which nobody knows what to do, Brighton is cheerful. Its stylish combination of Cockney energy and Sussex breeze is a tonic. It has some odd variants. To the east, Rhodean stands in majestic isolation before the dip into the older fashioned delights of Rottingdean in its valley. Then the coast road climbs to the bungalow paradise of Peacehaven perched suicidally on the cliff's edge, someone's dream of the common man's answer to the palaces of princes.

Westwards stands Hove, still trying to be aloof, where the later works of the Kemp Town architects met up with Decimus Burton. The promenade fades into pitch and putt and bathing huts and a sudden confrontation with Portslade power station, visible from almost every vantage point on the South Downs. Then it is all wharfs and quays and cranes and coastal shipping laden with cement and sand and lime and timber and oil lining the 7-kilometre haven of the River Adur, carrying a shipping tonnage nearly as great as that of Dover.

Amongst all this industry, the discovery of two superb Norman churches in close proximity is a major surprise. St Mary de Haura (of the haven) at New Shoreham and St Nicholas at Old Shoreham mark two distinct stages in the medieval growth of the old port; around the former a planned town of straight streets, around the latter the core of the original settlement at the mouth of the River Ardur. Even by the eleventh century, about 780 acres of land had gone under the sea and a new town was needed. The shingle spit continued to grow eastwards and almost made a complete bar by the eighteenth century. The solution in 1760 was to make an artificial gap in the shingle which is still the main entrance but it needs constant dredging. The growing trade of the harbour has put an intolerable strain on the roads inland, especially through Steyning and Bramber, which were, in their turn, early medieval ports. An unusual survival in Shoreham is the 1781 wooden bridge, due for replacement soon.

Between the Adur and the Arun the pattern repeats itself in a minor key, Worthing in the place of Brighton, Littlehampton in the place of Shoreham. Brighton had the prince, Worthing had the princess. Amelia arrived in 1798, guarded by 120 men of the Derbyshire militia fresh from Clapham Common. The town soon had its bathing machines and esplanade and its Steyne in 1807. The first six streets laid out between 1802 and 1805 were 'occupied by persons of the first-rate fashion and fortune in England'.* Amon Wilds of Brighton did some work here at Park Crescent. Most of Old Worthing is in the two parallel streets, the High Street and Chapel Road which run north-south towards the sea. The High Street is rather down-at-heel now and Chapel Road, which was not built over until the 1870s, now has all the attention. The museum and library there will tell the visitor more about the origins of Worthing than the present townscape. Where Chapel Road meets Montague Street is the focus of the town and the site of two new experiments. The Guildbourne Centre, opened

* J. D. Parry, op. cit.

in 1974, replete with indoor flower beds and water fountains, incorporates a bell from the old 1834 town hall and combines bright new shops with offices above. But even more successful is the closing of a long length of the shopping area of Montague Street to traffic. Just narrow enough to make people think they can walk down the middle of it, the street seems cosier and friendlier than the long Marine and West Parades on the sea-front. It is as if people emerge from the close confines of the town to make a short dash along the front to remind themselves of its beneficial breezes and then, for most of the year at least, hurry back into shelter. Worthing, however, boasts of its winter sunshine rate, a fact that is supported by the market garden industry that flourishes round its inland suburbs, much favoured by retired people. According to Worthing's archives, many people used to work in Brighton but chose to live in Worthing, a nice point in their mutual debate. It is not a place where you expect the smell of real fish but, like Brighton, it has its quota of inshore craft hauled up on the beach by the pier, selling the daily catch from the boats.

Grown so mightily, Worthing has swallowed up many villages with names as Saxon as its own – Goring, Tarring, Salvington, Durrington and Ferring. Lancing and Sompting are well within its growing orbit. Each village is marked by a church and a clutch of flint cottages and sometimes by a distinctive village centre as with the green at Angmering. They are the sweet currants in an otherwise unremarkable bun. The outskirts of Worthing have now reached Findon, the site of the age-old annual sheep fair. The rest of the coast is villa and semi-detached and bungalow determined to enjoy the 10-kilometre long beach and its gently shelving sands uncovered by a tide that can ebb more than a kilometre. 'Pleasant and sociable,' said Parry in the 1830s and Worthing still is, though each of its villages quietly claims to be the 'best' place. One lady assured me that Goring was 'much superior' and I am ready to agree if only for the lovely avenue of holm oaks that remains from the previous parkland landscape.

After the suburban anonymity of Worthing's outposts, Littlehampton is a relief. The lighthouse by the harbour mouth is matched with the Kursaal and the funfair, minor intrusions on the open space that sets the hotel front well back from the sea. Pleasure craft mix with the small cargo vessels but the tiny museum in the town has reminders of greater days when a packet boat plied to the Continent and sailing vessels traded with the West Indies. It even boasted of its canal links with London, being the southern terminal of the Arun–Wey Navigation. Littlehampton once had the prospect of a neighbouring town to be called Hothampton. But Sir John Hotham's schemes for developing his newly purchased estates at Bognor never matched his intentions. A London merchant, he saw the potential but his main contribution to the present landscape is Hotham Park and the unusually fine house he built in the 1780s, now boarded up, but a deserving candidate for restoration. His seaside retreat is now confronted by Butlinland, a large holiday complex designed by the founder himself in 1960. The ice-house that once stood within Sir John's grounds is now restored and stands at the main road entry to the town by the modern library, an imaginative touch. The best of Bognor as a resort lies a kilometre to the west of Hotham's town by Waterloo Place and the Steyne. The very names announce the period. The big hotels like the Royal Norfolk and the Carlton are grand enough to give the town its royal adjective but the 'regis' was not added until 1929, following the convalescence of King George V. As with Worthing, it is the shopping streets behind the sea-front that show most evidence of rebuilding and development and, like its greater rivals, it is a natural focus of an extensive area of the coast. Amongst the villages within its growth is Bersted, the original core from which it grew. Felpham, yet another of the pleasant flinty villages which gives the area variety, deserves fame if only for the residence of William Blake at the time when he was charged with sedition. His cottage, quite close to the sea, is a private residence. Beyond Felpham lie Middleton and Elmer, with yacht clubs and ever-increasing notices announcing the privacy of the area, making access to the shore difficult. The sea ignores such privacy and each year makes further inroads, removing large chunks of concrete and barbed wire, a sure winner in the battle of the beaches. It has time on its side.

The greatest success in the creation of a new resort town from a private estate was that of Eastbourne, one of the last to develop. In thirty years, from the coming of the railway in 1849, the seventh Duke of Devonshire created the Empress of watering places. His predecessors at Compton Place had eschewed the new developing fever and left the small villages of East and South Bourne comparatively untouched. A small hamlet had grown by the shore at Seahouses. From these three nuclei of stone and flint houses, which survive in the present town, an elegant Victorian town was laid out. Terminus Road in 1850 was followed by Grand Parade in 1851 with grand hotels such as the Burlington and the Claremont. The statues of the ducal family stud the gardens; the streets and hotels bear the family names, Devonshire Place, Cavendish Place, the Chatsworth Hotel.

Neatly poised between the Downs and the Pevensey levels, the town has a subtle gradient of status and style from the upper slopes at the west end to the new housing estates and light industrial estate on the low ground to the east. Between them lies one of the most pleasant towns in the region. The inland focus is still the railway station with the 1884 town hall nearby but a fair collection of pre-Victorian buildings remains around St Mary's church, centre of the old village – Norman church, medieval parsonage, timber-framed inns and an eighteenth-century manor house, now the Art Gallery.

Bexhill had a theatre and a circulating library, two of the essentials for a watering place, as early as 1830 but it really emerged from its village status only in the 1880s with the determined activity of its major landowners, the De La Warrs, although it never achieved the eminence of character of its earlier rivals. Furthest west, beyond Bognor, the bungalows and the caravans tread gingerly along the shingle towards Pagham Harbour and the Nature Reserve. The yachting caps which are a badge of honour throughout the south-east – even into Surrey, for they are as prominent along the Thames reaches at Chertsey as they are in Rye Harbour – make a final and impressive flurry around the Selsey Peninsula. For the most part, it remains a coastline of small villages on muddy creeks with yachts at rakish angles; West Wittering, Birdham, Itchenor, Bosham, Chidham and the packed pleasure fleet in Chichester Yacht Basin, once terminal of the Chichester–Arun canal. There is the usual non-descript development along the south shore, especially at East Wittering, but Selsey at least has a great past to recall. The origins of the present settlement lie partly to the north round the isolated church of Church Norton but mostly far to the south under the sea where the Romans first landed and the first Saxon bishops established their see. The sand dunes at East Head at the furthermost corner of the region are a good place to roam. There are moments there when you are aware of nothing more than sea and sky and sand and mud flats and sea birds. This is what the coast once was. Operation Neptune came a little late in the history of the south-east. The coast now is the most striking statement of what man will make of the natural world, with all his faults and virtues. It all depends which you prefer, Dreamland or Pagham Harbour.

In spite of the delights of fresh Dover sole, the fishing fleets of the south-east ports make a minor contribution to the total British catch, yet ten of the ports appear in the official statements. Eight of them are old Cinque Ports or their confederates – Dover, Hythe, Hastings, Folkestone, Ramsgate, Newhaven and Shoreham. Two 'newcomers' to the list are Eastbourne and Dungeness. The tenth, Whitstable, is the only one from the North Kent coast, famous since Roman times for its oysters though overfishing and pollution have caused a temporary setback to this succulent trade.

Whitstable began life as an outpost of Canterbury, an early link that was strengthened by one of the first railways in England, in 1830. Stephenson's pioneer steam engine, the Invicta, which ran on the line, is kept in trim condition in the Dane John Gardens within the walls of Canterbury, although the line is no more. Whitstable has been curtly dismissed by recent topographers, yet quite apart from the weather-boarded cottages and old net houses of Island Wall and Middle Wall and the beach, the High Street curling between comfortable, unpretentious shops and houses is as pleasant as most towns can boast. It has no outstanding individual building but the whole alignment is singularly free from modern despoiliation and well worth the efforts being made now to have it made into a conservation area with traffic excluded. The narrow alleys of the old port are matched with the prim red villas of the late Victorian period. Nothing startling but it is a real place, a centre in its own right with two later resort 'wings' of Tankerton and Seasalter. Seasalter is an ancient, honourable name but it has no visual reminder of its past. Herne Bay developed at the same time as the Canterbury railway, its new town being planned by a Canterbury speculator with the inevitable pier, Hanover Square, assembly rooms (now the Pier Hotel), promenade and simple grid of roads, focusing on a clock tower of 1837. Clock towers, like town halls, are a constant theme reflecting periods of civic pride. The earliest part of the town was the village of Herne more than a mile inland, a long walk to Sunday service from the bay town that led to vigorous protest and the erection of new churches.

By far the greatest port of the region, in terms of cargo tonnage, is the Medway. The name as it now appears in the shipping manuals is a reflection of the visual amalgamation of the towns and ports grouped round the estuary – Rochester, Chatham, Strood, Gillingham, Grain and Sheerness – creating an annual turn round of twenty-seven million tonnes of shipping that puts it in the same league as Liverpool and Southampton, although twenty-two million tonnes are of oil. The modern port dates from the founding of the Royal Dockyard in 1546. This was the third of Henry VIII's docks, the first two being at Deptford and Woolwich, close to his palace at Greenwich. The two latter closed in 1869, though both still bear ample signs of their maritime past. Chatham's rise to pre-eminence was obvious even to contemporaries. 'No Towns, nor Citie is there (I dare say), in this whole Shire, comparable in right value with this one Fleete,' wrote William Lambarde, a traveller with an affection for ports, for he had founded almshouses at Greenwich and owned an estate near by.

There was already another castle nearer the meandering mouth at Queensborough on the Isle of Sheppey, a borough since the reign of Edward III. To the north of the borough, Charles II developed a new dock on the swamps of Sheerness. Samuel Pepys walked there with the King, 'laying out the ground for a yard to lay provisions for cleaning and repairing of ships and a most proper place it is for the purpose'. The forts and docks did not prevent the Dutch fleet attacking in 1667 and occupying Sheppey for eleven days. Queensborough raised the flag of surrender, acknowledging the last occupation of English soil until the Germans overran the Channel Islands in 1940.

From small beginnings, Chatham dockyard grew to cover 200 hectares with 2 km of docks. Many of the present buildings date from the same period as the main gate built in 1720. The Admiral's House, the Officer's Terrace and other administrative buildings bear the same architectural stamp as the better known Royal Naval Hospital at Greenwich. Later came the warehouses, stores, ropery, tarring house, bell mast and hemp store and the slips for shipbuilding and repair, all names tanged with the smell of sailing days. The dockyard, in spite of its use until the present day, is a period piece, symbolizing the defence of the continental angle and the narrow approaches to London.

Gillingham became the residential area for 'dockyard persons', only the church and the green remaining from its village origins. The nineteenth-century spread of industry, lime and cement and engineering and, more recently, oil-refining at Grain has overlaid the old marine industries with a new industrial pall, blanketing Rochester's castle, Strood's house of the Knights' Templar and Gillingham's green. Under it lies the largest concentration of population outside the Greater London area. But there are older delights to discover. Queensborough's evocative High Street has a superb fourteenth-century church and a Guildhall of 1728 befitting its borough status. The yacht-lined creek parallel with the High Street stands cheek-by-jowl with steel works and chemicals and glass works, and the Victorian days when packet steamers plied to the continent seem far away.

The townscape of Sheerness, though faded and depressing by the headland, has an extraordinary development revealed by its localities known as the Blue Town, the Mile Town and the Marine Town. Blue Town, for example, is said to have gained its name from the blue paint stolen from Naval stores to paint local houses. An aquatic town grew up on abandoned hulks that was only swept away by the Grand Alleys built in 1794 and the new dockyard built by Sir John Rennie after 1813. It might so easily have become the main dockyard for the Royal Navy but floods and gales and its generally exposed site gave Chatham the advantage.*

The first sight of Sheerness for railway travellers is a sign saying Welcome to Sheerness and doing so with funfair and bingo. The unwarlike face of its leisure

* H. Harbour, *Sheerness and the Isle of Sheppey* (Warne, 1897).

shores was due to the Sheppey Light Railway in 1901. Bungalows and caravan sites cover the north shore, especially at Warden and Leysdown. The soft cliffs cut out of London Clay have a habit of disappearing into the hungry sea at regular intervals, taking many a happy holiday home to become a sea wreck. Sheppey was the scene of another dramatic venture in travel for the pioneers of aviation used Eastchurch aerodrome for their first testing flights – Moore-Brabazon, a circular flight of one mile, Charles Rolls, two miles. They are all commemorated together with bas-reliefs of their biplanes and triplanes in the village centre.

The smaller inlets on the Swale estuary sheltered by Sheppey reached inland as far as the main Roman highway of Watling Street and there at the junction of tidal water and land route the ports of Milton Regis and Faversham developed. Milton, once a royal manor, deserves a better fate than its present faded self suggests. Overtaken and submerged by the growth of Sittingbourne, it has lost its role. The narrow High Street winds up to an open space with Court Hall of the fifteenth century slap in the middle of it, a more interesting building than anything its larger neighbour has to show. Sittingbourne is remarkable mainly by its sheer length, stretching seemingly endlessly along the A2, a scattering of eighteenth- and nineteenth-century houses and hotels being lost beneath new shopping façades. But Sittingbourne has the business and a bright new central precinct; Milton has only its memories.

Ask a group of Kentish people for the best town in their county and the majority will plump for Canterbury. More than one voice will be raised for Tunbridge Wells. But after a little hesitation, someone will mention Faversham. Situated midway between Sittingbourne and Canterbury, it is one of the most interesting towns in the whole region, combining the bustle of a busy market town with as varied and fine a collection of buildings as a visitor could wish. It smells of hops and fruit and corn and the sea. Its structure is simple enough, a basic cross of streets with a small but delightfully compact market square at the centre dominated by the Town Hall-cum-market hall, built in 1604, enlarged and capped with a handsome cupola in 1819, two dates reflecting two main periods of prosperity. West Street and East Street lead direct from the market-place. To the north runs the axis of Court Street and Abbey Street parallel with the creek that was the lifeblood of the place. To the south, Preston Street leads straight to the railway station and the A2 which was turnpiked before 1750. East Street has its share of Tudor timber-framed jetty houses, of seventeenth-century ornamentation and plasterwork, of eighteenth-century elegance and nineteenth-century solidity. Edward Jacob's classic history written in 1774 was of the Town and Port of Faversham, reminding the inhabitants of their antiquity as the King's Port, a limb of the Cinque Port of Dover, with its early privileges confirmed by charter in 1252 and many times since. It supplied ship-service and goods such as gunpowder to the Crown. One of the gunpowder mills, more than two hundred years old, has been preserved by local enthusiasts in a housing estate on the west side of the creek. The oyster fisheries are recalled only by faded notices on the Swale bank and the days of the hoys carrying corn to London are recollected in the seventeenth-century warehouses down by Standard Quay. The mouth of the creek and the jetty at Oare are lined with rotting hulks from the sailing era. The other source of the town's greatness, its Cluniac Abbey, lies underground. Abbey Street, unusually broad, and tastefully restored in the last decade, stands comparison with North Street in Chichester and Mermaid Street in Rye. The outstanding house in it is the Tudor house of Thomas Arden, whose murder was the plot of an Elizabethan play. On a footpath at the back of the old abbey precinct is the Elizabethan Grammar School, now used as a public hall. West Street leads down to the creek in a gentle curve, giving an excitingly gradual revelation of its old buildings, like the Ship Inn. An outstanding medieval building, the Fleur-de-Lys, stands in Preston Street, headquarters of the active Faversham Society and one of the first Heritage Centres in England. Not the least triumph of Faversham's skyline is the spire of the parish church rising above the shops and the industry. Perhaps Sittingbourne would have been as well preserved as Faversham had the A2 not cut straight through its heart. Faversham lies to the north of the road, mercifully by-passed.

Upriver from the Medway the ports are found, not on tidal creeks but on the headlands where the chalk country bows out to meet the Thames, creating dry-points between the otherwise marshy flood plain. Each chalk bluff has its hythe – Gravesend, Greenhithe, Erith – and each settlement holds some of its early character intact beneath the industrial spread of the last two centuries. Gravesend, especially, has a history rich enough to match its surviving Georgian elegance. It lays some claim to be the first watering place, earlier even than Brighton or Margate. It has all the ingredients associated with better known resorts – piers, prom, planned Georgian town and a nineteenth-century fort. Its medieval hythe, recorded in Domesday, was a main ferry link with London, the long ferry avoiding the dangerous roads over Blackheath and Shooter's Hill. It was a royal route and Henry VIII's fort at Tilbury was built for the protection of shipping at the narrowing of the estuary. An unusual link with the Jacobean adventurers is the statue in the churchyard of St George's of Pocahontas, the Indian princess who died in England in 1617.

The great days of Gravesend came after the fire of 1727. St George's was rebuilt in brick and tall, four-storeyed houses lined the riverside. A few remain at the foot of the High Street but look to be in danger of demolition. The Customs House was built in 1815, the Town Hall by Amon Wild in 1836. Between those dates the new packet station and watering place grew up with theatre, sunken gardens (in a disused chalk quarry) and baths, hence Bath Street and Rosherville Gardens, the latter name the very epitome of a London resort. Harmer Street, Berkeley Crescent and the Grove retain their stately air, while the clock tower in the town centre, built in 1887, makes the final punctuation mark, the end of an era. The East Terrace followed the line of the old river cliff, overlooking the moated Fort Gordon, now set in a park and informatively labelled by the Kent Research Group. The basin of the Old Higham Canal which linked, albeit briefly, with the Medway in 1845, is now occupied by yachts, though the industrial area spreads beyond it.

A ferry link runs across the river to Tilbury Docks. Gravesend shares some of the activity of this major part of the Port of London dock series, being the centre of the Thames Navigation Service, supplying tugs and pilots for the big craft. At the very time that the Georgian town was being built, the seeds were being sown of the new industrial landscape that was to transform the whole of Thameside. In 1824, a brick-layer from Leeds took out a patent to make Portland cement near Gravesend. The close proximity of the chalk of the North Downs to tidal water made the area ideal for the production of one of today's major construction materials. The works at Northfleet just to the west of Gravesend is one of the largest in the world. Everything at Northfleet is on a grand scale, including the power station pylons. It also claims to have had the first electric tramway in the world. This is one of the most scarred landscapes in Britain, great pits and the overall blanket of chalk dust creating a moon landscape. Housewives watch the wind direction before doing any washing in these parts. Some of the quarries are so big that industrial plant has been sited in disused workings.

The twin landscape of port and resort is carried far inland along the Surrey bank by the highway of the Thames, even beyond tidal water at Teddington. Part of the Tudor dockyard at Greenwich was in the old administrative county of Surrey and the largest of the docks on the south bank was the Surrey Dock built in 1804 and linked with Croydon by the Surrey Canal. The warehouses of Bermondsey and Southwark are the inheritors of the medieval quays of Bermondsey Priory and the Bishop of Winchester's Palace near St Mary-Ovarie (now Southwark Cathedral). Lambeth was literally Lamb hythe. The royal barges not only linked Westminster with Greenwich and Gravesend but upstream with Richmond and Hampton. Most of the riverine settlements, like Kingston-upon-Thames, Walton and Chertsey used the river for goods and passenger traffic and, at Weybridge, the Thames Navigation was joined by the Arun–Wey canal which completed the sailing circuit by way of Guildford to Arundel and Littlehampton. Volunteers are clearing sections of this trans-Weald canal but I doubt if a small craft will ever again be able to leave London and do a full circuit of the south-east region, though the idea is very appealing. Schemes were laid in the early nineteenth century to link the Royal Military Canal to the Medway but that, too, proved abortive. For the moment, the land routes hold sway and the decline of coastal traffic continues. But the small ports are all there waiting for the historic pendulum to swing, ready to don their historically glorious maritime gear in place of the leisure-time habit. Perhaps the infestation of juggernaut lorries tearing the interior roads and settlements apart may hasten the day and the sea-lanes come into their own again.

10

The Pleasuring of London

Pleasure for the citizens of London has long been associated with the Surrey side of the Thames. Strolling through Vauxhall Gardens, doing a play at the Globe, baiting bears, drinking in the ale houses of Southwark, wandering through the murky alleys by the Bishop of Winchester's palace, the people sought their pleasure on the South Bank, beyond the city's walls.

A useful excuse for diversion was added in the seventeenth century by the discovery of spring waters with alleged medicinal properties in several sites to the south. In some cases, it was really a rediscovery, for holy wells had been an attraction in the medieval pursuit of health and advantage. St Blaise's at Bromley, St Edith's at Kemsing, the Lady Well at Lewisham, Our Lady of Boulogne at Carshalton, all had their pilgrims. The Bermondsey spa was almost certainly the site of a holy well which achieved new fame. A well at Lambeth rose to the grandeur of St George's Spa. But it was the more distant spas that gave the hills and open country of Surrey a new attraction and led to villages such as Streatham, Camberwell, Norwood, Dulwich and Sydenham achieving a reputation for health and pleasure that was to make them favoured areas of residence a century later.

John Evelyn, from his estate at Deptford, took the waters at Westwood on the hills dividing Kent and Surrey and remarked on the local gipsies camped on the common. George III visited the same spot, closely guarded by his soldiery. Pepys drank the waters at Shooters Hill, which were still in use in the late nineteenth century. Camberwell was reputedly rich in iron and Dr Johnson was a frequenter of the Streatham Spa which had crowned its discovery in 1659 with an assembly room and concerts to divert the health-seekers. Beulah, up on the fringe of the North Wood, in the same vicinity as Dulwich and Sydenham, was a late-comer to the pleasure scene, in 1831, but had Decimus Burton to design the pump room, the assembly room and hotels. Richmond began in 1696 and endured until the 1870s with the usual attractions of card-rooms and leafy promenades where anyone who was anyone could be seen and heard.

The most important discoveries of spa water that were to change the landscape of the south-east were on the chalk downs at Epsom in 1618 and in the Wealden sandstones of Rusthall Common, the future Tunbridge Wells, a decade earlier. An Epsom farmer declared that his cattle would not drink the stuff but the salts in the water soon attracted a daily post from London. Whether it was the quality of the water or the fresh Downland air that worked the cure for over-indulgence was never certain. The well that made Epsom famous is railed off, adorned with a plaque and preserved inconspicuously in a housing estate at Woodlands Road on the common. Barbara Villiers, having been given the Royal palace of None-such by Charles II, sold the building, stone by stone, to building speculators at Epsom. Many of the great houses such as Durdans are built of stone, therefore, that was first quarried for the medieval priory of Shene. The buildings come and go; the stone endures. 'Epsom thus became one of the first residential towns in England, developed for the benefit of the rich merchants of the new commercial age, who had become sufficiently prosperous to be able to afford two houses, one in the city and one in the country.'* Thus was established a pattern of the good life that was to affect the landscape of the whole region as the necessary affluence was achieved by more and more people. A new well at Epsom and a new town were laid out in 1754. The well failed but the town flourished, for amongst the many diversions of the spa were wrestling, foot-races and horse-racing on the common lands of Epsom and Walton. Following the example of the St Leger at Doncaster, the Earl of Derby established two new classic races on the Epsom track in 1779, the Oaks and the Derby. Thousands flock to the course for the races, the people's races, for the land is still common, criss-crossed by footpaths. The villas of the rich and not-so-rich dot the hillslopes below the common and the riders try their paces on the chalk turf but the commonalty fly kites, eat ice-creams, take picnics and enjoy the breezy air until the day of the annual flutter.

Tunbridge Wells, too, had its common and its race-course on the waste lands of Rusthall Manor. Perhaps because it was further afield, the spa at Tunbridge took a more sedate, even regal path. Lord North, riding in the country near Lord

* Nairn and Pevsner, *Surrey*.

Abergavenny's house at Eridge in Sussex, found a spring with a deposit of salts that gleamed, reminding him of similar spa water he had seen in Belgium. The water source was railed off, the area paved and the booths set up. As with the seaside resorts later, it was a royal visit that finally gave the spa its esteem and popularity; in this case, Henrietta, after the birth of the future Charles II, in 1630. Other queens followed, Catherine of Braganza and Anne. The promenade, now the Pantiles, was tiled, trees were planted, the temporary booths and tents became permanent shops. The Cromwellians, keeping an eye on royalist sympathizers, added the austerity of names like Mount Ephraim and Mount Sion to the surrounding hills but the wells went on their diverting ways, recalled now in the local museum, packed with theatre bills, Tunbridge Ware and other crafts that flourished to cater for the visitors. Beau Nash was enticed from Bath and remained for years as Master of Ceremonies. Royal Tunbridge Wells was already the wealthiest residential town in the country when Decimus Burton designed the Calverley Estate of elegant villas near the Pantiles. Despite the railway's arrival in 1845 and the extension of the town to the north, it has never lost its reputation as a superior residential area and its shopping facilities attract people even from its rival market towns. The wild, open spaces with rocky outcrops encroach into the heart of the town, just the right counterpoint to the rows of hotels, fine houses and offices that line the common.

The new fashion for sea water, both to drink and to bathe in, saw the decline of the inland spas. All roads led to Brighton and Worthing and Margate. But both Epsom and Tunbridge Wells slipped easily into their new residential roles, linked with London by train and road, a role that other towns such as Crowborough, with no spa to boast, could also adopt. As we have seen, it was the taste for Highland scenery, with the Victorian adoption of Balmoral, that gave the Weald its final flourish. The sandstone hills, clad in Scots pine, a favourite tree for Victorian planting, gave land agents a new advertisement, Scotland in Sussex, Scotland in Surrey. Burton built more villas, George Devey rebuilt estates and lodge cottages, as at Penshurst and Leigh, with a medieval flavour. Alfred Lord Tennyson moved to the wooded hills of Blackdown, and Ruskin could still find 'open fields animate with cow and buttercup'* at Dulwich when he walked the still-forested ridge from Herne Hill, much closer to London. The spoilation, for Ruskin, started with the new Crystal Palace, transferred to Penge Common in the 1850s, attracting a 'flood of pedestrians' down his sylvan tracks 'who left it filthy with cigar ashes'. The multitude was on the march.

* J. Ruskin, *Praetorita* (1899).

'The Great Exhibition could not have occurred before the Railway Age, at least on so large a scale and with such spectacular success.'* Six million people, nearly a third of the population, visited the exhibition on the Surrey hills, including '800 agricultural labourers in their peasant attire from Surrey and Sussex'. The new age of science and industry, glorified by the exhibition, was soon to consign the peasants and their attire to the museum and the history book. The railway was the catalyst. The official catalogue of the Exhibition noted the

54. *Victorian restoration by George Devey at Hall Place, Leigh.*

similarity between the Crystal Palace and the engineering structure of a railway station. Just as the stage-coaches were breaking new records along the turnpikes, the new competitor was showing its paces. The first horse-drawn public railway, the Surrey Iron Railway, linked Wandsworth with Croydon in 1803 and was extended to Merstham two years later. Whitstable was joined to Canterbury in a pioneer venture. More significant in its future effects was the London-to-Greenwich railway that strode on viaducts across the flood plains of South London to the Royal Dockyard at Deptford and Greenwich Park. Greenwich,

* H. Perkin, *The Age of the Railway* (David & Charles, 1970).

like Richmond upstream, was already linked with the city by steamer, but it was the railway that effectively annexed North-West Kent as a new suburb for clerks and tradesmen, the beginning of a process that was to culminate more than a century later with the electrification of the line right to Folkestone. By 1841, the railway tentacles had reached Brighton with a journey time of two-and-a-half hours, compared with six hours needed by the horse-drawn coaches. Sir Rowland

55. *Stephenson's locomotive 'Invicta', used on Whitstable line, now in Dane Park, Canterbury.*

Hill, of Penny Post fame, as chairman of the London, Brighton and South Coast Railway, introduced cheap excursion fares as early as 1843. In the same decade, the river steamers that had plied to Gravesend and Thanet (105,000 passengers in 1835) were subject to the same competition, faster, safer and more comfortable. The steamers faded away very gently. One of my fondest memories of boyhood was the steamer from Greenwich Pier down the estuary. My fascination then was for the gleaming machinery that churned us on our happy way to some distant pier, ice-creams and a day in the sun.

By 1851, the year of the Great Exhibition, the basic network of railways was established – London to the south coast, a coastal route from Chichester up to Ramsgate; London to Dover by way of a cross-country route, the Mid-Kent line, linking Redhill, Tonbridge and the new railway town of Ashford, using the low ground of the clay vales. The new terminus at Waterloo opened in 1848 to link Surrey with the metropolis. In the sixties, Victoria started with excursions to Crystal Palace and beyond, followed by Charing Cross and Cannon Street in the same decade. Finally, the London, Chatham and Dover railway crossed the North Kent plain.

Many towns on the main lines such as Ashford, Tonbridge, Folkestone and Sittingbourne, doubled their populations in the twenty years following the opening of the railway. A halo of Victorian building grew round the old market centres. The towns close to London, such as Erith, Beckenham, Bromley and Croydon, were especially affected.

The railway companies sought their trade not only in day excursionists but in the new commuters, London workers who had the aspiration and affluence to live in the cleaner air beyond the city. The companies negotiated with individual landowners, like Albemarle Cator of Beckenham. When the railway came in 1857, with the promise of new villas and new passengers, it was on the understanding that there would be no Sunday trains, for otherwise the place would be 'inundated by trippers coming down from London'. Beckenham wanted to preserve its quality. One of London's Lord Mayors had lived there travelling daily to the city by coach. But Beckenham, like Brighton, more than doubled its population in the next fifty years.

The *Railway Times* of 1850 listed 'salubrious sites' that were all within a half hour of the city, such as Banstead and Epsom, Reigate and Northfleet. Entirely new towns, essentially dormitory in their function, grew up, such as Haywards Heath and Burgess Hill. It was not only the modern holiday that was the product of the railway age; it was the whole pattern of nineteenth-century settlement and even its style. The railways brought mass-produced bricks for the use of the speculative builder and the open spaces fell before the red rash. The visual effect can be traced on a map by following the railway from Wimbledon on its straight course to Surbiton, Esher, Weybridge, Byfleet and Woking, an iron line flanked by an almost continuous built-up area with only five km of open space before reaching Guildford. From Croydon another route via Epsom, Leatherhead and Horsley approaches the county town like a second pincer. All the land between was brought under pressure in turn by the new mobility of the motor car.

'Like Southern California, Surrey is entirely directed to serving urban man – the Green Belt as much as anywhere else.'* Surrey, so long the Cinderella of the three counties in terms of population and commercial development, suddenly found its wild heaths and commons a new attraction instead of a negation. The piny smell of the miniature Highlands brought the clients and the architects. After making little contribution to the history of medieval architecture, Surrey became the proving ground for one Victorian architect after another, each reaching back in his own particular fashion to recreate for the delight of the newly rich, Regency, Italianate, Gothic, Tudor, Jacobean. Nowhere was this more noticeable than in the rash of new Gothic churches in the wake of Pugin, to cater for the rapidly growing population. The restorer's hand was more strongly laid on the medieval churches than was the case in Kent and Sussex. Pugin was a Ramsgate man and his concept that 'Gothic is Christian architecture' was realized in the church of St Augustine, built at his own expense, and in his own house, the Grange, built in 1844, as well as at Albury and other churches in Surrey.

The medieval spirit also animated William Morris and the pre-Raphaelites. Philip Webb was invited to design Morris's new house at Bexleyheath in 1859. At that time it stood in orchard country five kilometres from the nearest railway station at Abbey Wood. The Red House is now hemmed in by suburbs and its individuality is even more striking, conjuring up the romantic imagination so lacking in the surrounds. Webb soon followed his Kentish experiment in Surrey's spaces, building Fairmile at Cobham, Coneyhurst at Ewhurst, Hurlands near Puttenham and others. George Devey, whom we have seen at work at Penshurst, was more deeply imbued with local traditions and his most outstanding venture was the manor house for Lord Northbourne on the Betteshanger estate in Kent. It is now a school but the mullioned windows and Dutch gables can be seen from the Roman road that passes near by. Devey worked in Surrey, too, extending Durdans at Epsom and building villas such as Sendholme. The passion for villas spread, too, from the new resorts. C. A. Busby of Brighton produced *A Series of Designs for Villas and Country Houses adapted with Economy to the Comfort and Elegancies of Modern Life*, very much the theme for his contemporaries such as Amon Wilds and Decimus Burton. The same motifs were taken up in a modernistic style by Norman Shaw who, after designing a lodge gate at Kew, built a series of minor masterpieces in Surrey, as at Hopedene near Holmbury St Mary and the Onslow almshouses at Guildford.

* Nairn and Pevsner, *Surrey*.

The love of medieval restoration reached a climax at the end of the century with the work of Sir Edwin Landseer Lutyens, who was brought up on the Surrey heathland at Thursley. The restoration of the fifteenth-century mansion at Great Dixter in Sussex was one of his greatest works. Amongst his many new houses are Little Thakeham and Halnaker House (Sx), the latter a house of remarkably subdued delicacy fitting well alongside the ruins of the old castle. Lutyens was also concerned with the humblest of cottages and several of his designs figure in the *Country Life Book of Cottages* that appeared as a result of a competition in the early 1900s.

Cottages in abundance sprung up in the new towns like Burgess Hill which built over the commons and wastes of the Manor of Keynes after the enclosure of 1828. Haywards Heath followed in 1862. The visual effect alongside the older established village of Lindfield is striking. It is difficult not to prefer Lindfield. Yet these were called 'abodes of civilization' by contemporary builders. Crowborough on the highest land in the Weald, on the delectable edge of Ashdown Forest, extolled its clean air and grew rapidly with the energetic consent of its principal landowner, Lord Abergavenny. Only in recent years has the town achieved some sort of administrative centre, and the sense of a real place. Here, as elsewhere, the most important building is the railway station forecourt, packed with cars for the daily migration to London.

Common land was the main target for speculators, a landscape feature that seemed destined to pass into oblivion. The General Enclosures Acts of 1801 seemed to give Lords of the Manors the right of ownership under the Statute of Merton of 1235, to enclose the commons, either for building or for the extraction of gravel, sands, loam and other building materials. Those nearest London were in the greatest danger. The great forest of Northwood and Westwood, still recalled by the local names like Norwood and Westwood Hill, had been defended successfully by the local inhabitants against enclosure in the early seventeenth century. Opened up by the early spas, the hillslopes soon broke out in a rash of villas. Dr Maddox of Curzon Street wrote enthusiastically about the 'purity of atmosphere, natural facilities of drainage and charms of scenery'* near the new Crystal Palace and urged his clients to 'fly the rank city'. They did, and the common, enclosed in 1812, this time without popular outcry, was no more.

The railways saw the commons as convenient routeways out of London. Wayleave was negotiated with the manorial lord and Wandsworth, for example, was sliced up by the London and South-Western and by the London and

* Dr A. D. Maddox, *On Sydenham* (1860).

Brighton railways. The latter company also cut through Banstead Downs. The city merchants moved to gothicized villas at Norwood and Penge, Wimbledon and Beulah, Beckenham and Chislehurst. The clerks adopted New Cross and Clapham. Terraces were built near the stations for the railway workers.

As the commons were despoiled, so enlightened opinion was alarmed. 'They are natural parks over which everyone may roam freely,' wrote Lord Eversley. 'They are reservoirs of fresh air and health whence fresh breezes blow into the adjoining towns. They bring home to the poorest something of the sense and beauty of nature.'* By 1865, the Commons Preservation Society was formed, first of the conservation bodies that were the necessary antitheses to the urbanization of the south-east. In the years to follow, the Society fought expensive and prolonged legal actions against enclosing landlords. Plumstead and Bostall Heath were saved from Queen's College, Oxford, in 1871. What was left of Tooting Common was saved in 1870. Wimbledon, a 400-hectare waste belonging to four Surrey manors, was protected and put under the care of a board of Conservators. Dartford Heath was bought by the local authority in 1874, but the longest and most acrimonious battle was fought for a stretch of the North Downs at Coulsdon and Banstead. Coulsdon was eventually bought by the corporation of the City of London; Banstead, after sixteen years of lawsuits, during which time the landowners even stripped the turf to render the land barren, was finally saved. The Commons, Open Spaces and Footpaths Preservation Society is still active with its headquarters in London, for its work is not yet done. Orbital roads and by-passes threaten the spaces anew.

Many acres were bought up by the newly constituted London County Council and other local authorities. But this enlightenment was all due to the persistence and vision of people like Lord Eversley, Robert Hunter and Octavia Hill a hundred years ago.

One of the earliest members of the Commons Preservation Society, Octavia Hill was a pupil and friend of John Ruskin. They had walked together and enjoyed the wooded heights of Dulwich. During one of her many campaigns for the open spaces around London the idea of the National Trust was sown. It was a natural step for this dynamic woman to extend her horizons from the smaller spaces of working-class London, such as Deptford Park and Vauxhall, to the wider problem of the rural landscape. Amongst the first areas of land given to the National Trust, formed at the end of the nineteenth century, were parts of the greensand ridge near her new home at Crockham Hill in Kent. I

* Lord Eversley, *Commons, Forests and Footpaths* (Cassell, 1910).

make a regular pilgrimage from the stone seat bearing her name, at Ide Hill, to Toys Hill and Mariners Hill, all National Trust sites and all bearing physical witness to her vision. Toys Hill was, in her words, 'the first beautiful site in England given as a memorial'. Her grave at Crockham Hill is quite unremarkable. Her name appears under that of her sister, Miranda, in the shade of a yew tree, but inside the Victorian church is a more substantial tomb to her memory.

Another major threat to the Surrey commons came by chance from a surprising source, Queen Victoria. There is a large memorial on Chobham Common erected by eight thousand local parishioners to commemorate the Queen's review of her troops at the beginning of the Crimean War. The temporary encampment of the troops evolved into the permanent military establishment at Aldershot. The surrounding heathlands resound not only to names with a military ring but to the occasional sound of guns and rifles, Camberley, Pirbright, Bisley, Sandhurst and Farnborough create a military no-man's-land along the Surrey–Hampshire border, emphasized by constantly recurring signs of Danger Areas.

Whilst Surrey and North-West Kent were bearing the brunt of railway development and its associated residential growth, Sussex, apart from the major resorts, was comparatively unscathed. The isolation of the inland areas suited a different clientele. Nairn puts it succinctly: 'Sussex is a county of schools, colleges, convent schools and the houses of various orders, High Anglican and Roman Catholic.'* Ardingly, East Grinstead, Hurstpierpoint, Lancing, Roedean, Burwash, Wadhurst and Chailey all have their share of the solid though somewhat gloomy institutions in the Gothic style. There are light and lovely touches such as the Burne Jones windows in Rotherfield Church. The biggest single structure in this genre is St Bartholomew's in Brighton, 135 feet of solid brick.

What the trains began, the cheap, popular modes of suburban transport, the tram and the bus and the tube, extended. In the 1920s and 1930s there was an even greater loss of rural land in the vicinity of London. Large council estates of terraced houses with front and back gardens grew on the farming lands of Lewisham and Merton, followed by an enthusiastic rush of semi-detached houses and bungalows financed by building societies. They were all intended to create a better life for people moving out from the congested areas of the Victorian city. But they were great eaters of land. Garden suburbs of a superior kind with large detached houses and spacious gardens developed in Surrey, on the Wentworth Estate, Camberley, Woodcote, Camilla Lacey, Dormans Park and Whiteley Village. The houses were variants on the 'cottage' properties of rural England

* Nairn and Pevsner, *Sussex*.

designed by architects like William Clough-Ellis and Lutyens. Less expensive and more extensive property developments followed the opening of the tube to Morden in 1926.

Decentralization was increased by the new arterial roads and the light industrial estates liberated from traditional industrial areas by the new cheap electric power. The by-pass at Kingston in the 1930s, avoiding the congestion of the market town, cut through open land and attracted ribbon development. Each new road increased the potential catchment of London as an employment centre. The urbanization of the countryside followed the roads. Some of the commons may have been saved but farmland was under even greater pressure. The idea of a 'green girdle' of protected land surrounding London so as to preserve 'the fresh delights of the countryside' was conceived by Ebenezer Howard as early as 1902.*

The concept was not to be translated into reality for another half-century until Professor Abercrombie's plan for London, 1944, proposed a Green Belt about sixteen kilometres wide to contain the capital's growth. It was made effective by the Town and Country Planning Act of 1947. Recent legislation has increased the potential green belt, with its restrictions on building, to an extent of about forty-five kilometres, reaching the Medway to the east, virtually the whole of Surrey and West Kent down to the Sussex border. At least 8 per cent of the belt in Surrey is already covered by housing but agricultural land still covers about 70 per cent. In Kent, the figure is nearer 80 per cent. Despite restrictions, new building does take place and the Green Belt has been described as 'a blanket full of moth-holes'.† There is a large estate built by the Greater London Council, for example, by the village of Kemsing in Kent and government permission was given for the development of an entirely new 'village' at New Ash Green in Kent. It looks more like a mini New Town, with residential neighbourhoods and a two-storey shopping precinct in the middle. The architect-designed houses may look fine but the effect on the narrow lanes and the area generally has been savage. The wooded banks are bulldozed to make the passage of cars safer. The 'village' virtually coalesces with nearby Longfield and Hartley to make yet another sprawling suburb, about thirty kilometres from London's centre, an easy jaunt for motorists by way of the M2.

The concept of the New Town was launched in the same year as the Green Belt. Crawley, one of the first generation of such towns, established in 1947, has now 'grown up', with ten residential neighbourhoods, a new town centre, a

* E. Howard, *Garden Cities of Tomorrow* (1902; Faber, 1965).
† D. Thomas, *London's Green Belt* (Faber, 1970).

large industrial estate, a motorway by-pass and a mayor of its own. With 68,000 people, it has nearly reached its target population and is already one of the largest concentrations of population in the region, bigger by far than most of the older market towns. A new generation is growing up and they, too, will want houses of their own. With the siting of Gatwick, London's second airport, just to the north, the effect on the Wealden landscape has been immense. It is not just the 'noise-blanket' created by the aircraft but the demand for new warehousing facilities and commercial activities connected with this new inland port. Horley and all the surrounding villages are affected. The village of Worth with its superlative Saxon church is almost an anachronism in this brashest of urban landscapes. Tinsley Green in the same area persists with its famous marbles competition, with the jets screaming overhead.

Accepting the situation pragmatically, the new strategy for development in the south-east with the need to cater for an estimated addition of three million people envisages a corridor of growth along the main transport routes.* Crawley lies on one of the corridors created by the Brighton railway and the M23. The urban corridor from Croydon south to Reigate and Crawley is a visual fact. The Green Belt looks very pale in such circumstances.

Counter measures of conservation become even more important. Under the same Town and Country Planning Act of 1947, local authorities were urged to designate all rural land with Great Landscape Value. This was reinforced by the National Parks and Access to the Countryside Act of 1949. No National Park has been set up in the south-east but several areas have been designated as Areas of Outstanding Natural Beauty. Such areas in the south-east include more than 160 square miles of the Surrey Downland, almost all the chalk ridge of the North Downs from Dover to the Hampshire border and all of the South Downs. Parts of the Greensand Ridge are included, notably between Westerham and Ightham in Kent, including those areas saved earlier by Octavia Hill. The great arc of high greensand from Leith Hill in Surrey down to Hindhead and Blackdown is included. A lozenge of land in the High Weald, from Worth in Sussex eastwards to Tunbridge Wells and Goudhurst in Kent, is under consideration for similar status. Many of these areas are heavily wooded and woodland has an additional safeguard with tree preservation orders.

Yet another strand in the web of rural conservation was spun by the setting up of the Nature Conservancy in 1949, which had the duty of designating small areas of special interest to naturalists. They include Nature reserves and Sites of

* South-East Economic Planning Council, *A Strategy for the South-East* (HMSO, 1967).

Special Scientific Interest where public access may be limited by the need to conserve rare flora and fauna. The preservation may be more apparent than real when you see the housing estate at present devouring the fields right up to the edge of the heronry at High Halstow and the threat of another oil refinery on the marshland where the herons feed.

A significant change of attitude towards the rural landscape was expressed in the Countryside Bill of 1967. This launched the idea of the Countryside Park in which public access would be stimulated and controlled with parking sites, picnic areas, information centres and the like. Several small parks have been set up, as at Frensham Ponds in Surrey, the seven-hectare disused quarry at Dry Hill near Chevening and the Seven Sisters Park in East Sussex, where a great barn has been converted into an Interpretive Centre. Two well-established sites exist in West Sussex, the open-air museum of Wealden and Downland life at Singleton and the private venture in the Goodwood estate.

Frensham is already feeling the impact of over-use. The sandy tracks used by horses and walkers have been eroded with the possible loss of flora while the areas near the ponds, so popular with children, are becoming devoid of vegetation. The nature reserve on the chalk downs at Wye in Kent faces the same problem. The view and the steep slope of the Devil's Kneadingtrough attract hundreds of people and the initial purpose of preserving and restoring traditional downland flora is endangered. Disused pits of sand, gravel and lime, once a dangerous eyesore, are showing new potential for recreation. The Thorpe Countryside Water Park near Egham not only caters for angling, sailing and swimming but for water-skiing, with an arena of international status. A similar use is planned for a chain of lakes at Leybourne near the Medway.

The demands for leisure activities create new pressures on the limited land. Golf-courses alone occupy 2 per cent of green-belt land and they are being added to every year. Parks such as Lullingstone and High Elms have both been utilized by the local authority as golf-courses. Golf has a long pedigree in the region. It was introduced to Blackheath by James I from Scotland. The Royal Blackheath Club, now playing on what was once a royal park at Eltham, lays claim to be the oldest club in England. Golf-courses occupy some of the finest parkland landscapes in the region, such as Sundridge and Langley and Cobham where Repton worked. Three courses cover no less than ten km of the dunes and shingle ridges of the shore between Sandwich and Deal. Courses such as Wentworth are as much part of the Surrey landscape as the elegant villa. The mansion becomes the golf-house, the parkland vales are the fairways. The transformation has the merit of maintaining some of the visual beauty of the original landscape but golfers are sometimes intolerant of other's rights, especially walkers following ancient rights of way.

Cricket, another heavy user of land, can claim an even older lineage. The village greens and parks of the south-east were the first nurseries of the game, which was recorded at Guildford in the sixteenth century. A 'Kent' team played a 'Surrey' team as early as 1731. Lord Harris of Belmont is commemorated in Throwley church as much for his captaincy of England as for his empire-building. One set of the Ashes resides in Cobham Hall. For many years, the first match of the Australian tour was played in the grounds of Arundel. Lillywhite and Broadbridge introduced round-arm bowling in 1826 and the following year Sussex challenged an England team. One of the many historic 'fossils' is the Surrey County Cricket ground slap bang in the heart of London, at the Oval. Kent shares its splendours between the county ground in Mote Park, Maidstone and other towns such as Canterbury, Folkestone, Tunbridge Wells, with the occasional sally to the traditional home at Blackheath. Sussex, anchored more firmly at Hove, uses the aberrations of coastal mists and breezes to deceive its opponents but it also plays at Hastings, Eastbourne and Horsham. The effective home of tennis, too, is in the region, starting with the All-England Lawn Tennis Club at Wimbledon in the 1870s.

New avenues for countryside exploration and understanding are being developed in numerous nature trails. The Forestry Commission was one of the pioneers of the idea, trails being laid out in most of the Commission forests such as Bedgebury, Challock, Shipbourne and St Leonards in Sussex. Local authorities have laid out trails in much-used open spaces such as the downs at Banstead and Coulsdon in the Surrey Downs. Surrey is notable for the publicity the county gives its open spaces, publishing a map showing no less than 159 areas including 41 owned by the National Trust. They are mostly heaths and commons and they are all well signposted. Even this impressive number does not include the extensive spaces that were once in Surrey but now lie within the Greater London boundary such as Wimbledon Common, Richmond Park, Ham Common and Kew, spaces that give south-west London an unrivalled sense of openness and amenity. Many Londoners have more open space where they can walk at will than inhabitants of the high-farming areas.

Perhaps the most dramatic innovation in countryside access has been the opening of long-distance walkways, one of 150 kilometres along the crest of the South Downs and another potentially 225 kilometres long following the line of the North Downs, mostly using the traditional Pilgrims' Way but sometimes climbing to the old trackway on the ridge. The South Downs Way has the merit of linking many sites of antiquarian interest such as Cissbury and Chanctonbury Ring. In some stretches it is hemmed in by forest and high wire fences which detract from the intended sense of freedom and leisure and make the walker feel confined. Over half the North Downs Way is open, from Chevening eastwards to Dover, but it has lost some of the charm that Hilaire Belloc found when making his classic traverse of the Old Way. The stretch from Canterbury to Dover winds over the chalk plateau and is often impeded by plough, electric fencing and untended hedgerows.

56. *The North Downs Way above Godmersham.*

This is the story generally in the footpaths of the region. Some parishes I have surveyed have effectively lost half their paths. Landowners and farmers resent maintaining paths, fences, stiles and gates as an amenity for visitors who sometimes have little respect for the land and its produce. Footpaths on the whole have lost their original function in linking outlying farms and hamlets to the parish centre, in giving access to common grazing and in linking village with village. But they are amongst the oldest features of the landscape, showing man's colonization of the region, and are as much part of the historical record as church and manor. Most are medieval but some tracks have a pedigree at least as old as the Romans and the Iron Age people. Voluntary groups such as the Ramblers Association and the Youth Hostel Association walk the paths regularly and there are local parish committees that do sterling work but a path can be ruined as much by neglect as by deliberate obstruction. A new problem has arisen with the rapid growth of commercial stables and the number of horse-riders who do not confine their mounts to the bridlepaths.

Other great attractions for the leisure industry are the great houses and their grounds. The sites controlled by the Department of the Environment such as Dover Castle may receive more than a quarter of a million visitors in a year but even the private houses such as Hever, Knole, Petworth and Loseley have more than 50,000. Since its foundation in 1895, the National Trust has gained control of more than 132 sites in the south-east, many of them houses and gardens of major historical importance such as Uppark, Petworth, Slindon, Wakehurst, Sheffield, Sissinghurst, Nymans, East Clandon, Scotney and Knole. They are major targets for the pleasuring of London. Their attractions are a commercial proposition. Many private owners are developing their estates as at Goodwood as private countryside parks. Wild animals at Bekesbourne, Spanish imperial eagles at Chilham, farm visits at Hever, all help to gain revenue to keep the estates viable. But many of the mansions have become schools or are sub-divided as private flats as at Waldeshare, Oxenhoath and Lees Court.

The demands of leisure and pleasure are accepted in the new strategic plans for the south-east. New titles are invented. The Areas of Outstanding Natural Beauty become Main Country Zones and the bulk of the rural area becomes a Green Sector. The Country Zone along the North Downs becomes a slender infill sandwiched between two broad sectors 'for future growth'. One sector covers the whole of North Kent along the line of the A2 from London to Thanet. Another follows the A20 from Maidstone to Ashford and Folkestone. The 'strategic map' makes the garden of England look like a backyard. Sussex is more generously treated with the one main corridor of growth from Crawley towards Brighton. Another growth sector, almost inevitably, is that part of Surrey that is trapped between the M3 and the A3. People must live somewhere and estimates of another half a million houses needed for Londoners alone by the end of the century show the need for finding new land for building. And much of that land must be in the most favoured residential areas of the south-east. People must work somewhere, too, and the employment pattern for most of the coastal resorts, with its heavy dependence on a seasonal trade, has caused a loss of the younger generation. The migration of elderly people for retirement on

57. *Twentieth-century garden restoration – topiary work at Hever Castle.*

the coast has exaggerated the problem, putting stress on social services. In some towns, more than half the inhabitants are over 65. Hastings has arrangements with London for new housing for London's overspill population together with the necessary industry and commercial offices to give them work.

Being still the highway to the continent and to the Common Market, Channel Tunnel or no Channel Tunnel, the south-east has most pressure for new warehousing and distribution centres such as freightliner depots at Lenham and Paddock Wood. The effect of the juggernauts on village streets and country lanes needs no emphasis here. The steady rumble of thirty-three-ton lorries along B class roads makes little sense for lorry or lane and the siting of a fruit-collecting centre in a village like Horsmonden makes a mockery of planning in terms both of accessibility and amenity. An oil distribution depot at Wye, an equally perverse scheme, was only averted by local opposition.

The south-east has had little of the heavy industries of coalfield England, though it has a small coalfield of its own. The Kent coalfield was developed in the 1890s. The pithead gear of Tilmanstone, Betteshangar and Snowdown look incongruous in the rural setting of the East Kent plateau but some of the settlements like Easole Street, Eythorne and Elvington add a new variant to the village theme. Heavy industry has been confined to the docks and Thames-side. Cement, paper and oil-refining make the Medway the nearest approach to a 'black' country. The refineries at the Isle of Grain had the honour of refining the first oil from the North Sea. The skyline from Chatham to Gravesend is a phalanx of chimneys, cooling towers and pylons rising out of the marshes.

Fingers of industry poke along the river valleys such as the Ravensbourne, the Wandle and the Wey, part of the halo that makes the metropolitan area one of the major manufacturing zones in the country. Generally, unemployment in the south-east has been lower than the national average but declining activity in the dockyards, including the naval establishments, and seasonal unemployment in the resorts have led to needs for new sources of work and there are few resorts without a light industrial estate. For planning purposes, the Metropolitan region has nearly a 75-kilometre radius, reaching the Medway, Tunbridge Wells, the South Downs and the Surrey border at Farnham. It gives administrative reality to the essential truth that the growth of London has brought the entire south-eastern peninsula into its embrace. To assuage the daily migration of about half a million people, office development is being encouraged in market towns and coastal resorts such as Tonbridge, Tunbridge Wells, Sevenoaks, Reigate and Guildford. Along the Brighton sea-front, Georgian houses are being modernized as 'prestige' office blocks. The tallest building in Folkestone is an office block. Ashford is due for the sort of growth that has transformed the Crawley area.

The office block and the shopping complex are the twin pillars of town-centre redevelopment that has torn the old heart out of many a town. The loss of local identity has led, too late in many cases, to a realization of the need to preserve urban landscapes just as much as rural areas. Individual buildings have been protected, though not always effectively, by listing as places of outstanding historical or architectural importance, grades 1 and 2 comprising the statutary list. Some of the most outstanding are owned by the Department of the Environment, by the National Trust and thereby preserved for posterity. Now whole areas are designated for conservation due to the promptings of the Civic Trust founded in 1957. Ten years later, the Civic Amenities Act gave local authorities the power to designate whole groups of buildings as worthy of conservation. This has been most effective since the reorganization of local government in 1974. Kent has 252 areas, more than any other county in Britain. Surrey has nearly 100, West Sussex 47 and East Sussex 41. They include entire villages and town centres, such as Canterbury, Chichester, Rochester and Guildford. The Cinque Ports of Rye, Hastings Old Town, Faversham, Deal and Sandwich are included. So are the market centres of Farnham, Chertsey, Sevenoaks, Milton Regis, Lenham, Cranbrook and Lewes. Parts of Tunbridge Wells, including the Pantiles, and five areas in Brighton are only the forerunners of many more to come while we take breath to look at the damage done in the boom days of the 1960s.

The designation of villages as conservation areas comes just at the time when most villages have lost their original function. The parish has been retained as the smallest unit of local government but the people who live in the villages are frequently people who use them as a dormitory, as an escape from the town in which they spend their working day. The desire for the country cottage has been made realizable by the private ownership of cars which has brought almost every rural settlement within the reach of the London housing market. The value of small rural properties has escalated to the point where the farm worker, amongst the lowest paid group in the country, has to live in a tied cottage or a council house.

The situation is summarized most poignantly in the handbook in the church of St Mary and St Peter at Wilmington, one of the hundreds of such booklets that I have read with delight and benefit. 'Though some may regret the passing of the old farming community,' it reads, 'it could not have survived in this day and age, and Wilmington is in fact fortunate that it is now inhabited by those who appreciate and are prepared to preserve its heritage.' The heritage of that small Sussex community stretches back far into the past, across the broad arable fields to the mysterious figure of the Long Men carved in the chalk face, to the even more ancient burial mounds on Windover Hill. The wild flowers in the nature reserve on the summit of the Downs are preserved and protected like the giant yew in the churchyard.

Though much is changed, even despoiled, in this most humanized of regions, subject to every pressure of modern advance, the roots of the past are still there to be cherished as our links with the landscape we have helped to fashion. The earliest expression of the landscape survives most palpably in Ashdown Forest, last of the unenclosed wild. Ravaged by iron workers since the Iron Age, traversed by the Romans, hunted over by Norman lords, grazed by monastic flocks, including those of Wilmington, the common rights have persisted miraculously until the present day. 'The Forest is in everyone's mouth,' wrote Richard Jefferies. It still is. In 1961, the Friends of Ashdown Forest set up a society to protect it. Six hundred sheep, a herd of cattle and feral deer still graze the heath land, a link with the Forest's first use.

'And it will remain a place of beauty, if only people care,' said Garth Christian. If enough people care. All the measures of conservation, whether of forest or mill, of village or historic town, will only be effective if people care. Ashdown is the constant reminder of our own past, the first stage in the complex evolution of the landscape we inhabit and inherit.

58. *Jack-in-the-Green, carved on a pew in Charing church.*

Select Bibliography

Chapter 1

The Hampshire Basin, British Regional Geology (HMSO).

The Wealden District, British Regional Geology (HMSO, 1954).

London and Thames Valley, British Regional Geology (HMSO, 1947).

MARTIN, E. A., *Sussex Geology* (1932).

MARTELL, GIDEON DR, *The Geology of the South-East of England* (1833).

WOOLDRIDGE, S. W. and GOLDRING, F., *The Weald* (Collins, 1953).

WOOLDRIDGE, S. W. and LINTON, D. L., *Structure, Surface and Drainage in South-East England* (George Philip, 1955).

COLEMAN, A. M. and LUKEHURST, C. T., *East Kent* (Geographical Association, 1967).

HALE, W. J. C., *Romney Marsh* (Hale, 1953).

STEERS, J. A., *The Sea Coast* (Collins, 1953).

LINTON, D. L., 'The Sussex Rivers', *Geography*, November 1956.

MAY, V. J., 'Retreat of the Chalk Cliffs', *Geographical Journal*, June 1971.

SHEAIL, G. M., 'Coombes of the White Chalk Downs', *Geographical Magazine*, April 1971.

MERCER, V., 'The Tillingbourne', *Field Studies*, May 1959.

MACRAE, S. G., contributions on Geology and Physiography in *The Rural Landscape of Kent* (Wye College, 1973).

MILLWARD, R. and ROBINSON, A., *South-East England: The Channel Coastlands* (Macmillan, 1973).

MILLWARD, R. and ROBINSON, A., *South-East England: Thamesside and the Weald* (Macmillan, 1971).

MATHEWS, E. C., *The Highlands of South-West Surrey* (A. & C. Black, 1911).

Chapter 2

BARRINGTON, C. A., *Forestry in the Weald*, Forestry Commission Booklet No. 22 (HMSO, 1968).

MANNING, S. A., *The Naturalist in South-East England* (David & Charles, 1974).

BURTON, JOHN, *The Naturalist in London* (David & Charles, 1974).

SIMMS, ERIC, *Birds of Town and Suburb* (Collins, 1975).

WHITE, JOHN T., *A Country Diary: Kent* (A. J. Cassell, 1974).

SANKEY, J., *Chalkland Ecology* (Heinemann Educational Books, 1966).

CORNISH, VAUGHAN, *The Churchyard Yew* (Muller, 1946).

YATES, E. M., 'The Vegetation of Blackdown', *Geography*, Vol. XL Pt. 2, April 1955.

HARRISON, J. et al., *Breeding Birds of the Medway; Wildfowl of the North Kent Marshes; A Gravel Pit Wildfowl Reserve* (*Reports of the Wildfowlers' Association of Great Britain*).

Sussex Naturalists' Trust annual reports and occasional pamphlets on *Pagham Harbour*; *Woods Mill*; *Nap Wood*; *The Mens*; etc.

Kent Trust for Nature Conservation pamphlets on *Hothfield Common*; etc.

Nature Conservancy pamphlets on *High Halstow*; *Ham Street Woods*; *Lullington Heath*; *Kingley Vale*; *Wye and Crundale Downs*; etc.

National Trust Pamphlets on *East Head*; *Blackdown*; *Devil's Punch Bowl*; *Gibbet Hill*; etc.

Bulletin of the Dungeness Bird Observatory.

Report of the Surrey Bird Club.

Local authority pamphlets on local nature trails and country parks, e.g. *Coulsdon Down, Hastings Country Park.*

Frensham Country Park; *Signpost 2000* (Hambledon Rural District Council).

The Southern Heathlands (Surrey Naturalists' Trust, 1976).

Chapter 3

JESSUP, R., *South-East England* (Thames & Hudson, 1970).

COPLEY, G. J., *An Archaeology of South-East England* (Phoenix House, 1958).

MARGERY, I. D., *Roman Ways in the Weald* (Phoenix House, 1965).

MARGERY, I. D., *Roman Sussex* (Sussex Archaeology Society, 1971).

MARGERY, I. D., *The London–Lewes Roman Road* (Sussex Archaeology Society, 1967).

British Museum, *Guide to the Antiquities of Roman Britain* (3rd edn, 1964).

WINBOLT, S. E. and HERBERT, G., *The Roman Villa at Bignor, Sussex* (1935).

COTTRELL, L., *The Roman Forts of the Saxon Shore* (HMSO, 1964).

PEERS, SIR C., *Pevensey Castle* (HMSO, 1972).

CUNLIFFE, PROF. B., *Fishbourne* (Times Newspaper Ltd, 1971).

Lullingstone Roman Villa (HMSO, 1969).

CURWEN, E. C., *The Archaeology of Sussex* (1954).

BENNETT, F. J., *Ightham, the Story of a Kentish Village* (1913).

Research articles in *Archaeologia Cantiana*; and of Surrey Archaeological Society and Sussex Archaeology Society.

Reports of the Kent Archaeology Rescue Unit on *Archaeological Excavations in the Darent Valley*; *Roman Dover*; etc.

Chapter 4

EKWALL, E., *English Place Names* (4th edn Oxford, 1960).

WHITELOCK, D., *The Beginnings of English Society* (Penguin, 1952).

BEDE, *A History of English Church and People* (Penguin, 1970).

FISHER, E. A., *The Saxon Churches of Sussex* (David & Charles, 1970).

COX, J. C., *Kent* (revised by P. M. Johnston) (Methuen, 1927).

COX, J. C., *Surrey* (revised by P. M. Johnston) (Methuen, 1926).

MAWER, A., STENTON, F. M., GOVER, J. E. B., *The Place Names of Sussex* (Cambridge University Press, 1929).

GOVER, J. E. B., MAWER, A., STENTON, F. M., *The Place Names of Surrey* (Cambridge University Press, 1934).

FURLEY, R., *A History of the Weald of Kent*, 2 vols (1871).

DARBY, H. C., and CAMPBELL, E. M. J. (Ed.), *The Domesday Geography of South-East England* (C.U.P., 1962).

SHIRLEY, EVELYN, *Deer and Deer Parks* (John Murray, 1867).

WALLENBERG, J. K., *The Place-Names of Kent* (Uppsala, 1934).

BRANDON, P., *The Sussex Landscape* (Hodder & Stoughton, 1974).

HEARNSHAW, F. J. C., *The Place of Surrey in the History of England* (Macmillan, 1936).

BAKER, A. H. R., 'Field Systems in the Vale of Holmesdale', *Agricultural History Review*, Vol. XIV Pt. I (1966).

BAKER, A. H. R. and BUTLIN, R. A., *Studies in Field Systems in the British Isles* (C.U.P., 1973).

Chapter 5

EVERSLEY, LORD, *Commons, Forests and Footpaths* (Cassell, 1910).

SHIRLEY, EVELYN, *Deer and Deer Parks* (John Murray, 1867).

WHITE, J. T., *The Parklands of Kent* (A. J. Cassell, 1975).

LAMBARDE, WILLIAM, *A Perambulation of Kent* (1570, reprinted by Adam & Dart, 1970).

MASON, R. T., *Framed Buildings of the Weald* (Coach Publishing House Ltd, Horsham, 1964).

ARMSTRONG, J. R., *A History of Sussex* (Phillimore, 1974).

MORRIS, J. E., *The Churches of Surrey* (Allen, 1910).

HOSKINS, W. G. and STAMP, L. D., *Common Lands of England and Wales* (Collins, 1963).

BERESFORD, M., *The Lost Villages of England* (Luttleworth, 1954).

LINDSAY, P. and GROVES, R., *The Peasants Revolt, 1381* (Hutchinson, n.d.).

BRANDON, P., *The Sussex Landscape* (Hodder & Stoughton, 1974).

DU BOULAY, F. R. H., *The Lordship of Canterbury* (Nelson, 1966).

EMERY, F. V., 'Moated Settlements in England', *Geography*, Vol. 47 (1962).

BRANDON, P. F., 'Medieval Clearances in the East Sussex Weald', *Trans. of the Institute of British Geographers*, Vol. XLVIII (1969).

BAKER, A. R. H. and BUTLIN, R. A., *Studies of Field Systems in the British Isles* (C.U.P., 1973).

BAKER, A. R. H., 'Field Systems in the Vale of Holmesdale', *Agricultural History Review*, Vol. XIV Pt. I (1966).

BRANDON, P. F., 'Demesne Arable Farming in Coastal Sussex During the Late Middle Ages', *Agricultural History Review*, Vol. XIX Pt. II (1971).

SMITH, ANN, 'Medieval Field Systems in Some Kent Manors', *Liverpool Essays in Geography* (1967).

TATE, W. E., 'Open Fields, Commons and Enclosures in Kent', *Archaeolgia Cantiana*, Vol. LVI (1943).

YATES, E. M., 'A Study in Settlement Patterns', *Field Studies*, Vol. I (1961).

YATES, E. M., 'History in a Map', *Geographical Journal*, Vol. CXXVI Pt. I (1960).

Department of Environment Guides to *Pevensey Castle*, *Farnham Castle Keep*, *Dover Castle*, *Rochester Castle*, *Eynsford Castle*, *Maison Dieu*, *Ospringe*, *Eltham Palace*, *Bayham Abbey*.

National Trust Handbooks to *Bodiam*, *Scotney*, *Knole*, *Petworth*; etc.

Chapter 6

NEWMAN, JOHN, *West Kent and the Weald* (Penguin, 1969).

NEWMAN, JOHN, *North-East and East Kent* (Penguin, 1969).

NAIRN, IAN and PEVSNER, NIKOLAUS, *Sussex, The Buildings of England* (Penguin, 1973).

NAIRN, IAN and PEVSNER, NIKOLAUS, *Surrey, The Buildings of England* (Penguin, rev. ed. 1971).

STRAKER, E., *Wealden Iron* (1931, reprinted David & Charles, 1969).

RIDLEY, U., *The Story of a Forest Village, West Hoathly* (The Friends of the Priest's House, 1971).

CHRISTIAN, GARTH, *Ashdown Forest* (The Society of the Friends of Ashdown Forest, 1967).

KENYON, G. H., *The Glass Industry of the Weald* (Leicester University Press, 1967).

MASON, R. T., *Framed Buildings of the Weald* (Coach Publishing House, 1964).

FURLEY, R., *A History of the Weald of Kent* (1871).

CHALKLIN, C. W., *Seventeenth-Century Kent* (Longmans, 1965).

WOLSELEY, VISCOUNTESS, *Some of the Smaller Manor Houses of Sussex* (Medici Society, 1925).

KERSHAW, S. W., 'Refugee Industries in Kent', *Memorials of Old Kent* (Bemrose, 1906).

AUBREY, J., *The Natural History and Antiquities of the County of Surrey*, 5 vols (1719).

Official Guides of the Department of the Environment to Deal, Walmer and Upnor Castles (HMSO).

National Trust Handbooks on *Knole, Petworth, Uppark, Scotney, Sissinghurst, Batemans.*

Handbook on *Ham House* (Victoria and Albert Museum).

BAINES, J. MANWARING, *Wealden Firebacks* (Hastings Museum, 1958).

LAMBARDE, W., *A Perambulation of Kent* (1570, new edn by Adams & Dart, 1970).

CATTELL, C., 'Iron Bloomeries', *Griffin*, Vol. 1, April 1971 (Geography Dept., N.W. Polytechnic).

Kentish Sources, III: Aspects of Agriculture and Industry (Kent County Council, 1961).

Chapter 7

JAMES, WILLIAM and MALCOLM, JACOB, *General View of the Agriculture of the County of Surrey* (1794).

STEVENSON, WILLIAM, *General View of the Agriculture of the County of Surrey* (1809).

BOYS, JOHN, *General View of the Agriculture of the County of Kent* (1799).

YOUNG, ARTHUR, *General View of the Agriculture of the County of Sussex* (1813).

COBBETT, WILLIAM, *Rural Rides* (1821).

MARSHALL, WILLIAM, *The Rural Economy of the Southern Counties* (1798).

JESSE, R. H. B., *A Survey of the Agriculture of Sussex* (Royal Agricultural Society, 1960).

GARRAD, G. H., *A Survey of the Agriculture of Kent* (1954).

STAMP, L. D., *Report of the Land Utilisation Survey of Britain: Surrey*, Pt. 81 (1942).

MCRAE, S. G. and BURNHAM, C. P., *The Rural Landscape of Kent* (Wye College, 1973).

HARVEY, D. W., 'Fruit Growing in Kent in the Nineteenth Century', *Archaeologia Cantiana*, Vol. LXXIX (1964).

HARVEY, D. W., 'Locational Changes in the Kentish Hop Industry', *Transactions of the Institute of British Geographers*, Vol. 30 (1962).

FINCH, W. COLES, *Watermills and Windmills of Kent* (C. W. Daniell Co., 1935).

HEMMING, P., *Windmills in Sussex* (C. W. Daniell Co., 1936).

WHITE, J. T., *The Parklands of Kent* (A. J. Cassell, 1975).

HARRISON, F., *Annals of an Old Manor House* (Macmillan, 1899).

WEBBER, R., *The Early Horticulturists* (David & Charles, 1968).

KERRIDGE, E., *The Agricultural Revolution* (Allen & Unwin, 1967).

HYAMS, E., *The English Garden* (Thames & Hudson, 1964).

BRIDGE, J. W., 'Kent Hop Tokens', *Archaeolgia Cantiana*, Vol. LXVI (1953).

Royal Botanical Garden handbooks for *Kew* and *Wakehurst Place.*

Forestry Commission Guides, *Bedgebury Pinetum and Forest Plots* (HMSO, 1972).

National Trust, Handbooks for *Nymans, Sissinghurst, Scotney, Sheffield Park, Uppark, Petworth,* etc.

Chapter 8

NEWMAN, J., *West Kent and the Weald* (Penguin, 1969).

NEWMAN, J., *North-East and East Kent* (Penguin, 1969).

NAIRN, I. and PEVSNER, N., *Sussex. The Buildings of England* (Penguin, 1973).

NAIRN, I. and PEVSNER, N., *Surrey. The Buildings of England* (Penguin, 1971).

FITTER, R. S. R., *The Home Counties* (Collins, 1951).

PARKER, E., *Highways and Byways in Surrey* (Macmillan, 1908).

JERROLD, W., *Highways and Byways in Kent* (Macmillan, 1907).

LUCAS, E. V., *Highways and Byways in Sussex* (Macmillan, 1912).

ANON, *The Kentish Traveller's Companion* (1779).

CHALKLIN, C. W., *Seventeenth-Century Kent* (Longmans, 1965).

CHALKLIN, C. W., 'A Seventeenth-Century Market Town: Tonbridge', *Archaeologia Cantiana,* Vol. LXXVI (1961).

BERESFORD, M. and FINBERG, H. P. R., *English Medieval Boroughs* (David & Charles, 1973).

BUTLER, D. J., *The Town Plans of Chichester, 1595–1998* (West Sussex County Council, 1972).

TOWNSEND, W., *Canterbury* (Batsford, 1950).

Town guides to Guildford, Farnham, Tonbridge, Ashford, Canterbury, Horsham, Chichester, Maidstone, Lewes, etc.

MILLWARD, R. and ROBINSON, A., *South-East England: The Channel Coastlands* (Macmillan, 1973).

MILLWARD, R. and ROBINSON, A., *South-East England: Thamesside and Weald* (Macmillan, 1971).

Chapter 9

PARRY, J. D., *The Coast of Sussex* (1833, reprinted by E. & W. Books Ltd, 1970).

JESSUP, R. and F., *The Cinque Ports* (Batsford, 1952).

BURROWS, M., *Cinque Ports* (Longmans, 1895).

LEWIS, A. D., *The Kent Coast* (Fisher, Unwin, 1911).

HOLMES, E., *Seaward Sussex* (Robert Scott, 1920).

JACOB, E., *History of Faversham* (1774, reprinted by A. J. Cassell, 1974).

ANDREWS, J. H., 'The Thanet Seaports, 1650–1750', *Archaeologia Cantiana,* Vol. LXVI (1953).

BAINES, J. MANWARING, *Burton's St Leonards* (Hastings Museum, 1956).

VINE, P. A. L., *The Royal Military Canal* (David & Charles, 1972).

SUTCLIFFE, S., *Martello Towers* (David & Charles, 1972).

HADFIELD, C., *The Canals of South and South-East England* (David & Charles, 1969).
MARSDEN, C., *The English at the Seaside* (Collins, 1947).
Official Guides to Rye & Winchelsea, Sandwich, Dover, Folkestone, Ramsgate, Margate, Hastings, Brighton, Worthing, Bognore, Littlehampton, etc.
Annual Digest of Port Statistics, Vol. I (National Ports Council, 1973).

Chapter 10

MACKINDER, HALFORD J., *Britain and the British Seas* (Oxford, 1906).
CHRISTIAN, GARTH, *Ashdown Forest* (The Society of the Friends of Ashdown Forest, 1967).
ADDISON, WILLIAM, *English Spas* (Batsford, 1951).
EVERSLEY, LORD, *Commons, Forests and Footpaths* (Cassell, 1910).
RUSKIN, JOHN, *Praeterita* (1899, reprinted by Rupert Hart-Davis, 1949).
PINLITT, J. A. R., *The Englishman's Holiday* (Faber, 1947).
PERKIN, H., *The Age of the Railway* (David & Charles, 1970).
WEAVER, L., *The Country Life Book of Cottages* (Country Life, 1919).
HOWARD, EBENEZER, *Garden Cities of Tomorrow* (1902, reprinted by Faber, 1965).
BEST, ROBIN H. and ROGERS, ALAN W., *The Urban Countryside* (Faber, 1973).
The South-East Study, 1961–81 (Ministry of Housing and Local Government, 1964).
South-East Economic Planning Council, *A Strategy for the South-East* (HMSO, 1967).
Surrey Structure Plan: Alternative Strategies (Surrey County Council, 1975).
County Structure Plan: Progress Report (Kent County Council, 1974).
Surrey County Planning Department, *Antiquities and Conservation Areas of Surrey* (6th edn 1976).

Index

Index

Abbot's Wood, 48
Abinger, 64, 119, 128
Addington (K), 65
Addington (Sy), 55, 68
Adur, River, 26, 31, 91, 116
Agriculture, 146ff
Albury, 46, 72, 92, 136, 163, 166, 228
Alciston, 103, 126, 160
Alfold, 100, 130, 132
Alfriston, 72, 122, 179, 180
Allington, 113
Amberley Wild Brooks, 57
Ambersham Common, 47
Andred's Weald, 85, 87, 97, 100
Arable farming, 153ff
Area of Outstanding Natural Beauty, 233
Arun, River, 26, 30, 31, 178
Arundel, 118, 178
Ashburnham, 128, 130
Ashdown Forest, 44, 76, 125, 129, 171, 229, 241
Ashdown Sands, 19
Ashford, 148, 187
Assarts, 103
Atherfield Clay, 32
Aylesford, 84, 106, 113

Bagshot Beds, 29
Banstead, 227, 230
Barfreston, 108
Barrows, bell and disc, 67
Barrows, long, 66
Battle, 113, 131, 151
Bayham Abbey, 114, 164
Beachy Head, 17, 52, 58, 70
Beckenham, 227
Bedgebury, 144, 167
Bedham, 23
Beech woodland, 38, 41
Belgae, 74
Bethersden, 157
Bethersden Marble, 21, 106, 154
Bexhill, 215
Bexley, Hall Place, 143
Biddenden, 134, 135, 188
Bignor, 75, 79
Billingshurst, 188
Bird reserves, 55ff
Birling, 156
Bishopstone, 91
Black Rocks, 20, 210
Blackdown, 23, 37, 44
Bletchingley, 119, 182, 183
Bloomeries, 128
Bodiam, 120, 121, 164, 196
Bognor Regis, 32, 214
Boroughs, 96
Bosham, 89, 96
Botany Bay, 27, 28
Bough Beech, 57, 58, 124
Boughton Monchelsea, 55, 143, 171
Bourne streams, 31, 32
Bow Hill, 43, 67
Box Hill, 54, 55
Boxgrove, 115
Boxley, 71, 113, 159
Bracklesham Beds, 29
Bramber, 116, 123

Brickworks, 23, 136
Bridges, 105, 176, 212
Brightling, 164, 172
Brighton, 70, 96, 209ff, 226, 230, 231
Broadstairs, 198
Bromley, 113, 190, 191
Bronze Age, 67
Brook, 107, 149
Brookland, 106
Brown, 'Capability', 163
Burgess Hill, 227, 229
Burpham, 118, 178
Burton, Decimus, 207, 212, 223, 224, 228
Burwash, 129, 231
Buxted, 55, 129

Caburn, Mount, 69
Camden, William, 129
Canals, 153, 182, 201, 221
Canterbury, 77, 92, 111, 118, 133, 170, 172ff
Castles, 116ff
Caves, 61ff
Celtic people, 61ff
Chaldon, 107, 135
Chalk, 24ff
Chalk flora, 52
Chalk grassland, 49ff
Challock, 48, 107
Chanctonbury Ring, 49, 68
Charing, 113, 241
Charleston Manor, 123
Charlwood, 100, 130
Chatham, 189, 216
Chert, 46
Chertsey, 85, 86, 116, 192
Chevening, 86, 109, 143, 172
Chichester, 74, 77, 110, 173ff
Chiddingfold, 100, 132
Chiddingstone, 21, 86, 122, 131, 137
Chilham, 40, 57, 66, 119, 165
Chobham, 29, 231
Cinque Ports, 195ff
Cissbury, 63, 68
Clandon Park, 165
Claremont, 66
Clay-with-flints, 32
Claygate Beds, 29
Clayton, 66, 161
Cliff erosion, 17, 27, 34, 35
Cliffe, 57, 81, 95, 153
Cliftonville, 27, 199
Climping, 86, 108
Cloth halls, 134
Clover, wild white, 157
Coal, 19, 239
Coates, 109
Cob plantations, 151
Cobbett, William, 149, 155, 163, 172, 177, 184
Cobham, 40, 66, 93, 109, 143, 235
Cocking, 26, 32
Coldrum Stones, 65
Common land, 44, 47, 230
Conservation areas, 233ff, 240
Compton, 92, 110
Cooling Castle, 120
Coombes, 32
Copperas, 135
Coppice woodland, 38, 40
Coulsdon, 54, 230
Country Parks, 234
Cowden, 96, 100, 128, 129, 131
Cowdray, 46, 144, 161
Cranbrook, 96, 133, 135, 161
Cranleigh, 46, 80, 119, 188
Crawley, 36, 100, 171, 232, 233
Cretaceous rocks, 19ff
Cricket, 115, 190, 235
Crockham Hill, 41, 46, 231
Crowborough, 229
Crowhurst, 130, 131
Croydon, 113, 190, 191, 225
Crystal Palace, 224, 225
Cuckmere, River, 34, 52, 115, 177, 179

Danes, 87, 116
Darent, River, 78, 86, 135, 138
Deal, 138, 234
Deer, wild, 55
Deer parks, 55, 97, 124, 125, 137
Dene holes, 63
Dene Park, 40
Denns, 96ff
Deserted sites, 112, 126
Devey, George, 224, 225, 228
Devil's Dyke, 32, 69, 106
Devil's Jumps, 23
Devil's Kneadingtrough, 32, 33, 53
Devil's Punchbowl, 32
Dew ponds, 70
Doddington, 40, 42
Domesday Survey, 88ff
Dover, 49, 78, 92, 118, 170, 199
Dry valleys, 31, 32
Ditchling, 66
Dungeness, 35, 58
Dunsfold, 101, 110, 132, 145
Dutch influence, 141ff

Earth tremors, 20
Eashing, 93, 105

Eastbourne, 214
East Farleigh, 105
East Grinstead, 128, 131, 190
East Head, 35
Eastwell Park, 48
Edenbridge, 76, 100
Ellman, John, 155
Enclosure, 154, 229ff
Epsom, 76, 223, 227
Evelyn, John, 36, 46, 136, 141, 154, 163, 222
Ewhurst, 46, 100, 101
Eynsford, 119, 135, 167

Fairlight, 17
Farley Heath, 80
Farm museums, 158
Farnham, 119, 151, 171, 184
Faversham, 112, 135, 136, 218, 219
Felpham, 214
Fernhurst, 44, 100
Field systems, 66, 78, 80, 95, 103, 154
Findon, 156
Fishbourne, 80
Fishing ports, 215
Flemings, 133, 147, 152, 167
Flint, 27ff
Flint mines, 62, 63
Folkestone, 200, 226
Folkestone Beds, 23
Folkestone Warren, 24
Footpaths, 104, 236
Fordwich, 194
Forestry Commission, 48, 235
Forstals, 101
Frensham, 45, 234
Friston Forest, 41, 52
Fruit farming, 146ff
Fuller's earth, 24

Gatton, 182, 183
Gatwick, 233
Gault Clay, 24
Gavelkind tenure, 103
Gillingham, 217
Glass industry, 29, 132ff
Godinton, 36, 143, 151, 168
Godstone, 94, 100, 135
Golf, 234
Goodwood, 34, 41, 68, 154, 163
Goring-on-Sea, 49
Goudhurst, 106, 109, 133, 134, 151
Gravesend, 170, 172, 219, 220, 226
Gravetye, 38, 127
Great Bookham, 110
Great Dixter, 123
Great Tangley, 136
Green Belt, 232
Greens, village, 100ff
Greensand, Lower, 23, 61, 136
Greensand, Upper, 24
Greenwich, 36, 44, 77, 88, 136, 137, 141, 143, 217, 225
Groombridge, 141
Guildford, 119, 125, 134, 137, 171, 179, 235

Hadlow, 167
Hailsham, 188
Halnaker, 161
Ham Street Woods, 40
Hamlets, 102
Hammer ponds, 128
Hardham, 107, 116
Harrow Hill, 62, 63
Harting, 26, 159
Hascombe, 24, 69
Haslemere, 131, 132, 190
Hastings, 70, 96, 128, 131, 206, 207, 239
Hastings Beds, 19
Hawkhurst, 96
Haxted Mill, 132, 136
Haywards Heath, 188, 227
Headcorn, 36, 106, 134
Headley Heath, 30
Heathfield, 19, 166, 188
Heathland, 44ff
Hengist and Horsa, 84
Herne Bay, 34, 216
Heronries, 56, 216
Herstmonceux, 122
Hever, 44, 109, 122, 168, 237, 238
Heyshott, 47, 101
Hill forts, 67ff
Hill, Octavia, 230
Hindhead, 45
Hog's Back, 26, 27, 70, 125, 149, 159, 179
Hollow ways, 72
Holmbury, 46, 69
Holmesdale, 24, 95, 138
Holtye, 76
Holwood, 69, 163
Holy wells, 222
Hops, 149ff
Horam, 151
Horsham, 20, 171, 190
Horsmonden, 101, 128, 129, 164, 188
Hothfield Common, 45
Hythe, 119, 200
Hythe Beds, 23

Ice Age, 32, 34, 37, 63

Ide Hill, 46, 231
Ightham, 23, 46
Ightham Mote, 124
Iguanodon, 17, 20
Industrial zones, 220, 239
Innings, 126
Iping, 86
Iron Age, 61ff
Iron industry, 72, 126ff

Jevington, 91
Juniper Hill, 53
Jutes, 83ff

Kemsing, 55, 232
Keston, 68, 161, 163
Kew, 141, 167
Kingley Vale, 43, 53
Kingston-upon-Thames, 171, 184, 190, 191, 192, 232
Kit's Coty, 65
Knole, 138, 139, 166

Lambarde, William, 63
Lamberhurst, 130
Landscape gardening, 163ff
Leatherhead, 135, 171, 185, 227
Leeds Castle, 24, 119
Leith Hill, 23, 25, 46, 75, 166
Lenham, 24, 30, 113, 160, 239
Lewes, 67, 113, 118, 129, 131, 177
Limpsfield, 23, 86, 94, 123
Lingfield, 109
Littlehampton, 213
Livestock breeding, 155ff
Livestock fairs, 188
Livestock markets, 188
London Clay, 29, 218
Loseley Hall, 26, 141
Lower Halstow, 92, 107
Luddesdown, 93
Lullingstone, 36, 79, 122
Lullington, 126
Lullington Heath, 52
Lurgashall, 44
Lutyens, Sir E. E., 144, 229
Lydd, 93, 202
Lympne, 81

Maidstone, 112, 133, 135, 186
Marden, 96, 102, 171
Margate, 193, 198
Market gardening, 152ff
Market towns, 172ff
Marl, 63, 154
Marshland, 35, 56, 126
Martello towers, 202
Mayfield, 113, 131
Medway, River, 30, 65, 105, 149, 186, 189, 216
Megaliths, 64ff
Melbourne Rock, 24
Mens Nature Reserve, 38, 100
Meopham, 100, 161
Mereworth, 165
Mersham-le-Hatch, 40, 55, 109
Merton, 112, 231
Michelham Priory, 115, 125
Midhurst, 189
Milton Regis, 96, 102, 218, 240
Minster-in-Sheppey, 113
Minster-in-Thanet, 113
Mitcham, 152
Moated sites, 120, 124
Mole, River, 30, 31, 54, 185
Monasteries, 111ff

Nap Wood, 39
National Trust, 21, 44, 46, 47, 69, 75, 99, 118, 138, 168, 230, 237
Nature trails, 43, 235
New Ash Green, 232
Newchapel, 100
Newark Priory, 116
Newenden, 97, 108
Newgardens, 147
Newhaven, 208
New Romney, 202
Nonesuch, 112, 137, 223
Norman churches, 107
North Downs Way, 72, 235
North Foreland, 27
Northfleet, 220
Northiam, 132, 188
Northwood Hill, 56
Nymans, 168

Oak woodland, 36ff
Ockley, 38, 75, 87, 101, 130
Offham, 101
Oldbury, 46, 61, 69
Open fields, 103
Orchids, 53
Ospringe, 112
Otford, 125, 138
Ouse, River, 30, 68, 86, 208
Outwood, 99
Oxted, 145

Paddock Wood, 148, 150, 239

Pagham Harbour, 58, 87
Paper industry, 135
Parham, 55, 144
Parish boundaries, 93ff
Patrixbourne, 108
Peasemarsh, 20
Pegwell Bay, 29, 194
Penshurst, 36, 109, 124, 144
Peper Harow, 160
Petworth, 21, 47, 131, 144, 154, 163, 188
Pevensey, 82, 85, 116, 208
Pilgrims' Way, 66, 71, 100, 235
Place-names, 84ff, 99
Plateau gravels, 30
Plaxtol, 80, 123, 151
Pleasure grounds, 222
Plumpton Place, 144
Plumpton Plain, 66, 67
Polesdon Lacey, 165
Pulborough, 75, 188
Puttenden Manor, 124
Pyrford, 107

Queen Down Warren, 53
Queensborough, 216
Quex, 166

Rabbits, 55
Railways, 225ff
Raised beaches, 34, 61
Ramsgate, 197
Reculver, 81, 92
Redhill, 184
Reigate, 80, 119, 161, 167, 171, 182, 184, 227
Repton, Humphrey, 144, 164
Richborough, 81, 84
Richmond, 55, 116, 223, 225
Ridgeways, 69, 70
Ripe, 81
River terraces, 31, 34, 61
Robertsbridge, 129
Rochester, 77, 118, 176
Rolvenden, 36, 97, 161
Romans, 42, 68ff, 128, 152, 194
Roman forts, 81, 194
Roman roads, 74ff
Roman villas, 78ff
Romano-British fields, 78, 80
Romney, 157
Romney Marsh, 35, 96, 126, 153, 157, 200
Rother, River (K), 30, 35, 201, 202
Rother, River (Sx), 30, 105
Rotherfield, 97, 104, 231
Royal Military Canal, 200, 201
Royal dockyards, 136
Royal palaces, 137
Runnymede, 125
Rusthall Common, 21, 22, 223
Rye, 96, 151, 202ff
Rye Harbour, 58

St Leonards, 207
St Radegund's Abbey, 115
Saltwood, 119
Sandgate, 140
Sandgate Beds, 23
Sandown, 138
Sandwich, 133, 152, 195ff, 234
Sandwich Bay, 57, 58
Sarsen stones, 34, 65, 83
Saxons, 83ff
Saxon churches, 89ff
Scotney, 20, 120, 165
Scots pine, 38, 43ff
Seaford, 202, 208
Seasalter, 216
Selsdon Wood, 55
Selsey, 85, 87, 89, 126, 215
Seven Sisters, 27, 34, 52
Sevenoaks, 58, 134, 135, 171, 186
Shaws, 103
Sheep, 155ff
Sheerness, 216, 217
Sheffield Park, 164, 168
Sheppey, Isle of, 29, 57, 87, 88, 135, 171, 216ff
Shere, 145
Shoreham, 28, 36, 108, 169
Shoreham-by-Sea, 212
Silk industry, 135
Singleton Open Air Museum, 93, 124, 161
Sissinghurst, 144, 168
Sittingbourne, 218, 227
Slindon Forest, 41, 74, 167
Smallhythe, 88, 143, 196
Smarden, 134
Sompting, 91
Southease, 88, 93, 96
South Downs Way, 68, 235
Spas, 222ff
Squerryes, 69, 143, 167
Squirrels, 48
Staddle barns, 160
Stane Street, 74
Staplehurst, 21, 124, 130
Stelling Minnis, 101, 162
Steyning, 86, 178
Stone Age, 61
Stone-in-Oxney, 20
Stone-next-Faversham, 83
Stopham, 105, 109

Strategic plans, 237
Swanscombe man, 61
Suburban development, 231ff
Sussex Marble, 17, 21
Sussex Red cattle, 157
Sutton Place, 141, 142, 153

Tandridge, 41, 116
Tenterden, 21, 88, 135, 188, 196
Tertiary rocks, 20
Thames reservoirs, 59
Thanet, Isle of, 20, 27, 34, 57, 84, 88, 96, 153, 198, 226
Thanet Sands, 29
Thorpe, 192, 234
Thursley, 45, 128
Tilgate Forest, 20
Tonbridge, 120, 134, 135, 148, 189
Toys Hill, 46, 231
Trottiscliffe, 65, 94, 113
Trundle, 68
Tufa, 24, 83
Tunbridge Wells, 62, 69, 171, 223, 224
Tunbridge Wells Sands, 19, 21
Turnpikes, 170ff

Upnor, 140
Uppark, 144, 167, 172

Vineyards, 151

Wadhurst, 130, 132, 188, 231
Wadhurst Clays, 19, 128
Wakehurst Place, 167
Waldeshare, 167, 168
Walland Levels, 35, 162
Walmer, 138
Walton-on-Thames, 85, 192
Wantsum Channel, 35, 57, 81, 96, 126
Water mills, 95, 136
Watling Street, 77
Weald, definition of, 100
Wealden Dome, 19
Wealden house, 122
Wealden Lake, 17, 23
Westerham, 100
Westenhanger, 138
West Hoathly, 127
West Malling, 24, 112, 119
West Wittering, 29, 32, 35, 215
Wey, River, 30, 31, 45, 105, 153, 182, 184
White Horse, 84
Whitstable, 215
Wildfowl, 57
Wilds, Amon, 212, 228
Wilmington, 52, 115, 240
Wilmington, Long Man, 70
Winchelsea, 204, 205
Windmills, 161
Winkworth, 168
Wisborough Green, 102, 132
Wisley, 107, 168
Witley, 92
Woking, 86, 130, 137, 227
Woods Mill, 40
Woolbeding, 23, 73, 89, 105
Woollen industry, 133ff
Woolwich and Reading Beds, 29
Wonersh, 92, 134, 145
Worth, 30, 89, 90, 128
Worthing, 34, 86, 153, 212, 213
Wotton, 46, 92
Wrotham, 95, 100
Wye, 96, 158
Wye and Crundale Downs, 53

Yew, 41ff
Young, Arthur, 132, 149, 154, 155, 158